Readers say about DISCOVER WASHINGTON WITH KIDS:

This comprehensive book helps us discover the kid within us all. It's not just for children. From the sweetness of Cow Chip cookies to the warmth of Sol Duc Hot Spring to the rainbow of colors at Roozengarde, there are wonderful surprises in here for each of us, some right in our own back yards.
— **Patti Payne, Public Affairs Director, KIRO Newsradio/ Entercom Seattle, and Eastside Journal columnist.**

• •

This guide book on Washington features adventures in all shapes and sizes while providing detailed information on activities that are affordable, educational and fun for families, grandparents and friends traveling with children.
— **Robin Pollard, Director, Tourism Division of the Washington State Dept. of Community, Trade and Economic Development**

• •

On the go people who don't have time to keep up with places to go and things to do can find it all in *Discover Washington*. My dog-eared copy is beloved by out-of-town guests and family. Don't tell my kids—I even use it for adult-only outings. The comprehensive listings give me all the details I need to make a decision about where to go and how to ge there. A book I can't do without.
— **Sherry Grindeland, columnist, The Seattle Times**

DISCOVER
WASHINGTON
WITH
KIDS
· SECOND EDITION ·

Enjoy!

Rosanne Cohn &
Suzanne Monson

Rosanne Cohn

JASI

DiscoverWashington with Kids
Second Edition
© 1998 by Rosanne Cohn and Suzanne Monson

ISBN 1-881409-22-8

Cover design: Marge Mueller
Cover and frontispiece photos courtesy Yakama National Cultural Heritage
    Center, Northwest Trek/Metropolitan Park District of Tacoma, and
    The Seattle Mariners. Lower right cover photo and frontispiece ©Marge
    and Ted Mueller.
Production, typesetting, and layout by Gray Mouse Graphics
Maps by Gray Mouse Graphics

All entries in this book have been included at the decision of the authors and publisher. No advertising is accepted for *Discover Washington with Kids*.

Although diligent efforts have been made to confirm the accuracy of information contained in this work, neither the publisher nor the author is responsible for errors or inaccuracies or for changes occuring after publication. This work was not prepared under the sponsorship, license, or authorization of any business, attraction, park, person, or organization described, depicted, or discussed herein.

Post Office Box 313
Medina, Washington 98039
(425) 454-3490; FAX: (425) 462-1335; e-mail jasibooks@aol.com

Printed in the United States of America

Library of Congress Cataloging-in-Publication Data

Cohn, Rosanne.
    Discover Washington with kids / Rosanne Cohn & Suzanne Monson. -
- 2nd ed.
        p. cm.
    Includes index.
    ISBN 1-881409-22-8
    1. Washington (State) -- Guidebooks. 2. Family recreation -- Washington
(State) -- Guidebooks. I. Monson, Suzanne, 1961- II Title.
    F889 . 3 . C58   1998
    917.9704'43 -- dc21   98-38472
                                                            CIP

Contents

• •

Contents

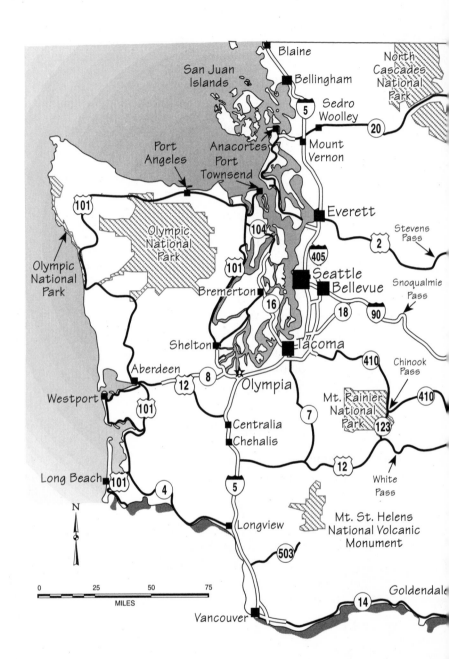

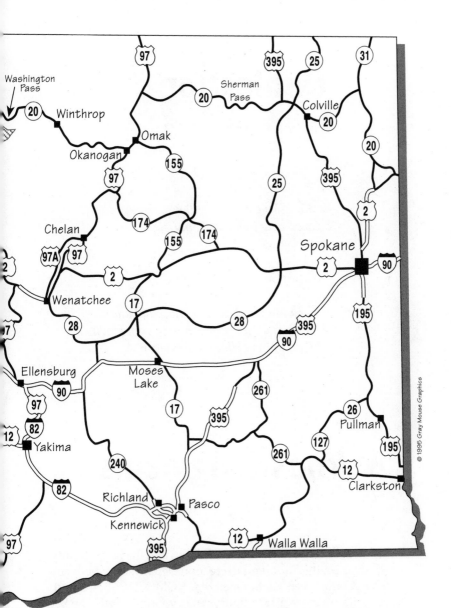

WASHINGTON

Dedication

From Rosanne Cohn:

To Kit Nicole and Joel Alan . . .
beloved new chapters in my life

From Suzanne Monson:

To my ever-ready band of explorers . . . husband and chief
stroller-pusher, Dori, and our "where are we going today"
daughters, Kelsey, Haley and Keegan.

Acknowledgments

Seattle Children's Theater, Jeanne Thorsen and the King County Library System; Seattle Parks and Recreation Department; Bellevue Chamber of Commerce; Kathi Goertzen, KOMO TV; Bill Yeend, KIRO Radio; Patti Payne, KIRO Radio; Sherry Grindeland, The Seattle Times; and Cathy Reiner, The Seattle Times

Foreword

● ●

Time with our families is so precious in this fast-paced world where it seems we're all headed in different directions. This book is a great tool for getting the family headed to one destination . . . together!

My daughters and my husband and I love to go on adventures, We find those special times are the ones we all remember. They bring us close. This book is a great reminder of the vast number of adventures just waiting for families in this gorgeous state we call home. Our favorites are anything that have to do with hiking, skiing, or swimming. We love the winter and summer in the areas around Snoqualmie Pass, we can't wait to get back to the Methow Valley, and the kids love anyplace with a beach.

This book is a collection of outings near and far that provide one thing we all need more of: FUN!

Enjoy your times with your loved ones.

— Kathi Goertzen
KOMO ABC 4

Bellevue's Robinswood Park. PHOTO COURTESY BELLEVUE PARKS AND RECREATION DEPARTMENT

Tips for Traveling With Kids

● ●

B e prepared! It's a great motto for the Boy Scouts and a good one for families, too. Getting ready for any family trip involves everyone—especially in the planning. Planning is the key to preventing—or being ready for—any of the small crises or misadventures that sometimes happen. Here are some ideas to help you plan a great adventure.

- Have a family conference to plan the trip. That way, everyone gets to share his or her ideas about where the family should go, and everyone feels like he or she has had a say in the planning.
- If you can't come to an agreement about where to go, have a lottery.
- After you've decided when and where, mark those dates on the calendar. The kids get a sense of when the big event will happen, and the anticipation builds as the days go by.
- Involve the children in making the plans. After a certain age (usually 6 or 7), they can make some of the phone calls to request information, maps, prices, availability, etc. You, of course, can do some role-playing in helping them prepare to make the call.
- Pack a travel bag with any and all items you might possibly need, especially those that can forestall a crisis. Let the kids help plan what goes in to the bag—and keep it handy for any occasion that involves leaving the house. Suggested items: clean plastic bags; aspirin or Tylenol (your choice); Band-Aids; extra toys and books; blankets or towels; canned foods and juices; coloring books and crayons; toilet paper and paper towels; change of clothing (old jeans are good here); disposable cameras; tape recorder or Walkman and cassettes (books on tape are great); quarters for pay phones; cell phone—you get the idea!
- Encourage your kids to start a scrapbook and show them how to collect memorabilia or write entries to record their memories.

Whatever you do to create some consensus or make your family trip a group event contributes to everyone's enjoyment. Planning ahead helps to avoid anything that might spoil this wonderful occasion. Enjoy!

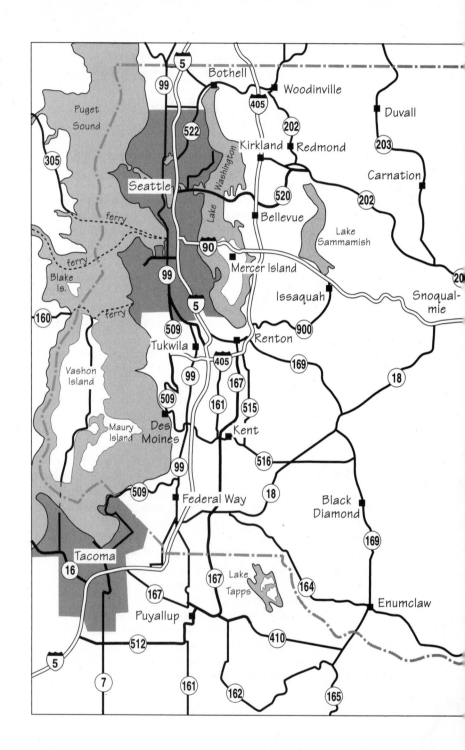

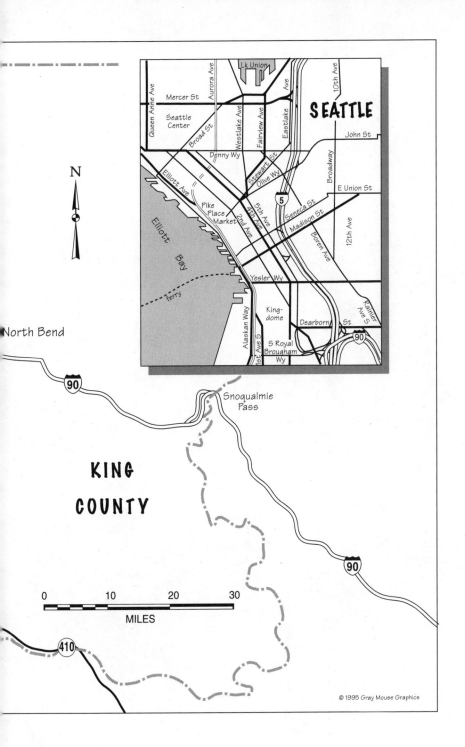

© 1995 Gray Mouse Graphics

CHAPTER
1

Downtown Seattle

• •

So much commends this extraordinary city of Seattle, and in many ways it speaks for itself. Our commanding skyline, a fascinating shoreline, the myriad of outdoor opportunities—all have brought new faces to Seattle and Puget Sound in increasing numbers. Fortunately the downtown core of Seattle—once in danger of losing its uniqueness—has done an about-face and started off in a vital new rebuilding phase. The diversity of our neighborhoods, complemented by sparkling and scintillating new faces in the retail sector, creates a living kaleidoscope for families, indeed everyone, to enjoy and treasure.

- **Pioneer Square:** The triangular park at First Ave. and Yesler Way marks Seattle's first settlement. Yesler Way was originally called "Skid Road" because logs were dragged down its steep slope to a steam-powered lumber mill (now Magic Mouse Toys!). Pioneer Square is fascinating to explore, both for its people and places, but it is not a place to let children explore alone.

- **International District:** Once called Chinatown, this community now encompasses a wide variety of Asian cultures. Restaurants of all sizes and types, and shops with exotic and unusual merchandise are attracting visitors (and tourists) from everywhere. Watch the newspapers in spring and summer months for several wonderful festivals with authentic foods, traditional dancing, and art.

- **Pike Place Market:** The oldest continuously operating farmers' market in the country, this is a favorite of all of Seattle's shopping

Seattle Reign vs. San Jose Lasers. PHOTO BY JOANIE KOMURA COURTESY SEATTLE REIGN destinations. It's an eclectic mix of local farmers, specialty shops, artisans, and street musicians, and a wonderful place to bring the family on weekends, especially if everyone in the family shares in the grocery planning and shopping. Open year-round, it's the perfect place to bring your visitors, and grandparents love to bring their small charges here for a day's outing.

A gentle reminder: Victor Steinbrueck Park is a lovely vantage point in daylight hours, but not for exploring after dark. This is true of many local parks now.

- **The Seattle Center:** Once a Northwest Native American tribal gathering spot for ceremonial feasts, the center now serves the same purpose for today's families. There is literally something for everyone here, from the huge annual festivals to the world-class Children's Museum. From science to culture to entertainment to sports, the center has something to challenge your imagination, stimulate your mind, or pique your curiosity.

- **The Waterfront and Alaskan Way:** Much has changed since 1897 when the waterfront was the city's primary working harbor. Most industry has moved south to Harbor Island now, but Alaskan Way piers have been refurbished for varied uses. At Pier 69, the high-speed catamaran Victoria Clipper sets sail between Seattle and British Columbia, while harbor excursion boats depart from Pier 55, and Seattle's fireboats dock at Pier 53. Pier 52 is the point of departure for Washington State Ferries to Bremerton and Bainbridge Island. It's fun to take the Waterfront Streetcar from the International District (Fifth Ave. at Jackson St.) or Pioneer Square (Main at Occidental) all the way to the north end of the waterfront for an overview, and then stroll back along the bay. Call 206-553-3000 for details. At Pier 57, the bright lights and music on the vintage carousel inside the Bay Pavilion dazzle youngsters.

- **Downtown Seattle:** With new shops, parks, and other features, the face of downtown is changing rapidly. December's holiday shopping season is especially exciting: In Westlake Park, a nineteenth-century carousel of painted horses offers free rides for all ages; across the street, at Westlake Center, a Christmas tree is illuminated by more than 10,000 lights beginning the first Friday after Thanksgiving. Metro's tunnel station at Westlake Center provides an underground bus link between Seattle's leading department stores and beyond. The over-the-ground Monorail connects downtown with the Seattle Center.

PIONEER SQUARE

Places to Go

Amtrak/Mount Baker International   *800-872-7245*

Location: King St. Station, one block northeast of Kingdome
Web Site: www.amtrak.com
Days/Hours: Daily at least once, departing for Vancouver, British Columbia,
   and Portland, Oregon
Admission: Round-trip prices can vary: average is $50/adults, $30/children.
Wheelchair/Stroller Access: Yes

Zoom from Seattle to Vancouver, B.C., or Portland, Oregon, within
four hours aboard this high-speed Spanish-made train. Its family-friendly
design offers some seating where riders can face each other for a board
game or game of cards. The state-of-the-art system literally glides up to
140 mph, but goes slower to meet U.S. regulations. Aisles are wide enough
for strollers; restrooms offer diaper-changing facilities. The Seattle-to-
Vancouver run takes a scenic waterfront route most of the way, making
brief stops in Edmonds, Everett, Mount Vernon, and Bellingham.

The Kingdome   *206-296-3128*

Location: 201 S. King
Web Site: www.kingdome.org
Days/Hours: Monday–Saturday, 11 a.m., 1 p.m., and 3 p.m.; mid-April
   through mid-September.
Admission: Public Tours: $5/ages 13 and older; $2.50/children 6-12 and
   seniors; free/children 5 and under. Group Tours: $3.50/ages 13 and older;
   $1.75/children 12 and under; $1.75/chaperones. Group tours of twenty-
   five people or more available during the rest of the year when appointments are made at least two weeks in advance.
Wheelchair/Stroller Access: Yes

Demolition of this behemoth is slated for the year 2000, but there's
still time to tour the 60,000-seat Kingdome. If you've seen a Home Show,
Boat Show, noisy monster truck rally, or Mariners game at the dome,
you'll be curious to see what goes on behind the scenes. Guided one-
hour tours take visitors through the sports locker rooms, press boxes,
arena floor, and sports museum. The museum displays collectibles from
one of the game's all-time great wide receivers, retired Seahawk Steve
Largent, and memorabilia from the former Rainiers and Pilots baseball
teams. Wear comfortable shoes because you'll cover a lot of ground.

Klondike Gold Rush National Historical Park

206-553-7220

Location: 117 S. Main
Web Site: www.gold-rush.org
Days/Hours: Daily, 9 a.m.–5 p.m.; closed Thanksgiving, Christmas, and New Year's Day
Admission: Free
Wheelchair/Stroller Access: Yes

This storefront museum has been getting more attention since the 1997 centennial celebration of the 1897 Alaska Gold Rush. The smallest national park west of the Mississippi, the exhibits here show how early-Seattle's economy boomed as nearly 100,000 miners shopped here on their way to pan for gold. Films featured in the auditorium include Charlie Chaplin's *The Gold Rush* (3 p.m., first Sunday of the month). Park rangers guide free one-hour walking tours of Pioneer Square Historic District at 1:30 p.m. on Saturdays, Memorial Day to Labor Day. Children younger than 12 must be accompanied by an adult; appointments required for large groups.

Seattle Mariners

206-622-HITS (to order tickets)

Location: 83 S. King St., Suite 300
Web Site: www.mariners.org
Days/Hours: Season is April–September; game times vary. Ticket offices open Monday–Friday, 9 a.m.–5:30 p.m.; gates open two hours prior to game time.
Wheelchair/Stroller Access: Yes, by ramps and elevators

With a line-up that includes all-stars, top rookies, and pitching aces, a Seattle Mariners ticket has become the hottest thing in town. And there's more than just baseball happening during a Mariners home game in the Kingdome. The three-wheeling Mariner Moose mascot is always good for laughs. Between innings, families love to compete in computerized games on the DiamondVision mega-screen. There's a kids' arcade for older children near Aisle 120, with video games and baseball card booths.

Many games offer free promotions, including jersey, ball, or bat give-aways. When ordering tickets, ask about discounts for kids on Level 300 and two-for-one family nights (on selected Mondays during the season). For about $10, fans 14 or younger can join the Sparkletts Junior Mariners' Club and receive posters, club newsletters, Baseball for Kids magazines and more. All ages may join a Mariners Fan Club for $25 to receive lots of extras. Two free tickets are included in both clubs. Batting practice and infield activity give autograph hunters a chance to attract their favorite players for signatures.

Seattle Seahawks

206-628-0888 (tickets)

Location: Home games in the Kingdome.
Web Site: www.seahawks.com
Days/Hours: Game times vary on Sundays. Preseason games begin in early
August and postseason play-offs are possible in early January
Wheelchair/Stroller Access: Yes; ramps and elevator

Bone-crunching action kicks off in the Kingdome when the Seattle Seahawks take on other National Football League competitors. The team's training field is in Kirkland, but practices are closed to the public. There are no discount admission prices for kids.

Edgar Martinez of the Seattle Mariners. Photo courtesy the Seattle Mariners

Smith Tower
206-682-4646; 888-608-6337

Location: 506 Second Ave.
Days/Hours: Daily, 10 a.m.–2 p.m.
Tours: Self-guided: $4/adults and youth 12 and older; $3/seniors and children under 12.
Wheelchair/Stroller Access: Yes

Built in 1914, the forty-two-story Smith Tower was the tallest building west of the Mississippi River until the early 1960s, and unlike today's high-rises, the Smith Tower still runs manual elevators. In the lobby on the first floor, look for art depicting Chief Seattle and other Native Americans important to Seattle's history. You'll watch the floors go by through glass doors as you soar to the thirty-fifth story; here an observatory offers a 360-degree view of the city, Elliott Bay, and Puget Sound. When the Chinese Room is open, look inside at antique furniture presented to L. C. Smith by the Empress of China during the 1910s.

Underground Tour
206-682-4646; 888-608-6337

Location: 610 First Ave., Doc Maynard's Public House
Web Site: www.seattleonline.com
Days/Hours: Daily year-round but schedule changes seasonally
Admission: $5.95/adults; $4.87/seniors; $4.33/children 13-17; $2.51/children 6-12; free/children 5 and under
Wheelchair/Stroller Access: Yes, for the lecture; not on the tour

Seattle's "ghost town" is here, lurking under the streets of Pioneer Square. The ghosts are part of the town's mystery and history, old Seattle after the fire of 1889. The town was rebuilt, but the mystery under the streets lingers on. The tour starts at Doc Maynard's Public House with a twenty-minute presentation. You'll then walk along sidewalks from the 1890s. It's five blocks of rough ground and steep flights of stairs . . . hard work for youngsters under 7. Guides on this amazing tour tell anecdotes, replete with details about the glue-pot fire and other legends of Seattle. Reservations recommended; bring along a flashlight and good walking shoes. It can get damp and cool down there. Note: The only restroom stop on the tour is at Doc Maynard's. This is a great experience for teens and preteens, especially good for birthday parties. Light lunches are available before and after the stroll.

Waterfall Park

Location: Main St. at Second Ave. S.
Wheelchair/Stroller Access: Partially

This park is a summer favorite, welcoming visitors with water cascading over massive rocks that drowns out all street noises. A glass-covered shelter with tables and chairs offers a serene place for a picnic. Privately built and maintained by the Annie E. Casey Foundation, the park commemorates the original offices of United Parcel Service.

Places to Eat

Cow Chip Cookies   206-292-9808

Location: 102 First Ave. S.
Days/Hours: Monday–Saturday, 10 a.m.–6 p.m.; Sunday, noon–5 p.m.
Wheelchair/Stroller Access: Yes

Here's a good snack stop to include in a Pioneer Square outing. Cow Chip Cookies means big crunchy cookies, some with melt-in-your mouth chocolate chips. Plan to bring some home.

Grand Central Baking Co.   206-622-3644

Location: 214 First Ave. S. in the Grand Central Arcade
Days/Hours: Deli: Monday-Friday, 7 a.m.–6 p.m., Saturday and Sunday,
    9 a.m.–5 p.m. *Restaurant:* Monday-Saturday, 11 a.m.–3 p.m.
Wheelchair/Stroller Access: Yes

Their popular cinnamon rolls, great desserts, hearty homemade soups, whole and half sandwiches (including pb and j), and now a rustic European Italian-style bread have created a devoted clientele. Eat upstairs or in the main entry at wooden tables with benches on a creaky floor.

The Iron Horse   206-223-9506

Location: 311 Third Ave. S.
Days/Hours: Sunday-Friday, 11 a.m.–9 p.m.; Saturday, 11 a.m.–6:45 p.m.
W1heelchair/Stroller Access: Yes

It's a great combination of model trains and yummy hamburgers. Your meal arrives courtesy of a toy train; portions are generous and the setting is vintage.

Old railroad collectibles and photographs cover the walls. Fun to eat and look at the same time.

Shops to Browse

Elliott Bay Book Company   206-624-6600

Location: *First Ave. S. at S. Main St.*
Web Site: *www.elliottbaybook.com/ebbco/*
Days/Hours: *Monday–Saturday, 10 a.m.–11 p.m.; Sunday and holidays,*
    noon–6 p.m.
Wheelchair/Stroller Access: *Bookstore's first floor only*

There is almost always a reading event or special program for children on Saturday mornings at this venerable old bookstore. Kids love the wooden playhouse; parents love the bargain loft and well-stocked shelves. The café downstairs is quiet and diners usually have their noses in books or magazines while eating. There's no children's menu, but soups and half-sandwiches can be had for the asking. Watch the papers for celebrity readings and other happenings here, some well suited for families.

Glass House Art Glass   206-682-9939

Location: *311 Occidental Ave. S.*
Days/Hours: *Monday–Saturday, 10 a.m.–5 p.m.; Sunday (May–December),*
    11 a.m.–4 p.m.; closed on Sunday, January–April
Tours: *Free for groups of twenty or less. Please call ahead.*
Wheelchair/Stroller Access: *Yes*

This is a hot place to be, with good reason. The glassblower is at work from 10 a.m. to 3 p.m. (lunch break is 11:30 a.m. to 12:30 p.m.) in front of a gas furnace heated to 2,000 degrees. Blowers use the same procedure artisans have used for nearly 3,000 years. Glass is little more than melted sand, but what exquisite shapes and pieces they produce. There are glass forms of all sizes here, from small perfume bottles to large sculptures.

Great Winds Kite Shop   206-624-6886

Location: *402 Occidental Ave. S.*
Days/Hours: *Monday–Saturday, 10 a.m.–5:30 p.m.; Sunday, noon–5:30 p.m.*
Wheelchair/Stroller Access: *Yes*

They have over 400 kites to tempt you and the right people to help you decide which kite will work best for you. Located just three blocks west of the new underground bus terminal, it's a popular place for both the serious and amateur kite flier. The vibrant colors, shapes, and textures are fascinating. Shop staff is happy to answer questions about flying or kite-building problems. Kite history, construction, and flying classes are available by appointment.

Magic Mouse Toys   206-682-8097

Location: 603 First Ave.
Days/Hours: Monday–Saturday, 10 a.m.–9 p.m.; Sunday, 10 a.m.–6 p.m.
Wheelchair/Stroller Access: First floor only

A Pioneer Square fixture, Magic Mouse is a superb collection of international games, puzzles, and playthings. Most visitors can't leave without hugging at least one of the furry stuffed animals. It's not limited to goodies for kids. Board games for serious competitors attract adults to this store, too.

Wood Shop Toys   206-624-1763

Location: 320 First Ave. S.
Days/Hours: Monday–Saturday, 9:30 a.m.–5:30 p.m.; Sunday, 11 a.m.–
   5 p.m.; some extended hours in November and December
Wheelchair/Stroller Access: First floor only

This family-owned shop offers an eclectic collection of toys not often found elsewhere. Jack the Woodman greets visitors at the door. Inside the shop, marionettes and colorful nutcrackers imported from Germany line the shelves. Besides the popular wooden and Russian toys, look for the delightful "furry folk" collection of nearly thirty-five animal puppets. A pair of bears known as Fred and Vinnie are favorites here. If stairs are a problem, staff members are happy to bring things down to you.

THE INTERNATIONAL DISTRICT
Places to Go

Chinatown Discovery Tours   206-236-0657; 206-583-0460 (fax)

Location: PO Box 3406, Seattle, WA 98114 for required reservations.
Web Site: www.seattleonline.com
Tours: By reservation only; write to the address listed above
Admission: Prices range from about $10/children 5 to 11 years and $15/older
   visitors to about $25/adults and $15/children
Days/Hours: Flexible schedule, usually after 10:30 a.m.; tours are ninety
   minutes to three and a half hours
Wheelchair/Stroller Access: No

Children can count with an abacus and watch how fortune cookies are made during one of several guided walking tours led by Seattle native Vi Mar. While the tour is best for children over 5, this knowledgeable guide tailors tours for families of all ages so they can discover hidden treasures in Seattle's International District. She'll describe how Asian delicacies are prepared and share the history of Seattle's Asian communities, which includes the Chinese, Cambodian, Vietnamese, Japanese, Filipino, Laotian, and Korean. Trip departures often hinge on the weather, but do include a dim sum lunch. Teachers and other youth leaders may be interested in the Asian Cultural Youth Program tours designed for first- through sixth-grade students.

International Children's Park

Location: Seventh Ave. S. at S. Lane St.
Wheelchair/Stroller Access: Yes

This little playground is among the most charming in the city. A slide spirals down a mound of rocks into a huge bed of sand while a delightful dragon stands guard.

Wing Luke Asian Museum   206-623-5124

Location: 407 Seventh Ave. S.
Days/Hours: Tuesday–Friday, 11 a.m.–4:30 p.m.; Saturday–Sunday, noon–4 p.m.
Admission: $2.50/adults; $1.50/seniors and students 12 or older; 75¢/children 6 to 11; free/children 5 or younger; Thursdays are free.
Tours: Free: may be self-guided or with a docent by appointment
Wheelchair/Stroller Access: Yes

Even young children enjoy this museum because there are so many things they can handle and create. In fact, guided tours are best for kids because they're designed with kid-friendly history. Children may try on colorful clothing lifted from trunks brought by Seattle's earliest Asian settlers. Students may sniff the spices and fragrant aromas from the Far East and watch a video of the Chinese New Year celebration with firecrackers and dancing dragons. Seattle's Asian community dates back to 1860; its rich history is reflected in many ways here.

Places to Eat

House of Hong   206-622-7997

Location: 409 Eighth Ave. S.
Days/Hours: Monday–Friday,11 a.m.–5 p.m.; Saturday–Sunday, 10:30 a.m.–
   5 p.m.
Wheelchair/Stroller Access: Yes

A restaurant with slightly more formal decor, House of Hong offers
seventy types of dishes of generous portions as well as dim sum. Lined
with comfortable booths, this place specializes in family gatherings.

King Café   206-622-6373

Location: 723 S. King
Days/Hours: Thursday–Tuesday, 11 a.m.–5 p.m.
Wheelchair/Stroller Access: No

Dim sum is served hot and fresh upstairs. Dishes come up on a dumb-
waiter and are quickly distributed. Seating is limited, but tables open up
quickly.

Ocean City   206-623-2333

Location: 609 S. Weller
Days/Hours: Dim sum served daily from 9 a.m. to 3 p.m.; "Hot Pot" dinner
   Monday-Friday, 5 a.m.–10 p.m.; reservations not necessary.
Wheelchair/Stroller Access: Yes, by elevator through the garage

Dim sum is something of a Chinese smorgasbord. Ocean City presents over thirty dishes and provides high chairs and booster seats for
little ones. The restaurant's outside decor is colorful with striking carvings. It gets crowded on weekends, but the food is worth waiting for. The
waitstaff pushes carts filled with small dishes of fried, steamed, or baked
beef, pork, fish, and vegetables past your table, pausing while you make
your selection. First timers may want to try fried Fun Gow, a crescent-
shaped type of egg roll (also available steamed); Gin Dau, a sweetish,
sesame-covered dough filled with red-bean paste; and steamed Hum Bow,
a white baked dough usually filled with a tangy barbecue sauce. Most
dishes contain two to four portions, easily divided among a family. Kids
get to take a bit of everything, and parents don't have to waste time with
the old "clean your plate" routine. They can accommodate any size group
here; the rooms are very large. You can also order regular dishes off the
menu. The "Hot Pot" dinner is quite an experience, too. With a selection

of uncooked vegetables and meats, you cook your own at the table in a heated broth. There is also a buffet with twelve to fourteen items. Price is all inclusive: $11.99 for adults, $8.99 for children ages 3 to 10.

Shops to Browse

Uwajimaya   206-624-6248

Location: Sixth Ave. S. at S. King St.
Days/Hours: June–Labor Day: Monday–Saturday, 9 a.m.–9 p.m.; Sunday,
    9 a.m.–8 p.m. Rest of the year: daily, 9 a.m. to 8 p.m.
Wheelchair/Stroller Access: First floor only

You'll feel as if you've flown to another country when you venture into Uwajimaya's electric atmosphere. This Asian department store is a colorful market filled with foods, gifts, art, and clothing. Cooking connoisseurs—and wanna-bes—come here for regularly scheduled cooking classes. Kids are quite taken with the colorful gift items and unusual foods they won't see in other stores. The deli offers take-out, with a good variety of hot and cold entrees.

ALASKAN WAY AND THE WATERFRONT

Places to Go

Argosy Cruises (formerly Seattle Harbor Tours)   206-623-4252

Location: Pier 55; Suite 201
Web Site: www.argosycruises.com
Days/Hours: Varies with cruise
Admission: Prices will vary according to cruise; Argosy does offer a combination ticket for the Lakes and Harbor tours, and an annual Cruise Pass

Argosy's narrated cruises take you around Lake Washington (departing from Kirkland's Marina Dock) or through Elliott Bay and the Duwamish waterway. From Pier 55 you'll see shipyards, cargo docks, freighters, tugboats, and almost every kind of water life that exists off Seattle's shores. For complete information on the various tours, prices, and accommodations, call for a brochure or specific information. It's often fascinating to locals when they take visitors out—and they find how much they don't know about the place they live! These are good for pre-teen and early-teen birthday parties.

Coast Guard Museum   206-217-6993

Location: 1519 Alaskan Way S.
Days/Hours: Monday, Wednesday, and Friday, 9 a.m.–3 p.m.; Saturday and
  Sunday, 1 p.m.–5 p.m.
Admission: Free
Wheelchair/Stroller Access: Yes

This small but very interesting museum is dedicated to the work and history of the U.S. Coast Guard. Navigational aids, including a magnetic compass, ship models, Arctic ivory, and a four-foot-high Fresnel lens made in France for a Puget Sound lighthouse are on display.

Coast Guard Vessel Traffic Center   206-217-6050

Location: Pier 36
Web Site: www.webcom.com./d13www/cgunit/vts/esvts.html
Days/Hours: Daily, 8 a.m.–4 p.m.
Tours: Yes, but hours are flexible; call for information. Tours are free.
Wheelchair/Stroller Access: Yes

Here you can observe the Coast Guard watching local waters. Even 5 year olds are fascinated by the radar sites and complex radio communication at this center. The Coast Guard monitors the waters from Cape Flattery (on the Pacific Ocean) to Olympia (at the south end of Puget Sound) round-the-clock by radio, preventing collisions, groundings, and other marine mishaps in Puget Sound. During the day, the guided tour includes a sixteen-minute video. Drop in and watch personnel through a viewing window anytime.

Omnidome   206-622-1868

Location: Pier 59, at the foot of Pike Place Market next to the Seattle
  Aquarium
Days/Hours: Varies; shows usually air between 9:30 a.m. and 9:55 p.m., daily
Admission: $7/adults; $6/seniors and youths 6 to 18; $5/children 3 to 5; free/
  children 2 and younger
Wheelchair/Stroller Access: Yes

If you like your entertainment on the big, big screen, this is the place to be. Waves of sights and sound flood your senses in the curved megascreen IMAX theater in the Omnidome. Most movies shown here have a nature theme, but they are exciting and almost larger than life. Best to call ahead for schedules as shows and times change frequently.

Combination tickets are available if you're planning a same-day visit to the aquarium. Arrive ten minutes before show time.

Pier 54 Adventures   206-623-6364

Location: Pier 54
Days/Hours: Varies; call ahead for schedule
Admission: $12/adults; $10.80/seniors; $7/children 12 or younger; prices are subject to change
Wheelchair/Stroller Access: Limited

Even without lessons, as many as forty passengers can lend a hand in sailing The Spray, a two-masted tall ship replica. From about mid-May through September, this ship takes two-hour tours four times daily starting at about 10:15 a.m. through mid-September. Adult fares are $20; children pay $12.50; prices are subject to change. Three-hour sunset cruises cost a bit more.

For a little faster action, put your thrill-seeking family aboard the sixty-foot high-speed Seattle Rocket. This 124-passenger vessel leaves others in the mist as it reaches up to 45 knots. The Seattle Rocket takes riders on thirty-minute tours daily mid-May through mid-September; after that it's weekends only, weather permitting. Trips typically leave every forty-five minutes from 10 a.m. to 7:45 p.m.

Pier 70

Built in 1901 by Elton Ainsworth and Arthur Dunn, Pier 70 was a full-fledged ocean terminal for steamship lines until 1910. The Coast Guard leased it until 1954, and since then it has become a place to browse and explore. The ambiance is dim and cavern-like, but there are a number of places to eat and interesting shops that capture the Pacific Northwest flavor. Don't miss the main level restrooms with their nostalgic flush chains.

Seattle Aquarium   206-386-4320; 206-386-4300

Location: Pier 59
Web Site: www.seattleaquarium.org
Days/Hours: Memorial Day–Labor Day: daily, 10 a.m.–7 p.m. Labor Day to Memorial Day: daily, 10 a.m.–5 p.m.
Admission: $7.50/adults 19 and older; $6.75/seniors; $5/students 6 to 18;

$1.90/children 3 to 5; free/children 2 and younger. Discounts available for King County residents, Metro pass holders, and groups of ten or more. Ask about a combination Woodland Park Zoo/Seattle Aquarium annual pass.
Wheelchair/Stroller Access: Yes

Pacific Northwest sea life is at its best at the Aquarium, easily one of Seattle's most popular rainy day outings. From behind the safety of viewing glass, children can go nose to nose with sharks, rays, eels, and more. Even the outdoor exhibits, featuring lively sea otters, playful seals, and chipper sea birds are under cover; these are especially popular in the summer months. Older children enjoy looking under the microscope at the tiniest creatures, which start the food chain. If your child is eager to reach into the touch tank to stroke the starfish, a hand-washing faucet is nearby.

Don't miss the domed aquarium room, surrounded on all sides and overhead by tanks filled with other large sea creatures. When you first arrive, check to see what time divers are in the dome to feed the fish. Self-guided tours take anywhere from one to several hours. Another highlight is their Nightwatch program for thirty-five to fifty visitors. After an evening of marine science activities, you'll sleep overnight in the underwater dome. Rates are $600 for up to thirty-five people, $17 per person for each guest up to fifty.

Spirit of Puget Sound
206-443-1442

Location: Leaves from Pier 70
Days/Hours: Lunch cruises noon to 2 p.m.; dinner cruises Monday through Saturday, 7 p.m. and 10 p.m. and Sunday, 6 p.m.–9 p.m., during the summer months; schedule shortened during cooler months; call ahead for required reservations
Wheelchair/Stroller Access: Yes; alert the staff when you make your reservation

Especially popular with tourists and locals entertaining visitors, this narrated harbor tour cruises to Magnolia Bluff, Todd Pacific Shipyards, Alki Point, and Blake and Bainbridge islands. There's fascinating data about the inner workings of the Port of Seattle and Seattle's teeming waterfront activities from the water. Families on a budget may prefer the lunch cruise, which runs about $33 for those 13 and older; children 3 to 12 are half price; those 2 or younger cruise for free. Dinner cruises range from about $56 to $61; children cost about $42 to $50. Christmas ships sail in December on Fridays and Saturdays for about $60.

Tillicum Village on Blake Island   206-443-1244

Location: Sail from Pier 56
Days/Hours: Runs year-round; mid-October–April: weekends only. May–
   mid-October: daily. Call ahead; schedules vary
Admission: $50.25/adults; $32.50/teenagers; $20/students 6 to 12; $10/
   children 4 and 5; free/children 3 and younger
Wheelchair/Stroller Access: Yes

This is a nice opportunity to sample Native American hospitality.
You'll cruise across Elliott Bay to Tillicum Village on Blake Island; your
welcome includes a bowl of clams, a typical Northwest delicacy. It's a
four-hour outing, and no matter what the age, children take something
special away with them from the experience. After eating the clams, children learn to crush the white shells into the beach to recycle them. For
the main course, visitors are treated to an Native American-style salmon
dinner, tribal dancing, and forty-five minutes of free time to explore the
pristine island's totem poles, masks, and carvings. If you're lucky, a tribal
artist will be designing a new piece during your visit. The artists enjoy
taking time to tell you about their works. Tillicum Village also is accessible through Kitsap Harbor Tours from Bremerton. Reservations are recommended.

Washington State Ferries   206-464-6400; 800-84-FERRY

Location: Pier 52
Web Site: www.wsdot.wa.gov/ferries
Days/Hours: Schedules vary; call ahead
Wheelchair/Stroller Access: Yes

Riding a Washington State Ferry is a never-ending adventure for kids.
Whether it's the bellow of the ship's horn as it nears the dock, the seagulls
diving for handouts, or the rush from spray in your face, any of the three
Sound routes is worth the trip. The one-hour ride to Bremerton allows
time to explore the ship, watch the skyline disappear, or enjoy an onboard
picnic. If your destination is Bainbridge or Bremerton, you can walk-on
and leave the car behind. With or without kids, the evening ferries are
romantic as the city lights begin to sparkle. The $80 million Tacoma, new-
est on the Bainbridge Island–Seattle route, carries 2,500 passengers—500
more than the next largest ferry. Fares vary according to the season, but
summer rates are usually slightly higher. Fare information will vary
according to destination. For answers to your questions, call the number above; they will also mail you a brochure. Brochures also available
at the Public Information Desk at Pier 52. Special note: When calling for

information, be forewarned that working your way through the system can be tedious. Have paper and pencil ready and allow lots of time; the agents are very helpful and patient.

Places to Eat

The Frankfurter   206-622-1748

Location: Pier 55
Days/Hours: Memorial Day–Labor Day: daily, 9 a.m.–9 p.m. The rest of the year: daily, 9 a.m.–5 p.m. (they may stay open later on weekends if business is brisk).
Wheelchair/Stroller Access: Yes

Wieners, franks, hot dogs, or foot-longs—no matter what you call them, this place has them. Eat them plain—plump and juicy inside a bun—or slap on anything from the condiment bar. In summer months, their fresh-squeezed lemonade is very refreshing

Ivar's Acres of Clams   206-624-6852

Location: At Pier 54
Days/Hours: Memorial Day–Labor Day: daily, 11 a.m.–11 p.m. The rest of the year: Sunday–Thursday, 11 a.m. –10 p.m.; Friday and Saturday, 11 a.m.–11 p.m.
Wheelchair/Stroller Access: Yes

Seagulls and children adore the statue of the late Ivar Haglund, one of Seattle's most colorful characters, which stands outside this waterfront eatery. There's a children's menu with seafood and other choices for less than $3. Adults may prefer to sip a warm cup of red or white clam chowder before ordering clam nectar or another fish dish. The waterfront trolley stops across the street at "Clam Central Station."

The Old Spaghetti Factory   206-441-7724

Location: 2801 Elliott at Broad; across from Pier 70
Days/Hours: Lunch served Monday–Friday, 11:30 a.m.–2 p.m.; dinner served Monday–Thursday, 5 p.m.–10 p.m.; Friday, 5 p.m.–11 p.m.; Saturday, noon–11 p.m.; Sunday, noon–10 p.m. Reservations not accepted.
Wheelchair/Stroller Access: Yes

This pasta place is frequently crowded on weekends. It's a great favorite with families, especially if they can be seated in the 1917 Birney

Car. Diners savor the spaghetti and sauce while relaxing on velvet-covered sofas under red Tiffany lamps. Crayons and menus to color on go a long way in keeping restless spirits busy. Bring your own cake if you're celebrating a birthday; the waitstaff will sing "Happy Birthday." Spumoni ice cream is served with all orders.

Shops to Browse

Sandpiper Gift Shop   206-624-2835

Location: Pier 59 next to the aquarium
Days/Hours: Labor Day to Memorial Day: daily, 10 a.m.–7 p.m.; Memorial
    Day to Labor Day: daily, 10 a.m.–6 p.m.
Wheelchair/Stroller Access: Yes

Kids on a budget can find affordable souvenirs for only a few dollars at this Pacific Northwest specialty shop. Look for postcards, bookmarks, games, and puzzles in a child's price range.

Waterfront Landmark   206-622-3939

Location: Pier 55
Days/Hours: Labor Day–Memorial Day: daily, 9 a.m.–6 p.m.; Memorial Day
    to Labor Day: daily, 9 a.m.–9:30 p.m.
Wheelchair/Stroller Access: Yes

Admittedly a tourist destination, the Waterfront Landmark still has some inviting things to see and buy. Run your fingers through thousands of colored, tumbler-polished stones in an open display case or talk to the very big stuffed bears huddled in the corner. Look for the authentic Native American headdress on the wall. You can munch on thirteen varieties of fudge made on the premises or admire a display of totems by Northwest carvers.

Ye Olde Curiosity Shop   206-682-5844

Location: Pier 54
Days/Hours: May–mid-October: daily, 9 a.m.–9:30 p.m. The rest of the year:
    Monday–Thursday 9:30 a.m.–6 p.m.; Friday–Saturday, 9 a.m.–9 p.m.;
    Sunday, 9 a.m.–8 p.m.
Wheelchair/Stroller Access: Yes

Part museum, part curio shop, part gift shop, this establishment has been in the hands of the Standley family since 1899. Four generations later, the family still scours the earth for the strange and unusual. Even those with perfect vision will probably need a magnifying glass to read one of the finest exhibits here: the Lord's Prayer carved on a grain of rice. Hosts and chief residents of this honest-to-goodness curiosity shop are Sylvester and Sylvia, a pair of six-foot-tall mummies. You're sure to find other things you think are amazing.

PIKE PLACE MARKET

Pike Place Market

Location: First Ave. and Pike St.
Days/Hours: Daily, Monday-Saturday, 9 a.m.–6 p.m.; Sunday, 11 a.m.–
5 p.m.
Tours: 206-682-7453. Family walking tours of the market are slated the last
Saturday of each month; reservations are required. These tours vary from
thirty minutes to an hour, depending on the ages of the children.

One of the most memorable parts of the market is the "flying fish." When a visitor buys a salmon or other large fish at the seafood shop under the massive clock near the foot of Pike St., the fish "fly" around in an entertaining toss-and-catch game before it's wrapped for purchase. The main entrance at First Ave. and Pike St. is gateway to stands run by dozens of local farmers selling the finest in fruits and vegetables, more than 250 shops and restaurants, and nearly 200 artisans. Don't miss the market pig; she loves to be photographed.

Places to Eat

Chocolate and Ice Cream Delight   206-441-8877

Location: Soames Dunn Building
Wheelchair/Stroller Access: Yes

Just the place on a warm summer day! They sell delicious ice cream treats by the cone or by the dish, plus wonderful sodas, sundaes, and floats.

The Crumpet Shop   206-682-1598

Location: 1503 First Ave., Corner Market Bldg.
Days/Hours: Monday–Saturday, 8 a.m.–5 p.m.; Sunday, 9 a.m.–4 p.m.

If you show up between 7:30 a.m. and noon, you can watch from the sidewalk as the baker pours the batter into the ring molds; the crumpets are cooked right there on a griddle. It's a perfect midmorning or midafternoon stop, or a mini-meal at lunch. They're best when they're fresh. Just a warning: They stop serving a half hour before closing.

Cucina Fresca   206-448-4758

Location: 1904 Pike Place
Days/Hours: Daily, 9:30 a.m.–6 p.m.
Wheelchair/Stroller Access: From arcade side

Pasta, antipasto, and regional entrees are made fresh daily. Everything is take-out, and all but the bread is sold by the pound. Kids love to order the "aglio olio," a spaghetti dish with roasted garlic and fresh Parmesan.

Procopio Gelateria Italian Ice Cream   206-622-4280

Location: On the Hillclimb
Days/Hours: Monday–Friday, 10 a.m.–6 p.m.; Saturday–Sunday, 9 a.m.–
    11:30 p.m.
Wheelchair/Stroller Access: Take the elevator from Western Ave.

This popular summer stop serves up yummy gelato.

The Shy Giant   206-622-1988

Location: Corner Market Building
Days/Hours: Monday–Saturday, 10 a.m.–5:30 p.m.; Sunday, 11 a.m.–5 p.m.
Wheelchair/Stroller Access: Yes

A long-time market favorite for yogurt, waffle cones, and ice cream.

Three Girls Sandwich Shop and Bakery   206-622-1045

Location: Sanitary Market
Days/Hours: Restaurant open daily, 7 a.m.–5:30 p.m.; bakery open until
    6 p.m.
Wheelchair/Stroller Access: Yes

Families on a casual swing through the market will find a delicious array of baked goods here. Perch on a stool to eat or carry your meal with you.

Shops to Browse

Craft Emporium   *206-622-2219*

Location: Minus 1 Level
Days/Hours: Monday–Saturday, 10 a.m.–6 p.m.; Sunday, 10 a.m.–5:30 p.m.
Wheelchair/Stroller Access: Yes

There's a kids' section in this shop devoted to crafts for young hands. Look for beading, needlework, origami, face painting, and more. In the general shelves, crafters of all ages will find thousands of colored stones in countless shapes, colored and metallic pipe cleaners, miniature collectibles, craft ribbon, and unusual supplies for the craft-minded or creative party giver.

Golden Age Collectables   *206-622-9799*

Location: Minus 1 Level
Days/Hours: Monday–Saturday, 10 a.m.–6 p.m.; Sunday, 11 a.m.–5 p.m.
Wheelchair/Stroller Access: Take the elevator from Western Ave.

If comic books, posters, or baseball cards are your passion, this is the place. They've added a number of games from which to choose, too.

The Great Wind-Up   *206-621-9370*

Location: Economy Market
Days/Hours: Monday–Saturday,10 a.m.–5 p.m.; Sunday, 11 a.m.–4 p.m.
Wheelchair/Stroller Access: Yes

You don't have to be a kid to play with the myriad of wind-up, blow-up, animated, stuffed, and movable toys at this compact little shop.

Market Magic Shop   *206-624-4271*

Location: Minus 1 Level
Days/Hours: Memorial Day through Labor Day: Monday–Saturday, 9 a.m.–
    6 p.m.; Sunday, 10 a.m. to 5:30 p.m. After Labor Day: Monday–
    Saturday, 9:30 a.m.–6 p.m.; Sunday, 10 a.m.–5 p.m.
Wheelchair/Stroller Access: Yes

Before you can say, "abracadabra," you'll be drawn into this shop of prestidigitation. This store sells everything imaginable for the magician in all of us. For youngsters just entering the world of magic, it's a good starting place.

DOWNTOWN SEATTLE

Freeway Park

Location: Seneca at Sixth Ave., next to the Convention Center
Wheelchair/Stroller Access: Yes

This garden-style park was designed to restore pedestrian access between First Hill and downtown, but children may think it was built for them. That's because 27,000 gallons of recycled water rushes over the fountains each minute providing a splash of fun for youngsters. A peaceful place by day, it's not considered safe early morning or after dark. At the park's east end, children may romp in the grassy area known as Freedom Plaza. During the summer, watch for weekly concerts at noon.

GameWorks   *206-521-0952*

Location: 1511 Seventh Ave.
Web Site: www.gameworks.com
Days/Hours: Monday–Thursday, 10 a.m.–12:30 a.m.; Friday–Saturday, 10
    a.m.–1:30 a.m.; Sunday, 11 a.m.–11 p.m.
Admission: Free
Wheelchair/Stroller Access: Yes, but there are lots of stairs, too

This indoor virtual reality games extravaganza has been packing in visitors since opening in 1997. It's magnetic to preteens, teens, and their families who want to test their skills in riding computerized skateboards, motorcycles, Wave Runner watercraft, and more. Kids get a kick out of watching adults play Ms. PAC Man, now considered almost a prehistoric version of contemporary video games. Per-game prices start at 50¢ to $1. Players must buy a magnetized "Smart Card" which is used like debit card to be inserted into games. After the game is played, the cost is deducted from the card's value. It's a popular birthday party destination; call for arrangements.

King County Library System   *425-462-9600; 684-4494 (TTY)*

Location: 300 8th Ave. N.
Answer Line: 425-462-9600 (for all branches)
Web Site: www.kcls.org (for all branches)

There are forty branches in the King County Library System, now the country's second busiest library system. All have access to the World Wide Web and participate in an extensive schedule of year-round reading programs and special activities. These include a summer reading program, and midweek and evening programs that may focus on many different entertaining events, including science, magic, drama, and dance. The KCLS Answer Line is a lifesaver for youth tracking down homework answers or adults looking for answers to trivia questions. The three busiest branches in the system are Bellevue, Shoreline, and Federal Way.

Bellevue Regional Branch   425-450-1765

Location: 1111 110th Ave. N.E., Bellevue
Children's Program Line: 206-684-6622; 425-450-1775
Days/Hours: Monday–Thursday, 11 a.m.-9 p.m.; Friday, 10 a.m.-6 p.m.;
   Saturday, 10 a.m.-5 p.m.; Sunday, 1 p.m.–9 p.m.
Wheelchair/Stroller Access: yes

As the busiest branch in the King County system, Bellevue Regional Library circulates more than 1 million items a year.

Shoreline Regional Branch   206-362-7550

Location: 345 N.E. 175th St., Shoreline
Days/Hours: Monday–Thursday, 11 a.m.-9 p.m.; Friday, 10 a.m.-6 p.m.;
   Saturday, 10 a.m.-5 p.m.; Sunday, 1 p.m.–9 p.m.
Wheelchair/Stroller Access: yes

Shoreline is the second busiest branch, circulating more than 700,000 items annually. Midday readings for toddlers and preschoolers are very popular here. The branch's summer reading program awards prizes in age groups for those reaching their goals.

Federal Way Regional Branch   253-838-3688

Location: 34200 First Way S., Federal Way
Days/Hours: Monday–Thursday, 11 a.m.–9 p.m.; Friday, 10 a.m.–6 p.m.;
   Saturday, 10 a.m.–5 p.m.; Sunday, 1 p.m.–9 p.m.
Wheelchair/Stroller Access: Yes

As the third busiest branch in the system, Federal Way circulates almost 700,000 items a year. With the entire system offering full Internet access, parents can keep up with their computer-literate kids through free Internet classes.

Seattle Art Museum

206-654-3100 (recorded information);
206-654-3137 (TDD)

Location: *100 University St., between First and Second avenues*
Web Site: *www.sam.tripl.org*
Days/Hours: *Tuesday, Wednesday, and Friday–Sunday, 10 a.m.–5 p.m.;*
Thursday, 10 a.m.–9 p.m.; closed most Mondays except Labor Day,
Fourth of July, Presidents Day, Memorial Day, and Martin Luther King
Jr. holidays; closed Thanksgiving, Christmas, and New Year's Day
Admission: *$6/ages 13 or older; $4/seniors; free/children under 12 when*
accompanied by an adult. Boeing provides free admission to all visitors
the first Thursday of each month. Admission tickets for the Seattle Art
Museum can be used at the Seattle Asian Art Museum if used within
one week.
Tours: *Guided tours are Tuesday–Saturday at 2 p.m.; Sunday at 2:30 p.m.;*
and Thursday at 7 p.m.
Wheelchair/Stroller Access: *Yes, from First Ave. store entrance; not from*
museum entrance

Comfortably known around town as SAM, there's a vast world of art waiting for visitors to this four-story art museum. A good way to view the exhibits with kids is with a family guidebook, available in the lobby. The guide, probably best for 6 to 10 year olds, suggests museum routes using photographs of the displays that will be of interest to children. Other pages recommend activities children can complete as they're strolling the museum or at home. Often there are hands-on activities available for children. The museum store is on the first floor, special exhibits on the second floor. The third floor is dedicated to art from Asia, the Near East, Africa, and the Americas; European and U.S. art is on the fourth floor. The fine collection of Northwest Coast Native American pieces on the third floor is outstanding, and the masks on display often fascinate youngsters. And of course, don't miss Hammering Man, a daunting sculpture just outside the museum.

SAM offers a sign language program the first Sunday of each month. Sign language interpreters are available for other programs with two weeks' notice. The former SAM site at Volunteer Park now houses the Seattle Asian Art Museum.

Seattle Public Library

206-386-4636 (Quick Information);
206-386-4190 (general info)

Location: *1000 Fourth Ave.*
Web Site: *www.spl.lid.wa.us*
Days/Hours: *Monday–Thursday, 9 a.m.–9 p.m.; Friday–Saturday, 9 a.m.–*
6 p.m. During the school year also on Sunday, 1 p.m.–5 p.m.

Seattleites check out nearly 6 million books, audio selections, and other materials from the library each year. The Children's Department alone circulates about 2,500 videos a month, plus providing many other services for school-age children. There is usually an excellent summer program with professional performers and workshops, which makes vacation much more bearable. There are two computers in the department that children can sign up to use. Regular tours are no longer available due to changes in staff and scheduling, but tours will be booked on request. When you call, have several options in mind. Special note: Use the Quick Information line when you have a pressing question you can't find an answer to—the staff is amazing at uncovering all kinds of information.

Westlake Park

Location: *Fourth Ave. at Pine St.*
Wheelchair/Stroller Access: *Yes*

This red-brick park in the heart of the retail shopping core lures children to run through its water walls in the warm weather months. Youngsters old enough to read can check out the magical tale printed on tiles near both the fountain's entrance and exit. A narrow bridge through the center of these fountains is a favorite for kids who can't resist getting wet. In December, it's the site of the holiday carousel, offering free rides.

Places to Eat and Stay

Four Seasons Olympic

206-621-1700

Location: *411 University St.*
Wheelchair/Stroller Access: *Yes*

For a stroll or a stay, there's an elegant world inside the Four Seasons Olympic Hotel. For many families, a year-round favorite is the Children's Afternoon Tea in the Garden Court restaurant, daily between 3 p.m. and 5 p.m. It features a selection of petit fours, fruit breads, scones with Devonshire cream and strawberry preserves, and a pot of brewed tea for

$8.75 per person. Before the Christmas holidays, walk the lobby to see festive Yuletide trees, each adorned with decorations marking the names of patients at Children's Hospital and Regional Medical Center.

Another December favorite is the annual Teddy Bear Suite. The concierge will direct you to this room decorated with a multitude of bears. Bear ornaments, a tea table with cookies and other delightful holiday dÉcor adorns the room. Sneak a peak inside the bathroom: Teddies are even in the tub!

Overnight guests will find everything from Nintendo games to infant bathtubs. Cribs arrive with teddy bears ready for hugging. Guests also may ask for special hotel tours for children, including a peek inside the pastry kitchen.

Westin Hotel   206-728-1000

Location: 1900 Fifth Ave.
Days/Hours: Varies per restaurant or service
Wheelchair/Stroller Access: Yes

The posh Westin Hotel does welcome kids as visitors and guests. For guests staying in the hotel, the Westin Kids Club does have some privileges, such as express meal service by advance request, special children's menu, lock-out service on in-room movies, special laundry prices for children's clothing, children's bicycle seats, jogging strollers, and emergency diapers (all where applicable). Another advantage: Most rooms are child safety-proofed. Roy's is the main restaurant at the hotel; for lunch they do offer a pb and j and banana sandwich and other junior foods. For quicker meals, the Golden Bagel (open 6 a.m. to 9 p.m.) has breakfast and lunch choices, plus a long list of smoothies and juices. Would you believe Fresh Wheat Grass Juice?

Stores to Browse

Channel 9 Store   206-682-8198 (Seattle);
425-861-1899 (Redmond)

Location: In Rainier Square at 1308 Fourth Ave., and at Redmond's Town Center
Web Site: www.kcts.org
Days/Hours: Seattle: Monday–Saturday, 10 a.m.–6 p.m., Sunday, noon–5 p.m.
Redmond: Monday–Saturday, 10 a.m.–8 p.m.; Sunday, 10 a.m.–6 p.m.
Wheelchair/Stroller Access: Yes

Young fans of *Sesame Street, Barney the Dinosaur, Bill Nye the Science Guy, Magic School Bus, Wishbone, Arthur,* and other educational children's programs will most certainly like this store. It features a vast collection of books, puzzles, games, instructional toys, and more from their favorite PBS shows seen locally on KCTS/Channel 9. Late November is a festive time to visit because more than a dozen Christmas trees decorated with animated themes enliven Rainier Square. The trees are a Children's Hospital and Regional Medical Center fund-raiser.

FAO Schwarz   206-442-9500 (Seattle); 425-646-9500 (Bellevue)

Location: 1420 Fifth Ave; also at Bellevue Square in Bellevue
Web Site: www.faoschwarz.com
Days/Hours: Seattle: Monday–Saturday, 10 a.m.–7 p.m.; Sunday, 11 a.m.–
*   6 p.m. Bellevue: Monday–Saturday, 9:30 a.m.–9 p.m.; Sunday,*
*   11 a.m.–6 p.m.*
Wheelchair/Stroller Access: Yes

Seattle's trendiest toys can be found in this shop. Some of the stuffed animals talk to visitors, there are dozens of glamour dolls to choose from in the Barbie wing, and an FAO Schweetz has been added inside to sell candy, candy, and more candy.

REI: Recreational Equipment Inc.   206-223-1944

Location: 222 Yale Ave. N.
Web Site: www.rei.com
Days/Hours: Monday–Friday, 10 a.m.–9 p.m.; Saturday, 9 a.m.–9 p.m.;
*   Sunday, 9 a.m.–6 p.m.*
Wheelchair/Stroller Access: Yes, in most places

Outdoorsy persons come here to hide for hours. Although indoors, it's make-believe outdoors, with lots of opportunities to try out equipment in relatively real situations. Small ones can slide down a mountain, crawl through a cave, or wade through an imaginary river. Older kids can test hiking boots by trekking across an indoor path or scale a three-story boulder simulating rock-climbing lessons. There's even an outside bicycling path (around the store's perimeter) if you're bike-shopping. If you become an REI member, you'll become aware of many other values as well.

THE SEATTLE CENTER

The Seattle Center

Location: Denny Way and Fifth Ave. N.
Events Line: 206-674-8582
Web Site: *www.seattlecenter.com*

The Seattle Center is open year-round, but some exhibits and areas operate seasonally. Daily information is available by calling the events line listed above; this is a wise way to decide on your parking options. Watch the newspapers for the popular annual festivals that take place here; almost all have something to attract families. In early May, more than 70,000 people flock to the annual Seattle International Children's Festival. This week-long cultural arts event is the largest of its kind in the country, with nearly 300 performances from almost a dozen countries. Dance, theater, and musical productions with young and adult performers are geared to children and their families. Tickets range from $5 to $13, depending on the performance.

As you stroll the grounds, be sure to set aside some time for the International Fountain, a lighted, musically synchronized waterworks extravaganza.

Places to Go

Boeing IMAX Theater   *206-443-IMAX*

Location: Pacific Science Center
Days/Hours: *Daily from 11 a.m., plus evening shows on weekends*
Admission: *Matinee admission is $5.50/ages 14 or older; $4.50/seniors and students 6–13; $3.50/children 2–5; free/children 2 and younger*
Wheelchair/Stroller Access: *Yes*

On a screen three and a half stories high and sixty feet wide, viewers are nearly engulfed in the nature and science films shown here. Shows change periodically and most are an hour long; best to call for a current schedule. By late 1998, the Boeing IMAX Theater will feature three-dimensional technology.

The Children's Museum   206-441-1768 *(reservations)*

Location: Lower level of Seattle Center House
Days/Hours: Monday–Friday, 10 a.m.–5 p.m.; Saturday–Sunday, 10 a.m.–
   6 p.m.
Admission: $4/adults; $5.50/children over 1 year; free/children younger than
   12 months. On the first Tuesday of each month, between 4 p.m. and 8
   p.m., visitors are admitted on a "pay what you can" basis.
Wheelchair/Stroller Access: Yes, on the first level from the east and west
   sides

The centerpiece of the museum is a mountain forest so large it grows from the lower level of the Seattle Center House into the main floor dining area. It's amazing the global ground they cover here. Children may explore nature in one corner . . . and a few yards away take an entertaining lesson in culture from Africa, China, or some other part of the world in the Global Village exhibit. Rotating exhibits frequently reflect different nations and their food, dance, architecture, art, and music. The exhibits are hands-on, participatory learning, and meant to challenge the imagination, too.

Permanent displays include Cog City, where children can track the route of ping-pong-sized balls as they roll varying paths through tubes and pipes, and a child-size neighborhood with a firetruck, grocery store, restaurant, and more. Even infants and toddlers become explorers in the Discovery Bay, a padded toy area for climbing and romping.

Fun Forest   206-728-1585

Location: Seattle Center Grounds
Days/Hours: Memorial Day through Labor Day: daily, 11 a.m.–midnight.
   Pavilion open year-round, but outside attractions open weekends only,
   spring and fall; outside rides typically are closed during the winter
   months.
Admission: Free but tickets to rides run about 95¢; rides vary in the number
   of tickets required.
Wheelchair/Stroller Access: Yes

The center's had a facelift, and the makeover provides a new layout for family games and activities. Amusement rides for preschoolers and younger tots are separated from the head-spinning, stomach-turning, thrill rides for older children and adults. And a pavilion designed for arcade games and miniature golf has some open-air walls, ideal for our varying climate. The eighteen-hole mini-golf course is somewhat challenging, good for all ages; rounds cost $4 per person.

Laser Show   206-443-2850

Location: Pacific Science Center
Days/Hours: Most shows are after 7 p.m., Tuesday–Saturday; weekend
    matinees vary for younger children
Admission: $3 to $6.75, depending on the show's time and day.
Wheelchair/Stroller Access: Yes

It's important to check the schedule for the musical laser light shows
here because while most weekday and weekend night shows are geared
for teens and adults, Saturday and Sunday matinees may feature The
Beatles and *The Wizard of Oz*, which are much more appropriate for
younger children. Many visitors bypass the reclining chairs and opt for a
seat on the floor to get the full view of the ceiling production set to 4,500
watts of compact disk-quality sounds. For a few more dollars, laser show
admission is included in the price of a Pacific Science Center ticket.

Monorail

Location: Terminals at Fifth Ave. and Pine St. at the third floor of Westlake
    Center and at the Seattle Center near the Space Needle
Web Site: www.seattlecenter.com
Days/Hours: Summer: daily, 9 a.m.–midnight. The rest of the year: Sunday–
    Thursday, 9 a.m.–9 p.m.; Friday–Saturday, 9 a.m.–midnight.
Admission: One-way: $1/adults; 75¢/children 5–11; free/children 4 and
    under
Wheelchair/Stroller Access: Yes

This quick two-minute connection between the Seattle Center and
Westlake Center is fast, but not too fast for the small set. The large windows on the glass car give children a view of the city as they rush past on
their way to the downtown retail shopping area.

Pacific Science Center   206-443-2001

Location: Under the white arches
Web Site: www.pacsci.org
Days/Hours: Mid-June–Labor Day: daily, 10 a.m.–6 p.m. The rest of the
    year: Monday–Friday, 10 a.m.–5 p.m.; Saturday and Sunday, 10 a.m.–
    6 p.m.
Admission: $7.50/ages 14 or older; $5.50/students 6–13 years; $3.50/children

2–5; free/children 2 and younger. For $2 more per person, see an IMAX or laser matinee. All prices are subject to change.
Wheelchair/Stroller Access: *Yes*

Children can always spot the Pacific Science Center, with its eye-catching white arches over large reflecting pools. Here there are dozens of hands-on activities for all ages. Toddlers will find a special room just for them, complete with bubble and water play, drums, and climbing/crawling toys. School-age children are more attracted to the Tech Zone's virtual reality games, robotics, and computers. Many locals visit several times a year to catch the rotating exhibits. Favorite times to visit include the August Bubble Festival, the Halloween weekend haunted science center, and—most popular of all—Thanksgiving weekend's Model Railroad show. Exhibit admission includes all exhibits plus a planetarium show.

SeaDogs   206-28C-DOGS

Location: KeyArena
Web Site: Available only on a seasonal basis
Days/Hours: June–September: 7 p.m. on game nights
Admission: $9.50/adults; $6.50/children 12 and younger
Wheelchair/Stroller Access: Yes

Half-time shows with kicking contests and other interactive games make young soccer fans feel like they're part of the action. This local indoor soccer team has worked hard to build an audience, and it's growing each year. After the match, children may go on the field to practice kicking like the pros do. Special birthday party packages are available for groups of fifteen or more.

Seattle Children's Theatre   206-441-3322 (tickets)

Location: Charlotte Martin Theatre on the west side of Seattle Center
Web Site: www.sct.org
Days/Hours: Call ahead for performance schedules
Admission: $18/adults; $12/children (single tickets—prices subject to change)
Wheelchair/Stroller Access: Yes

Considered one of the country's finest children's theaters, SCT attracts award-winning productions to its two stages at Charlotte Martin Theater. Most plays are designed for youngsters 6 to 12 years, but several appeal to children as young as 4 years. Look for one Shakespeare or other classic production each season, too. Some theatergoers love to sit on the carpeted area in the front of the comfy seats, getting as close as they can to the stage. Season ticket holders receive advance-show guides that help parents prepare their children with tips on what to watch for in the production.

Check the schedule for performances that are signed for the hearing impaired. Director Howie Seago and his acting brother, Billy, also present special productions here for deaf and hearing audiences. Off stage, classes in mask-making, comedy, movement, and dance for children 4 1/2 to 19 years are available each quarter.

Seattle Reign

206-628-088 (tickets)

Location: *Home games in the Mercer Arena*
Web Site: *www.seattlereign.com*
Days/Hours: *Mid-October–mid-March: most games are 7 or 7:30 p.m.*
Admission: *Ranges from $11–$35; groups of fifteen or more receive a $3 per ticket discount; babies admitted free.*
Wheelchair/Stroller Access: *Yes*

This professional women's basketball team has captured Seattle hearts and is attracting wonderful crowds. The players are excellent role models for young athletes. and spend time signing autographs after every game. The team mascot is Triumph, a very special kind of bird; half-time shows often feature performances by youth groups.

Seattle Sonics

206-283-DUNK (season tickets);
206-628-0888 (single tickets)

Location: *190 Queen Anne Ave. N.*
Web Site: *www.nba.com*
Days/Hours: *Preseason games begin in early October; regular season starts in November and runs through mid-May. Game times vary.*
Admission: *Vary according to seating; call ticket office for current information*
Wheelchair/Stroller Access: *Yes*

Now at home in the KeyArena, the Seattle Sonics provide slam-dunking action for all ages. During breaks in the game action, children love trying to catch the prizes dropped by the radio-controlled mini-blimp. At half time, fans compete in hoop shoot contests to win prizes.

Seattle Symphony

206-215-4700

Location: *Seattle Center, Mercer St.; the Symphony's new home, Benaroya Hall, opens in late 1998*
Wheelchair/Stroller Access: *Yes*

Classical music is fast becoming de rigueur for the younger set. With new studies showing that classical music can enhance a newborn's learning ability, parents and educators are looking at the world of classical music with new eyes. Seattle Symphony has long been a proponent of "start 'em young!" There are a number of new programs available to

A production of the Seattle Children's Theatre. PHOTO BY CHRIS BENNION
COURTESY THE SEATTLE CHILDREN'S THEATRE.

youngsters and families, including open rehearsals for students and Symphony on Wheels—a cargo van visiting elementary schools. Immensely popular for families is the "Discover Music" five-concert series for children ages 6 to 10. Concerts are one hour long and begin at 11 a.m., but parents and kids can arrive early to participate in preconcert lobby activities. This is fun! But don't be afraid to bring your child to an adult concert, even if you only stay until intermission. It is necessary to discuss the "rules and regs" prior to the concert. Call the Symphony office for information.

Seattle Thunderbirds

206-728-9124 to order tickets

Location: 2505 Third Ave.
Days/Hours: Office: September–March: Monday–Friday, 9 a.m.–5 p.m.
Wheelchair/Stroller Access: Yes

For a team that plays on ice, this semi-pro hockey team can get really hot. Some fans like sitting right behind the players box to hear the coach bark orders. The season runs October through March. Watch for cross-state rivalries in Spokane and Tri-Cities.

Space Needle

206-443-2100

Web Site: www.spaceneedle.com
Days/Hours: Monday–Saturday, 8 a.m.–midnight; Sunday, 8 a.m.–midnight
Admission: $8.50/adults; $7/seniors; $4/students 5 to 12; free/children 4 and younger.
Wheelchair/Stroller Access: Yes

The Needle is a magnet to both visitors and natives, especially those locals treating out-of-town guests. The glass elevators whisk you in seconds to the Observation Deck or restaurant for a 360-degree view of the city, sound, mountains, and outlying islands (weather permitting). Four gift shops at street level sell local and regional souvenirs. See the Space Needle Restaurant listing for dining information.

Places to Eat

Seattle Center House

Days/Hours: Labor Day–Memorial Day: daily, 11 a.m.–6 p.m. The rest of the year: Sunday–Thursday, 11 a.m.–8 p.m.; Friday–Saturday, 11 a.m.– 9 p.m.
Wheelchair/Stroller Access: Yes

From hot dogs to fish-and-chips, pizza or Chinese food, the food court on the main floor of the Seattle Center House offers more than a dozen dining choices. Come to buy or nibble or just wander and watch activities in the performing arts area on the main level. Surrounding shops carry traditional and funky souvenirs. Almost daily entertainment often includes local bands, energetic youth dance groups, square dancers, and other cultural performances.

Space Needle Restaurant   206-443-2100

Days/Hours: Daily, 8 a.m.–10:30 p.m.
Wheelchair/Stroller Access: Yes, except restrooms. There's a restroom for the disabled on the 100-foot-deck; take elevator.

Your eyes aren't playing tricks on you. The restaurant on top of the 605-foot-tall Space Needle is revolving constantly to give you a 360-degree view while you remain seated. Prices are somewhat upscale, but locals and out-of-town visitors find it worth those special-occasion visits with children. Consider ordering the Space Needle punch for children; it comes in a plastic Space Needle cup kids can take home as a souvenir. Otherwise, the children's menu features burgers, fish, and pizza.

Store to Browse

Champion's   206-284-1980

Location: 124 Denny Way
Days/Hours: Monday–Friday, 9 a.m.–7 p.m.; Saturday, 9 a.m.–6 p.m.;
Sunday, 11 a.m.–5 p.m.
Wheelchair/Stroller Access: No

On Denny Way, a few blocks above Elliott Bay, this party palace offers the wildest costumes around. Selection is amazing, from Halloween goblins and ghouls to some of your favorite celebrities. Get-ups can be rented or purchased, but it's wise to get in early for Halloween. Party supplies include piñatas, stickers, balloons, party favors, and more.

Helpful Phone Numbers:

Seattle Public Library Quick Information: 206-386-4636

Seattle/King County Convention and Visitors Bureau: 206-461-5840

Seattle Parks and Recreation Department information and recreation scheduling: 206-684-4075

Seattle Parks and Recreation Department Youth Sports Information: 206-684-7091

King County Library System: 425-462-9600 (the "answer line"); 206-684-4494 (TDD)

Storytime at a branch of the King County Public Library. PHOTO COURTESY KING COUNTY LIBRARY SYSTEM

CHAPTER
2

In and Around Seattle

• •

- **Magnolia**, north of downtown, was named by early settlers who mistook the elegant madrona trees for magnolias. The stroll along Magnolia Blvd. is most appealing for its view of the Sound and of the ships and ferries that ply the waters. Nearby Queen Anne was named for the architectural style favored by early residents in the neighborhood. Today's residents often walk to the Seattle Center for entertainment.

- **Ballard, Wallingford, Fremont, Green Lake, Greenwood**, and several other neighborhoods are north of Lake Union and the ship canal. Public art is a distinctive feature here, especially the great Viking statue on Ballard's Shilshole Ave. and "Waiting for the Interurban," a fascinating sculpture of bus riders in Fremont. The Troll emerges from under the north end of the Aurora Bridge between Wallingford and Fremont.

- Also north, but separated from Lake Union by I-5, are the **University District** and **Sand Point**. Here much of the University of Washington's community resides. Second-guessing the Montlake Bridge's raising and lowering has become an art form.

- Northeast lie **Lake City, Bothell**, and **Kenmore**, home to the Kenmore Air Harbor and connected to much of the Greater Seattle area by the Burke-Gilman Trail.

- East of the city center are **Madison Park, Capitol Hill, Montlake**, and **Madrona**. At the foot of Madison St. on your way to Lake Washington, the Washington Park Arboretum is one of the city's most popular focal points, housing walking trails, athletic fields, and the lovely Japanese Garden. Capitol Hill's Broadway district can be a cosmopolitan twenty-four-hour bustle of activity; Madison Park is more sedate. Driving through Washington Park, you'll see some of the city's oldest, most elegant homes.

- In South Seattle, **Mount Baker, Seward Park, Beacon Hill,** and **Rainier Valley** are melting pots, housing much of the city's diverse ethnic mix. In summer, Seward Park is humming with walkers, bikers, and swimmers, and literally taken over by Seafair crowds in early August.

- **West Seattle**, west of the downtown area, has both the new and the old to commend it. The Fauntleroy ferry (to Vashon Island) is sequestered in this neighborhood, while industrial growth sprawls along the water, and one of the city's most magnificent views can be seen from Alki Beach (or at the end of a gravel road off West Marginal Way at Dakota St.). Alki is easily one of the most popular meeting and greeting places, with multitudes coming to fly kites and walk the shores. It was at Alki that the Arthur Denny party arrived in 1851, with some of the first white women to live in Seattle.

For other opportunities for family activities, see Trip Planning Resources in Washington State in the Appendix at the back of the book.

MAGNOLIA AND QUEEN ANNE

Places to Go

Bhy Kracke

Location: On Queen Anne at Bigelow Ave. N. and Comstock Pl.
Web Site: www.pan.ci.seattle.wa.us/seattle/parks/home.htm

Neighborhood children love the playground here, and parents watching them enjoy the lattice-laced arbor at this little park (pronounced "by cracky"). The steep, ivy-covered hillside is lush with azaleas and rhododendrons. Some visitors come here at night to catch a splendid view of the city's lights.

Daybreak Star Art Center/United Indians   206-285-4425

Location: North side of Discovery Park
Days/Hours: Monday–Saturday, 10 a.m.–5 p.m.; Sunday, noon–5 p.m.

Tours: *$2/visitor; group must be at least fifteen people; reservations needed prior to visit; discount rates are available for children.*
Wheelchair/Stroller Access: Yes

The upper level of this Native American center houses a collection of artwork from Northwest Native Americans as well as many other North American tribes. You'll find beadwork, baskets, Kachina cornhusks, Seminole and Miccosukee dolls, plus a major collection of contemporary works by Native American artists featuring large murals and sculpted pieces. On the second Saturday of the month, November through April, organizers host an Indian Art Mart between 11 a.m. and 4 p.m. Crafts created by Native Americans are sold here.

Discovery Park   206-386-4236

Location: 36th Ave. W. and W. Government Way, Magnolia
Web Site: www.pan.ci.seattle.wa.us/seattle/parks/home.htm
Days/Hours: Daily, dawn to dusk. Visitors Center: 8:30 a.m.–5 p.m.; closed major holidays
Tours: Yes, called Nature Walks, led by park naturalists, 2 p.m. on Saturdays; reservations needed by the morning of the walk
Wheelchair/Stroller Access: Yes

With five hundred acres and four parks in one—cliffs, beach, meadows, and forest—there's always something to explore here. Visit the Wolf Tree Nature Trail, a self-guided educational quarter-mile walk; there's a brochure at the Visitors Center near the park's entrance. Discovery Park has many nesting birds, some quite rare, and many small wildlife. Educational programs include "Bird Observation Tours" and "Meet the Ranger." Call for a schedule of modestly priced group programs about polliwogs, spiders, and snakes planned for preschoolers through eighth graders. Daybreak Star Art Center/United Indians is located in Discovery Park.

Interbay Family Golf Center's Garden Golf   206-285-2200

Location: West side of 15th Ave. W. near Wheeler St.
Days/Hours: Vary, best to call ahead
Wheelchair/Stroller Access: Strollers are easy to maneuver on course; wheelchairs are difficult. Pro shop is accessible to both.

Not your traditional miniature golf course, this garden golf layout appeals to golfers eager to improve their putting skills. Set on a lighted eighteen-hole layout, the course offers natural contours and hills with no artificial obstacles; landscaping is exceptional. Each hole features a par, and the course is designed with two eight- to ten-foot-high waterfalls, with streams, ponds, or water cascading down rocks near every green.

Course designers hope golfing parents will teach their children putting skills here. An adjacent, full-size eighteen-hole course is slated to open in 1998.

Seattle Funplex   *206-285-7842*

Location: Near Magnolia at 1535 15th Ave W., just west of the Magnolia
    Bridge
Days/Hours: Daily; hours change seasonally
Admission: None; each game is individually priced
Wheelchair/Stroller Access: Yes

Families with children with a wide range of ages will find dozens of indoor games inside this center. There's mini-golf, video games, batting cages, go-karts, and laser tag for older children and adults. Younger children like the toddlers' play area and "jungle bouncer," an inflatable arena of soft plastic floors and mesh walls designed for jumping kids. There's also a full-service concession area. Special group rates and birthday party packages are available. Afternoons and early evenings are the best time to visit with younger children; teens and young adults play here later. An eighteen-hole round of mini-golf is $3.50 for adults and $3 for those 12 or younger; unlimited golf play is $4.50 for adults and $4 for kids.

Places to Eat

Chinook's at Salmon Bay   *206-283-HOOK*

Location: At Fisherman's Terminal, just south of the Ballard Bridge
Days/Hours: Sunday, 7:30 a.m.–10 p.m.; Monday–Thursday, 11 a.m.–
    10 p.m.; Friday, 11 a.m.–11 p.m.; Saturday, 7:30 a.m.–11 p.m.
Wheelchair/Stroller Access: Yes

Their great view of the Seattle Fishing Terminal is a drawing card here, as is the popular menu specializing in seafood. Little Chinooks get a placemat menu with crayons and a choice of fish 'n chips, prawns, burgers, or a grilled cheese sandwich. Breakfast scones are a favorite, plus a scrumptious blackberry cobbler (in season).

Zi Pani (formerly Bruegger's Bagels)

206-284-9684 (Mercer St.); 206-524-3369 (Greenlake);
425-867-5720 (for other locations)

Locations: 23 Mercer St., near Seattle Center; 7200 Green Lake Dr. N.
Days/Hours: Monday–Friday, 6 a.m.–7 p.m.; Saturday–Sunday, 7 a.m.–7 p.m.
Wheelchair/Stroller Access: Yes

There are numerous Zi Pani locations in the Greater King County area; these two are especially popular. The $2.99 special meal deal here is attractive—a bagel, chips, soft drink or milk, and a prize provided by one of this restaurant's education partners: the Seattle Aquarium, Northwest Trek, Woodland Park Zoo, Pacific Science Center, and Museum of Flight. The meal comes with a trading card and a coupon for free admission to one of these destinations when a paying adult accompanies a child. If they're baking while you're there, you can watch through a window to see the bagels boiling in the big kettle and the baker slide the bagels into the oven (this will vary from store to store).

NORTHWEST NEIGHBORHOODS

Fremont, Wallingford, Green Lake, Bitter Lake, Ballard, Carkeek, and Phinney Ridge

Places to Go

The Bathhouse Theater

206-524-9108;
206-524-9109 (recorded information)

Location: 7312 W. Greenlake Dr. N.
Days/Hours: Box Office: Tuesday–Sunday, noon–7 p.m.
Wheelchair/Stroller Access: Four steps at entry; staff will assist

This theater group shows at least two productions a year suitable for children, including a musical in the summer. Admission prices vary; call for information. No babies, please. Adequate free parking.

Bitter Lake Community Center Wading Pool 206-684-7524

Location: 13040 Greenwood Ave. N.
Days/Hours: Varies, usually open daily, June through Labor Day
Wheelchair/Stroller Access: Yes

Open most summer days when it's not raining, this splash-around pool is hot weather heaven for toddlers. It's emptied at night and refilled daily with chlorinated water. Just off N.E. 130th St., you'll find parking and play-climbing equipment, too.

Carkeek Park

Location: North of Greenwood at N.W. Carkeek Park Rd. and Ninth Ave.
N.W., near N.W. 110th St.
Web Site: www.pan.ci.seattle.wa.us/seattle/parks/home.htm

A wilderness park of 180 forested acres, Carkeek rests on a hill above its Puget Sound beach. European-style playground equipment attracts young children. The swings near the picnic shelter are among the most popular; on a clear day, they offer incredible views of the Olympic Mountains. A hiking trail with an Olympic Mountains view runs to the hill's edge. Just inside the main gate is an Archery Range; bring your own bows and arrows. Model airplanes are welcome on the grassy area; check with the Park Department for competitions in the spring and summer. Permanent fire pits are located on the beach. Dangerous railroad tracks running through this park have been fenced off, but be aware of them. A pedestrian bridge links the beach and park land.

Gas Works Park

Location: Near Wallingford at Northlake Way and Meridian; from Aurora
Ave., take Northlake Way east and follow Lake Union's north shore.
Wheelchair/Stroller Access: Yes
Web Site: www.pan.ci.seattle.wa.us/seattle/parks/home.htm

Gas Works Parks is one of Seattle's favorite play places for kids. Outside, children can climb up the park's highest hill to study the sundial, then roll down the grassy mound to the bottom. Under cover, they can scale the wheels and gears of an old gas works' plant equipment. Breezes at the north shore of Lake Union make this park one of the best kite-flying destinations in the city. It's the place to be to catch the annual Fourth of July fireworks show; it's also a popular entry to the paved Burke-Gilman Trail for bicyclists, pedestrians, and in-line skaters.

Green Lake

Location: E. Green Lake Dr. N. at W. Green Lake Dr.
Days/Hours: Dawn to dusk
Wheelchair/Stroller Access: Yes
Web Site: www.pan.ci.seattle.wa.us/seattle/parks/home.htm

This tree-lined, lakefront park is the city's busiest meeting place for active Seattleites of all ages. They come from all over to skate, bike, walk, jog, and stroll the meandering 2.8-mile asphalt path that encircles the lake. A line down the middle of the path dictates pedestrians on one side, skaters and bicyclists on the other.

On the northeast side are tennis courts, playfields, an indoor swimming pool, gymnasium, canoe rentals, a sandy beach with a lifeguard in the summer, and a community center. Classes for swimming and other recreation and leisure activities are taught by city parks department staff. Behind the community center is a playground with a dozen swings, climbing toys, and slides.

The northwest side of the park is home to the Bathhouse Theater and an island game preserve, as well as fishing piers where anglers reel in some of the trout stocked here annually. Picnic tables, lawn bowling, horseshoes, and a pitch-and-putt course take up the park's south side.

One of the most beautiful events during the winter holidays is the Luminaria, in the first or second week of December—when literally hundreds of candles sheltered within paper bags line the path around the lake, and carolers fill the night air with holiday music.

Green Lake Boat Rental   *206-527-0171*

Location: 7351 E. Greenlake Dr. N.,
Days/Hours: Hours will vary; usually open from April–September

If the urge to hit the water at Green Lake in a canoe, paddleboat, kayak, or rowboat is irresistible, rent one here. Teens as young as 14 with experience may rent their own boats, perhaps for a trip to the lake's island; younger children less experienced are advised to try it with an adult in a boat. Paddleboats, rowboats, and canoes rent for $8 an hour; kayaks are $10 an hour; wind surfboards and sailboats are $12 an hour. Life jackets are provided, but parents of children weighing less than twenty-five pounds may want to bring their own for the best fit.

Green Lake Wading Pool

206-684-7796 (Seattle wading pool hotline)

Location: *N. 73rd St. and W. Green Lake Way*
Days/Hours: *Varies, but typically open June–Labor Day*

Parking is not easy here—the closest is on-street along W. Green Lake Way. But when the weather is warm, this pool is filled daily with clean, chlorinated water for lots of splashing. There's little shade for shelter during midday sun, so many families often show up later in the day.

Lake Washington Ship Canal and Hiram Chittenden Locks (also known as the Ballard Locks)

206-783-7001; 206-783-7059 (tours)

Location: *In Ballard at 3015 N.W. 54th St. From Elliott Ave., cross the Ballard Bridge to 15th Ave. N.W. Turn west on Market St. and drive about fifteen blocks.*
Days/Hours: *Daily, 7 a.m.–9 p.m. Visitors Center: June–September: daily, 11 a.m.–7 p.m. October–May: Thursday–Monday, 11 a.m.–5 p.m.*
Tours: *Yes; appointments required for group tours, which usually last about an hour. Summer tours are daily at 1 p.m. and 3 p.m. From October–May, tours are Saturdays and Sundays at 2 p.m.*
Age Minimum: *5 years old*
Wheelchair/Stroller Access: *Yes; there are ramps to the fish ladder to help physically challenged visitors.*

It looks as though you could almost reach out and grab the fish as they migrate through the fish ladders at these boating locks, which is easily one of our city's most popular tourist attractions.

Your tour begins in the Visitors Center with the history of the locks, then takes you to the immaculately landscaped gardens, and finally to the locks. You'll learn about the fish cycle at the fish ladder, which has underwater viewing designed to allow you to watch salmon returning to their spawning grounds. It's quite exciting at the height of the season—many families visit annually.

Thousands of boats pass between Lake Washington and Puget Sound via these locks. Commodore Park, adjacent to the locks on the south side, is a delightful park setting, completely fenced. The park and grounds at the north side of the locks close at 9 p.m. daily. Grounds adjacent are well-lit, with convenient restrooms and bike racks. It's a good walk, so wear comfortable shoes and warm outer clothing in cool weather.

Nordic Heritage Museum   206-789-5707

Location: 3014 N.W. 67th, Ballard
Days/Hours: Tuesday–Saturday, 10 a.m.–4 p.m.; Sunday, noon–4 p.m.
Admission: $4/adults; $3/seniors and college students; $2/students 5 to 17;
   free/children 4 and younger.
Tours: Yes; self-guided
Wheelchair/Stroller Access: Yes

Scandinavian Americans take great pride in the story of the immigration that brought their families to this country. Displays cover Sweden, Denmark, Norway, Finland, and Iceland; exhibits retrace local Scandinavians' steps across the Atlantic to Ellis Island. Each nationality has its own display room on the second floor. Lively holiday celebrations, including Christmas and summer Tivoli events, are hosted here with hands-on activities and crafts for children. During tours and special children's events, curators share fascinating history-come-to-life lessons. Exhibits highlight the fishing, farming, and logging work immigrants performed when they arrived in the U.S. Watch local papers for weekend performances and art and music demonstrations, or call ahead for a current schedule

Northwest Outdoor Center   206-281-9694

Location: 210 Westlake N.
Days/Hours: Varies; call for a schedule
Wheelchair/Stroller Access: Yes

Weather willing, children strong enough to paddle a two-person kayak can team up with an adult at this boating facility on Lake Union. Different trips have different rates, so it's wise to call ahead. For many families with children 10 or older, the guided "full moon paddles" during the summer are a hit.

Stone Gardens (also known as Kids Climb at
Stone Gardens)   206-781-9828

Location: 2839 N.W. Market St. in Ballard
Web Site: www.stonegardens.com
Days/Hours: Kids Climb: Friday, 6 p.m.–8 p.m.; Saturday, 10 a.m.–1 p.m.
Wheelchair/Stroller Access: For observation only

The kids who drove you crazy climbing places from which they couldn't get down will love the challenges at this indoor rock climbing center. Instructors provide equipment and safety instruction as they teach the proper ways to climb. Novel idea for a birthday party—celebrate with a two-hour class with three to four children per instructor; all gear is provided. Prices are about $20 per session per child. Most parents have to peel their kids off the wall after a session.

The Troll

Location: Under the north end of the Aurora Bridge, between Wallingford and Fremont
Wheelchair/Stroller Access: Up to the base on the city sidewalk

Tots like to play "Three Billy Goats Gruff" with this oddball sculpture tucked under the base of the Aurora Bridge. Scope out the Troll before letting the kids start climbing—some visitors leave garbage on this whimsical guy.

Woodland Park

Location: N. 50th at Green Lake Way N.
Web Site: www.pan.ci.seattle.wa.us/seattle/parks/home.htm

There's more here than just the city's zoo. You can play tennis, soccer, softball, or just let the kids run within the greenbelt, which is as large as the zoo. The park's upper and lower sections, on the east side of Aurora Ave., are linked by three pedestrian bridges. Wooded trails and pleasant picnic areas with grassy hills overlooking Green Lake are accessible from parking lots off Aurora Ave. and from N. 50th St.

Woodland Park Zoo   *206-684-4800 (recorded general information)*

Location: Between Green Lake and Ballard on Phinney Ridge at Fremont Ave. N.
Web Site: www.zoo.org
Days/Hours: April–mid-October: daily, 9:30 a.m.–6 p.m. Mid-October–March: 9:30 a.m.–4 p.m.
Admission: $8/adults; $7.45/seniors; $7.25/college students with school ID; $5.50/disabled visitors and students 6–17 ; $3.25/children 3–5; free/children 2 and younger. Ask about a 50¢ to $1 discount for King County residents. Admission may be charged to credit cards. A $3.50 car or van fee or a $10 bus fee is charged in the parking lot.
Wheelchair/Stroller Access: Yes; strollers to rent are $3, wheelchairs $5 at South Gate Visitors Center

Everyone loves to visit the Woodland Park Zoo again and again—there's always something new. Kids go buggy over the indoor Bug World Adventures with Arthropods exhibit which opened in fall of 1997. Twenty different species of insects live here, from those in your own backyard to those from the temperate forest, desert, savanna, and tropics. Just prior to Bug World, the Trail of Vines exhibit debuted, with its catwalk around the animated orangutan exhibit. The six-acre Northern Trail of Alaska exhibit features river otters, brown bears, wolves, and elk, and offers kid-sized caves for spying on the bears. Near the Family Farm, 3 to 10 year olds can burn off energy climbing on the "spider web," inside the "turtle shells" or on some of the other animal-style toys.

Ranked one of the top ten zoos in the country, Woodland Park Zoo has created realistic habitats for its creatures. A specially designed and nationally acclaimed Asian tropical forest houses the elephants; ask about schedules for the elephant shows. Bats and other night creatures live in the Nocturnal House. Giraffes and zebras roam in the Africa-like savanna, and jumbo hippopotami lurk under water. We can't resist telling you about the gardener's delight—Zoo Doo, the most excellent mulch you can find, available by calling their hotline, 206-625-POOP.

Please note two important rules here: No pets except Seeing Eye Dogs are allowed; and don't feed the animals, because their diets are strictly controlled. Visitors without diet restrictions can buy hot dogs, popcorn, and soft drinks here.

Places to Eat

Honey Bear Bakery   *206-545-7296*

Location: Near Green Lake at 2106 N. 55th
Days/Hours: Weekdays, 6 a.m.–10 p.m.; weekends, 6 a.m.–11 p.m.
Wheelchair/Stroller Access: Yes

Visitors to Woodland Park Zoo and Green Lake often include the Honey Bear in their outing. Some of the most delicious coffee break and dessert treats are here, and most are made from whole wheat ingredients and honey. Wonderfully hearty soups and chili are served daily. During cold winter days, hot spiced cider and hot chocolate are perfect.

Stores to Browse

Archie McPhee and Co.   *206-545-8344*

Location: 3510 Stone Way N., Fremont
Days/Hours: Monday–Saturday, 9 a.m.–7 p.m.; Sunday, 10 a.m.–7 p.m.
Wheelchair/Stroller Access: Yes, but aisles are narrow
Web Site: www.mcphee.com

This gag gift shop is a magnet for practical jokers—and anyone with a corny sense of humor. It's so popular that the store's mail-order catalog has thousands of customers around the world. For a few dollars, kids can buy fake eyeballs, Groucho Marx glasses-and-nose, glow-in-the-dark plastic bugs, and hundreds of other goofy things.

Painted Fire
206-545-2816

Location: 3601 Fremont Ave. N. in Fremont
Days/Hours: Monday–Wednesday, 9 a.m.–9 p.m.; Thursday, 9 a.m.–11 p.m.;
    Friday and Saturday, 9 a.m.–midnight; Sunday, 10 a.m.–7 p.m.
Wheelchair/Stroller Access: Yes

Open for artists of all ages, this pottery and ceramics shop gives children special classes in creating charming artworks of their own. Class times and fees vary; the usual fee is $6 an hour. The staff here will help you design a birthday party, too.

Secret Garden
206-789-5006

Location: 6115 15th Ave. N.W. in Ballard
Days/Hours: Monday–Wednesday, 10 a.m.–6 p.m.; Thursday– Saturday,
    10 a.m.–8 p.m.; Sunday, 1 p.m.–5 p.m.
Wheelchair/Stroller Access: Yes

Some parents began visiting this cozy bookstore when its home was near Green Lake. Now in Ballard, it still attracts youngsters with the same inviting atmosphere. The "talking bricks" in the alcove are a favorite; otherwise there are carpeted places to sit and read. Ask about midweek readings for preschoolers and Thursday's "jammie" night where little ones come for a reading dressed in their pajamas.

University District and Sand Point
Places to Go

The Burke Museum of Natural History and Culture
206-543-5590 *(recorded information)*; 206-543-7907

Location: At the University of Washington, at N.E. 45th St. and 17th Ave.
    N.E.
Web Site: www.washington.edu/burkemuseum
Days/Hours: Daily, 10 a.m.–5 p.m., and Thursday, 10 a.m.–8 p.m.
Admission: $5.50/adults; $4/seniors; $2.50/students; free/children 5 or
    younger.
Tours: Yes, self-guided, but you can request a docent by calling at least two
    weeks in advance
Wheelchair/Stroller Access: Yes

Walk through a twenty-foot rumbling, glowing volcano in this newly remodeled family museum on the University of Washington campus.

Most of the exhibits on the top of this two-story center are interactive. In the Discovery Center, kids can use a working seismograph and periscope, and then touch real fossils. The museum boasts exhibits spanning 545 million years, from the region's earliest dinosaur residents to a thousand bugs calling Washington home. In the Pacific Voices exhibits, visitors can learn about seventeen different Pacific Rim cultures and experiment with authentic mask replicas or learn a few words in an international language. Exhibits are geared for children 5 and older and best suited to older grade-school and middle-school-age kids. If time allows, stop at the Burke Museum Café on the ground floor for a light snack; lots of campus characters for people-watching.

Burke-Gilman Playground Park

Location: North of Laurelhurst at N.E. 52nd St. and Sand Point Way N.E.

This playground near Children's Hospital and Regional Medical Center is totally accessible to the physically challenged. Look for the innovative water-play equipment, picnic tables, and restrooms. The park is a stop along the Burke-Gilman Trail.

Burke-Gilman/Sammamish Trail

Location: From the north side of the ship canal in Fremont to Redmond
Web Site: www.pan.ci.seattle.wa.us/seattle/parks/home.htm and
www.metrokc.gov/parks/
Wheelchair/Stroller Access: Yes

The twenty-eight-mile Burke-Gilman/Sammamish Trail is the second most used urban recreation trail in the country. It's a flat, paved route for bicycling, in-line skating, and stroller pushing, ten to twelve feet wide in most places, and very attractive to families who are active together. The trail officially begins in Fremont on the north side of the ship canal and extends along the north shore of Lake Union, then continues along the abandoned Burlington–Northern Railroad route for 12.5 miles to Kenmore's Tracy Owen Station (previously named Log Boom Park). The trail then meanders another six miles along the Sammamish Slough to northeast of Bothell where it meets the Sammamish River Trail, a route that follows into Redmond. Maps are available from the City of Seattle's Bicycle and Pedestrian program; call 206-684-7583.

Civic Light Opera   206-363-2809

Location: *South of Lake City neighborhood at Jane Addams Theatre, 11051*
    34th N.E.
Days/Hours: *Box office: Monday and Wednesday, 1 p.m.–4 p.m.*
Wheelchair/Stroller Access: *Yes*

The premium musical productions performed here are terrific entertainment for children 6 and older or those who can sit through a two-
hour show. Performers are local talent. They offer summer workshops
for children 6 to 12 in acting, dancing, and singing. Call for a class listing.

George Pocock Memorial Rowing Center   206-328-0778

Location: *3320 Fuhrman Ave. E.*
Days/Hours: *Monday–Friday, 10 a.m.–6 p.m.*
Wheelchair/Stroller Access: *Yes*

The center was built in memory of Pocock, who was a master builder
of racing shells, used by rowers of all ages. If anyone in the family has an
interest in rowing, the artwork and photos here will be quite exciting.
There are many photographs of rowing celebrities, teams and events that
have made history in Washington state, many shot by nationally known
photographers.

Henry Art Gallery/Faye G. Allen Center
for the Visual Arts

> *206-543-2280; 206-616-8772 (information about upcoming workshops);*
> *206-543-2281 (for tour guides)*

Location: *University of Washington campus, 15th Ave. N.E. at N.E.*
    Campus Parkway
Web Site: *www.henryart.org*
Days/Hours: *Tuesday and Friday–Sunday, 11 a.m.–5 p.m.; Wednesday–*
    Thursday, 11 a.m.–8 p.m.
Admission: *$5/adults; $3.50/seniors; free/U.W. and high school students*
    with student identification and students 13 and younger. Free to
    everyone Thursdays from 5–8 p.m. Ask about group discounts.
Tours: *Guides available; see number above. Please allow at least one adult to*
    each group of ten children.
Wheelchair/Stroller Access: *Yes*

After a long closure for remodeling, the revamped Henry Art Gallery on the University of Washington campus has reopened with greater

opportunities for children. Those ages 8 to 18 will find workshops and classes with artists in varied media—from photography to cut paper silhouettes. Best suited for older children, the gallery specializes in fine art and is noted for featuring local artists, pieces from collections within the state, and important exhibitions of national scope. The $15 million underground addition creates even more space to exhibit American paintings and sculptures. Fees are charged to park in the underground garage next to the museum or at any of the U.W. parking lots.

Laurelhurst Community Center

Location: 4554 N.E. 41st St.

The big play structure here is a barrel of fun. It has tire swings, two slides, arch climbers, trapeze rings, and climbing platforms installed over a safe bed of sand.

Magnuson Park

Location: N.E. 65th St. at Sand Point Way N.E.
Web Site: www.pan.ci.seattle.wa.us/seattle/parks/home.htm

The paved paths at this park near Lake Washington attract families who enjoy bicycling and in-line skating. Part of the former Sand Point Naval Air Base, the site features tennis courts, softball fields, picnic tables, boat launch, and more. Young children are mesmerized by The Sound Garden, a sculpture of pipes that makes music in the wind, a favorite attraction here; look for it just inside the park's gates. There's a wading pool open during the summer, too.

Matthews Beach

Location: N.E. 93rd St. at Sand Point Way N.E.
Web Site: www.pan.ci.seattle.wa.us/seattle/parks/home.htm

Many north-end families consider this their favorite playground because of the innovative bridges and climbing equipment for toddlers and challenging play equipment for older children. This park also boasts Seattle's largest freshwater beach, where lifeguards usually are on duty between Memorial Day and Labor Day. During warm weather months, families on bicycles make this their picnic destination via the Burke-Gilman Trail, which runs through the park.

Medicinal Herb Garden   206-543-1126

Location: University of Washington campus (on Stevens Way across from
    the Botany greenhouse). From I-5, take the N.E. 45th St. exit (exit 169);
    travel east to the campus.
Days/Hours: Daily during daylight hours
Admission: Free
Tours: Free guided tours on the second and fourth Sundays at noon during
    the growing season; special tours by arrangement for a small fee.
Wheelchair/Stroller Access: Limited

This fascinating little garden was established in 1911 on one acre. It
has grown and shrunk over the years due to university expansion, but
today almost 600 species of medicinal herbs and shrubs are grown on
two acres, making it the largest such garden in both North and South
America. Many of the plants have been grown from seeds gathered from
around the world; it is maintained by the Friends of the Medicinal Herb
Garden. While you're there, look for the Cascara Circle, a circular garden
with a raised pool and charming wooden monkeys perched on pillars.
Early summer is the best time to visit.

North Acres Park Wading Pool

206-684-7796 (Seattle wading pool hotline)

Location: 12800 First Ave. N.E.
Days/Hours: Varies, but usually open daily, June–Labor Day
Wheelchair/Stroller Access: Yes

Tots may splash around in this shallow pool on warm weather days.
The pool is filled daily with clean water.

Northwest Puppet Center   206-523-2579

Location: 9123 15th Ave. N.E.
Days/Hours: Varies depending on scheduled weekend performances
Admission: $7.50/adults; $5.50/children 16 or younger.
Wheelchair/Stroller Access: Yes

Enchanting puppets and marionettes from all over the world come
alive on this stage. Some shows are performed by Seattle's own Carter
Family Marionettes; other performers come from as far away as Tashkent
(in the former Soviet Republic, Uzbekistan) and China. Before or after a
show, visit the center's puppet museum, featuring rotating exhibits from
throughout the world. Performances are designed for those 3 years and
older. The first Saturday matinee in each series is signed for the hearing-
impaired. For $8.50 per child, you can reserve a birthday party here. Each

guest receives admission to a puppet play and a puppet to take home; the birthday kid gets a crown.

Seattle Youth Symphony 206-362-2300

Location: 11065 5th Ave. N.E, Suite E (box office)
Days/Hours: Box office: Monday–Friday, 9 a.m.–5 p.m.
Wheelchair/Stroller Access: Depends on the location of the concert

For families who enjoy listening to music together, these concerts are a good introduction to classical music. Young musicians here play a fairly sophisticated repertoire and have gained a reputation for very professional performances. The recommended age for concert-goers is 7 and older as most performances are at least ninety minutes long. The performers play in four symphonies and perform at sites throughout the area, including the Opera House at the Seattle Center and Meany Hall at the University of Washington. Call ahead for schedules and tickets, which start at about $10.

University of Washington 206-543-2100

Location: 15th Ave. N.E. and 45th Ave.
Web Site: www.washington.edu
Days/Hours: Call for a brochure
Tours: Self-guided tours only; guided tours are for prospective students
Wheelchair/Stroller Access: Yes

The U.W. campus is worth a stroll, especially on autumn afternoons when the fall colors are brilliant or spring when the cherry blossoms in the Quad are bursting out. Pick up a map from the Visitors Information Center at 4014 University Way N.E. and a brochure on the university's history, and you're on your way! You can stop for a snack at the HUB (the student union building, also known as the Husky union building) or wander down to Drumheller Fountain. Include the Burke Museum or the Henry Art Gallery in your tour, if time allows.

University of Washington Waterfront
Activity Center 206-543-9433

Location: Behind Husky Football Stadium off Montlake Blvd.
Days/Hours: February–October: Monday–Friday, 10 a.m.–dusk; Saturday–
*   Sunday, 9 a.m.–dusk*
Wheelchair/Stroller Access: Yes

A great place for families, especially on a sunny afternoon! Canoes and rowboats rent here for about $5 an hour. Go exploring through the waterways around Foster Island and through the arboretum. You'll find water lilies, cattails, weeping willows, and lots of exuberant overgrowth. It can be very peaceful and relaxing. Reservations are not available, so you might want to plan for a wait with either a picnic or some activity that will keep the whole family involved. Life jackets are provided, but children must weigh at least twenty-five pounds to assure the tops of their life jackets don't cover their chins. Valid ID will be required for each boat rental.

Places to Eat

Pagliacci's   206-632-0421

Location: 4529 *University Way N.E. (other locations throughout the city)*
Days/Hours: Sunday–Thursday, 11 a.m.–11 p.m.; Friday–Saturday, 11 a.m.–
    1 a.m.
Wheelchair/Stroller Access: Yes

From the front of the restaurant, you can watch pizza makers toss dough high above their heads as they spin it out for pies to be laden with sauces, cheeses, and dozens of other toppings. The menu features salads, too. Buy it by the pie or by the slice.

Stroll through the restaurant and see how many cinema posters tacked to the walls your child can recognize. The posters are printed in Italian with many familiar words and pictures.

Stores to Browse

Display and Costume Supply   206-362-4810

Location: 11201 *Roosevelt Way N.E., Seattle (See Chapter 6 for their second
    location)*
Web Site: www.displaycostume.com
Days/Hours: Monday–Friday, 8:30 a.m.–8:30 p.m.; Saturday, 9:30 a.m.–
    6 p.m.; Sunday, 10 a.m.–5 p.m.
Wheelchair/Stroller Access: Yes

Not only are they on the Web, they're into webs—especially at Halloween. Everything's here but the invitations; they have a full line of party accessories and costumes for all occasions. Past "hot buttons" for Halloween included Batman Forever, Robin, and Cat Woman—who knows what the future brings! Face painting and makeup, tiaras and crowns even in toddler sizes, and plenty of free parking. They also rent helium tanks; you'll need them for the balloons!

MADISON PARK AND CAPITOL HILL

Places to Go

Cornish College of the Arts   206-726-5066

Location: On Capitol Hill at 710 E. Roy St.
Days/Hours: Monday–Friday, 9 a.m.–4 p.m.
Wheelchair/Stroller Access: Yes

At Cornish College for the Arts, student artists and performers offer several presentations each year that are wonderful attractions for children interested in the creative arts. Ask about Cornish Junior Dance Company performances and the school's Fisher Gallery, which hosts visual art exhibits between noon to 5 p.m., Monday through Friday. Admission to this gallery is free. Works on display are by professional artists with occasional student shows.

Museum of History and Industry (MOHAI)   206-324-1126

Location: Between University District and Madison Park at 2700 24th Ave. E.
Days/Hours: Daily, 10 a.m.–5 p.m.
Admission: $5.50/ages 13 or older; $3/seniors and students 6–12; $1/children 2–5; free/children under 2
Wheelchair/Stroller Access: Yes

Dedicated to the history of Seattle and King County, MOHAI features various programs for families. There are interactive games and hands-on for kids throughout the year, and each December the museum highlights international holiday traditions with an exhibition and activities. Ask about Family Fest weekend with special activities for children. Outside the museum, two nature trails belonging to the arboretum offer pleasant places to observe nesting birds, ducks, geese, and fish, or drift through in a canoe with a picnic lunch. One trail winds under the Montlake Bridge and meanders before ending at the Seattle Yacht Club. Another trail goes to little Marsh Island, crosses a bridge, and continues to Foster Island. The walk around Foster Island is long for small children. The trails have no restrooms, and the path can be muddy, so it's wise to bring boots.

Peppi's Playground

Location: 32nd Ave. at E. Spruce

Named by Leschi schoolchildren for a first grader who was killed in an auto accident, Peppi's Playground offers a wading pool and excellent new play equipment.

Pioneer Cemetery

Location: On Capitol Hill at 1554 15th Ave. E.
Days/Hours: Monday–Saturday, 8 a.m.–8 p.m.; Sunday, 9 a.m.–8 p.m.
Wheelchair/Stroller Access: Yes

A walk though an old cemetery may seem an odd way to see Seattle's history, but many of the city's earlier pioneers have their final resting places here. Some of the grave sites belong to more contemporary celebrities, including martial-arts film star Bruce Lee, buried here in 1973.

Roanoke Park

Location: Slightly north of Capitol Hill at 10th E. and E. Roanoke

Here's a nice place to spread a picnic on a blanket and let kids romp in a small neighborhood playground. It's especially pretty in spring when the flowering trees are in bloom.

Seattle Asian Art Museum   206-654-3100

Location: On Capitol Hill's north end in Volunteer Park at 14th Ave. E. and
*   E. Prospect St.*
Web Site: www.sam.tripl.org
Days/Hours: Tuesday, Wednesday, and Friday–Sunday, 10 a.m.–5 p.m.;
*   Thursday, 10 a.m.–9 p.m.*
Admission: $6/adults; $4/seniors and students 13–19; free/children 12 and
*   younger. Admission tickets for the Seattle Asian Art Museum can be*
*   used at the downtown Seattle Art Museum if used within one week.*
Wheelchair/Stroller Access: Yes

Formerly the site of the Seattle Art Museum, this facility has been remodeled to showcase numerous galleries of Asian art. Six galleries are devoted to Chinese works; another six feature Japanese pieces. Look for masterpieces from the Himalayas, India, Korea, and Southeast Asia.

Seattle Mime Theater 206-324-8788

Location: 915 E. Pine, No. 419 (ticket office only)
Days/Hours: Box office: Monday – Friday, 9 a.m.–5 p.m.
Wheelchair/Stroller Access: Yes

The only noise you'll hear at one of these performances is the sound of laughter. The unique talent of this small troupe of mime performers is enchanting to their audiences; many parents bring their children to enjoy this art form together. The troupe schedules many of its performances at schools, so it's wise to call ahead to learn where to find a show. Performances are geared to audiences of all ages, but kids especially relate to the magic of mimes.

Volunteer Park Conservatory 206-684-4743

Location: 15th Ave. E. at E. Galer; in Volunteer Park on Capitol Hill
Days/Hours: Daily and holidays, 10 a.m.–4 p.m.
Wheelchair/Stroller Access: Yes

Just by using your imagination, you can travel from the desert to the tropics inside this Victorian-style greenhouse conservatory. The Bromeliad House, where the temperature is fixed at seventy-two degrees, is home to just about every relative in the pineapple family—there are more than two thousand species. In the Fern House, you'll see a Sago Palm, a small pond (no coins, please; metal kills the fish) and many tropical and subtropical flowers. The tropical climate Palm House contains a permanent display of orchids that bloom year-round. The Seasonal Display House, at sixty-five degrees, is slightly cooler. Here, as the seasons change, you'll find begonias, coleus, fuchsia, geraniums, gardenias, and poinsettias. Large groups require an appointment.

Volunteer Park Wading Pool

206-684-7796 (Seattle wading pool hotline)

Location: 1400 E. Galer St.
Days/Hours: Varies, but typically open 11 a.m.–8 p.m., mid-June–Labor Day

When the weather is warm, this pool is filled daily with clean, chlorinated water for lots of splashing. You'll enjoy the tree-shade during hot weather. Parking is limited; nearby 15th Ave. E. is an option.

Volunteer Park Water Tower

Location: Volunteer Park
Web Site: www.pan.ci.seattle.wa.us/seattle/parks/home.htm
Days/Hours: Daily, 8 a.m.–5:30 p.m.
Wheelchair/Stroller Access: No

Put those energetic legs to work climbing the 106 steps to the top of the Observation Deck at Volunteer Park. From the top there's a beautiful view of the city. The park is a great place to visit during the day, but should be avoided at night.

Washington Park Arboretum   206-543-8800

Location: On Lake Washington Blvd., between E. Madison St. and the 520 Bridge; Graham Visitors Center is at 2300 Arboretum Dr. E.
Days/Hours: Daily, dawn to dusk. Visitors Center: September–April: Monday–Friday, 10 a.m.–4 p.m.; Saturday–Sunday, noon–4 p.m. May–August: daily, 10 a.m.–4 p.m.
Admission: Free
Tours: Yes, Saturday and Sunday, 1 p.m. (most weekends except December); reservations not necessary
Wheelchair/Stroller Access: Yes, at the Visitors Center, but limited on the trails

Many Puget Sound families have a favorite time of year to visit this sprawling park. Autumn offers the brilliant colors of turning leaves, while winter displays a refreshing collection of camellia and witch hazel. During snowfall, the textures and landscapes are dramatic. Spring showcases the well-loved (and often photographed) azaleas, rhododendron, and cherry trees. The arboretum is a living museum of woody plants, one of the finest collections in western North America, but all suitable for the Puget Sound region. There are over 5,000 species to admire and learn about here; the collections are well marked, but you can pick up a brochure at the Graham Visitors Center that will help you identify specimens. The arboretum staff offers guided tours, all designed to include the most interesting areas for the particular time of year. It's important that children be able to walk the distance. One- to two-hour tours may cover several acres.

Washington Park Arboretum/Japanese Garden

206-684-4725

Location: Lake Washington Blvd., two blocks north of Madison St.
Days/Hours: June through August: daily, 10 a.m.–8 p.m. September–October: 10 a.m.–6 p.m. November and March–May: 10 a.m.–4 p.m. Closed December–February.

Admission: $2.50/adults 19 and older; $1.50/children 6 and older and full-time university students; free/children under 6.
Tours: Group tours available with two weeks advance notice; appointment required; $8.50 charge for groups.
Wheelchair/Stroller Access: Yes

This garden is beautiful year-round, but most colorful in April and May when the shrubs are in bloom. Especially beautiful are the water irises in late spring and early summer. Children's Day in early May is an excellent time to visit with children. Japanese drums, storytelling, koi (carp) feeding, origami making, Japanese games, and martial arts demonstrations are all part of the day's festivities.

Founded in 1960, the three-acre Japanese Tea Garden was designed and created by a Japanese landscape architect who was considered a national treasure in Japan. A fire destroyed the teahouse in the 1980s, but

A gardening project fascinates a youngster at the Washington Park Arboretum. PHOTO COURTESY THE ARBORETUM FOUNDATION

local Japanese architects, artists, and volunteers helped restore it. A thirty-minute public tea ceremony (for observation only) is held in the teahouse at 1:30 p.m., the third Saturday of the month, April through October. With a brochure available at the garden's gate, you can interpret this authentic garden by understanding how the various elements in the garden—mountains, water, and fire—represent nature. Plantings in the garden are tended and pruned according to the original design. For children, one of the highlights here is the view from the small bridge where they can watch the elegant koi moving through the pond. If you visit the garden midafternoon, the staff often invites the children to help feed the koi. Turtles and frogs have a comfortable home here as well, threatened only by the large blue heron that visits from time to time. No smoking or food is permitted.

Places to Eat

Fran's   206-322-6511

Location: In Madison Park at 2805 E. Madison
Days/Hours: Tuesday–Friday, 10 a.m.- 6 p.m.; Saturday, 10 a.m. - 5 p.m.
Wheelchair/Stroller Access: Yes

This is, indeed, candy heaven. Fran's always has a sample of something wonderful on the counter, which may help you make your selection. Her chocolates—milk, dark, and light—are now popular nationally. Holidays are really irresistible here—Easter bunnies and eggs, Christmas Santas, and Hanukah dreidels are almost too good to eat—but, of course, you will. In summer the incredible hand-dipped ice-cream bars are delicious; in cooler weather a mug of rich hot chocolate is perfect. (See Eastside for Fran's Bellevue location; a third store is planned for University Village.)

SOUTH SEATTLE

Places to Go

Beer Sheva Park

Location: Seward Park South at South Henderson
Web Site: www.pan.ci.seattle.wa.us/seattle/parks/home.htm

This park's name honors Seattle's sister city in Israel, a site of great historical and religious significance. In the autumn, it's a colorful place for a family stroll among the park's chestnut trees; some are more than 100 years old.

Goodwill Memory Lane Museum 206-329-1000

Location: 1400 S. Lane St.
Tours: Monday–Friday; by appointment only. Tours last about forty-five
minutes. Schedule one week ahead.
Wheelchair/Stroller Access: Yes

Located in the back of a huge Goodwill Store is the Memory Lane Museum, showcasing special donations reflecting Seattle's history between World War I and II. The items are not for sale, and the exhibits change periodically. Highlights include "Miss Bardahl," one of the favorite Seafair hydroplanes of the '60s, and an eleven-foot-tall grizzly bear named Bruce, gifted by retailer Eddie Bauer.

Kubota Gardens 425-725-5060

Location: Renton Ave. S. at 55th St. S.
Web Site: www.pan.ci.seattle.wa.us/seattle/parks/home.htm
Days/Hours: Daily, dawn to dusk
Admission: Free

Even in one of the busiest parts of the city, you will find a quiet place in this historical and cultural garden. Part of the city's open-space protection program, it covers twenty acres and features an exquisite display of plants, waterfalls, ponds, and prayer stones tended by Japanese families in this area. This is an environmental education site for the new children's forest school program, too. Originally designed and created by Fujitaro Kubota, the garden was maintained by the Kubota family for many years and purchased by the City of Seattle in 1987.

Mount Baker Rowing and Sailing Center 206-386-1913

Location: 3800 Lake Washington Blvd. S.
Days/Hours: Call for information
Wheelchair/Stroller Access: Yes

Adult, child, and family water classes at this center on Lake Washington are very popular, with summer the busiest time of year. The sailboarding and sailing camps are for children 10 years or older. During the rest of the year, kids must be 13 to 18 to participate in the sailing, rowing, canoeing, and kayaking lessons. Courses are six to twelve weeks long. Children who have not taken a class may ride in a watercraft with an adult who has passed a class if the child can pass a float test: ten minutes floating in the water while fully dressed. At nearby Mount Baker Beach, lifeguards are on duty during the summer.

Museum of Flight   206-764-5720; 206-764-5712 (tours)

Location: 9404 E. Marginal Way S. Take I-5 exit 158, turn right on E.
Marginal Way S. and follow this road one half mile.
Web Site: www.museumofflight.org
Days/Hours: Friday–Wednesday,10 a.m.–5 p.m.; Thursday, 10 a.m.–9 p.m.
Admission: $8/adults; $4/students 6–15; free/children 5 or younger. Thanks
to PEMCO, admission on the first Thursday of each month is free from
5 p.m.–9 p.m.
Tours: Guided tours are ninety minutes; appointments required. Call at least
two weeks ahead. Small groups can go on hourly tours.
Wheelchair/Stroller Access: Yes

The Red Barn, formerly Boeing's first manufacturing plant, is now
an integral part of the Museum of Flight. Two floors of exhibits capture
visitors' imaginations with flight displays dating back to the replica of
the Wright Brothers' 1902 glider. A hands-on exhibit for kids called The
Hanger includes a plane they can climb into. The exhibit includes a life-
size replica of an actual FAA control tower, with a control panel that leads
you through all the stages of the FAA air traffic control system. This is a
wonderland for kids of all ages, but older kids are really captivated by
the history and a panorama of flight development. Parking is free. Most
of the docents are Boeing retirees, so you will get a personal flavor and
sense of what Boeing has meant to Puget Sound families.

Pratt Fine Arts Center   206-328-2200

Location: 1902 S. Main St.
Days/Hours: Monday–Friday, 9 a.m.–5 p.m.; call for class and tour times
Wheelchair/Stroller Access: Yes

Almost hidden behind the Wonder Bread plant in Pratt Park is the
Pratt Fine Arts Center. Teachers here are professional artists offering
classes in printmaking, jewelry casting, and all disciplines of glass-mak-
ing. Elementary school-age youngsters can learn some of these talents in
the Kids Artworks program offered each Saturday, September through
November. There's a $10 registration fee. The school emphasizes artwork
teams between artists and students. Pratt is one of the few nonacademic
visual arts facilities in the country offering beginning and advanced classes
and studio space.

Pratt Wading Pool   *206-684-7796 (Seattle wading pool hotline)*

Location: 1800 S. Main St., near Yesler and 20th Ave.
Days/Hours: Usually open June through the summer, but hours vary

This wading pool is shaped like the continent of Africa. Its creative and innovative design attracts children like a magnet; they delight in playing in the water spraying from spouts that resemble a menagerie of African animals. This pool is unlike any other in the city and is admired for its artistic imagery.

Seward Park

Location: South Juneau at Lake Washington Blvd.
Web Site: www.pan.ci.seattle.wa.us/seattle/parks/home.htm

In the summer, this park pulsates with activities: music concerts in the amphitheater, kids running on the playground, and families dining at picnic tables in the water. Bicycling families pedal around the lake;

Waterguns at Pratt Wading Pool are great fun on a hot day. Photo courtesy Seattle Department of Parks and Recreation.

serious walkers and joggers move along very intent on their pace. Others come for the beach, where lifeguards are usually on duty during the summer. Lovely flowering cherry trees at the entrance were a gift from Seattle's Japanese community.

Skyway Park Bowl and Miniature Golf   *206-772-1220*

Location: 11819 Renton Ave. S., Seattle. From Martin Luther King Jr. Way, drive south to Renton Ave. S.
Days/Hours: Daily, 9 a.m.–2 a.m.
Admission: $4.50/adults; $4/children 12 years and younger and seniors 50 and older. All players play $3.50 from 9 a.m.–1 p.m. at the daily discount session.
Wheelchair/Stroller Access: Yes

Tucked between South Seattle and Renton, this indoor Caribbean-style eighteen-hole layout is one of the area's newest mini-golf courses. Engulfed by tropical blue, red, and yellow lights, the course features a wrecked hull of a pirate ship and bridges over bubbling water. Ask about birthday party rates. No smoking at this facility.

Vintage Telephone Equipment Museum   *206-767-3012*

Location: 7000 E. Marginal Way. From I-5, take the Corson Ave. exit; turn left into the museum parking lot.
Days/Hours: Tuesday only, 8:30 a.m.–2:30 p.m.
Admission: Free; donations gratefully accepted
Tours: Available by request
Wheelchair/Stroller Access: Yes; both entrance ramp and elevator

This small museum is a tribute to the energy and loyalty of the Telephone Pioneers, retirees who wanted to see their history preserved. There are three floors of antique telephone and telegraph gear, and everything works! You'll see a British Call Box, from Derby, England, a piece from the Timbuktu Telephone Company, and a panel server testboard which, when placed in service in 1923, marked the start of dial tone and dial service in the Seattle area. Visiting hours are limited; this a great destination during a vacation or for a school-group field trip.

Places to Eat

Ezell's Fried Chicken   *206-324-4141*

Location: 501 23rd Ave.

*Days/Hours: Monday–Thursday, 10 a.m.–10 p.m.; Friday–Saturday, 9 a.m.–
11 p.m.; Sunday, 11 a.m.–10 p.m.*
Wheelchair/Stroller Access: Yes

The fried chicken here is so good that TV's Oprah Winfrey sometimes breaks her diet and has it shipped cross-country. Kids may want to
select two drumsticks and a melt-in-your-mouth roll for about $4. Give
the sweet potato pie a try, too.

WEST SEATTLE
Places to Go

Alki Beach Park

Location: Alki Ave. S.W.
Web Site: www.pan.ci.seattle.wa.us/seattle/parks/home.htm
Wheelchair/Stroller Access: Yes

The waters of Elliott Bay may be chilly, but that doesn't discourage
children from playing on the shores of this two-mile gently sloping stretch
of beach. On spring and summer evenings, it's a popular place for teens,
but walkers and joggers of all ages come here to enjoy the spectacular
view. Watch for the annual sand-sculpting contest in August; it's a lively
time to be here.

Camp Long   206-684-7434

Location: 5200 35th Ave. S.W. (West Seattle's Delridge neighborhood)
Web Site: www.pan.ci.seattle.wa.us/seattle/parks/home.htm
Days/Hours: Tuesday–Sunday, 8:30 a.m.–5 p.m., except holidays
Admission: Free
*Tours: Choose a self-guided trail or a ninety-minute nature hike led by a Camp
Long naturalist, Saturdays, 2 p.m. Call for reservations ahead of time or
during the same week as the hike you want to attend. No age minimum,
but they request that groups of children be accompanied by an adult.*
Wheelchair/Stroller Access: Yes

Camp Long is a wilderness experience within the city limits. It's especially good for families who love the outdoors and don't want to travel
far to enjoy it. The tours are educational and guides are quite knowledgeable.

Ten cabins provide overnight accommodations. Each has six double
beds and can sleep as many as twelve people. Three cabins are wheelchair accessible. Cabin rentals are $30 per night.

Ask about the rock-climbing program for those 7 or older. Students learn how to scale a twenty-five-foot artificial rock with safety harnesses and ropes. It was the first manmade climbing rock in the country. Rock climbing is free the fourth Saturday of each month, otherwise there's a small fee. Climbing rates for student groups of fifteen or more is about $45 per group.

Delridge Wading Pool

206-684-7796 (Seattle wading pool hotline)

Location: 4501 Delridge Way S.W.
Days/Hours: Varies, but usually open 11 a.m.–4 p.m., late June–Labor Day

When the weather is warm, this pool is filled daily with clean, chlorinated water for lots of splashing. Summer months bring lots of sunshine (we hope). The Delridge Community Center nearby brings lots of visitors to the area.

Ed Munro-Seahurst Park

Location: 12th S.W at S.W. 144th. Turn west off Ambaum Blvd. to S.W. 144th. Turn north on 13th S.W. Access road leads to beach.
Web Site: www.pan.ci.seattle.wa.us/seattle/parks/home.htm

At Seahurst, you'll find 185 acres of saltwater park land with lots of activities. The south part offers great beachcombing; the north end is both sand and grass. There are fire pits on the beach, picnic tables with individual grills, a Marine Skill Center at the north end, freshwater holding ponds and a fish ladder. All pets must be leashed within the park. Parking near the beach is available only to the physically challenged.

Lincoln Park

Location: Fauntleroy S.W. at S.W. Webster
Web Site: www.pan.ci.seattle.wa.us/seattle/parks/home.htm

In the summer, treat the kids to something rare in Seattle: swimming in heated seawater at the Colman Pool at Point Williams, found only in Lincoln Park. This beautiful beachfront park stretches along the coast from Southwest Webster to Trenton St. Playgrounds, a restroom, picnic tables, and a few picnic shelters are located throughout the park. Paths wind through groves of madrona, fir, and redwoods. Other activity areas include tennis courts, eleven acres of playfields, and horseshoe pitching pits. The beach has no lifeguard, but offers beachside barbecues, an Olympic Mountain view, and a vantage point for watching the Vashon-Southworth ferries.

Log House Museum   206-938-5293

Location: 3003 62nd Ave. S.W. (corner of 61st S.W. and S.W. Stevens)
Days/Hours: Tuesday, noon–7 p.m.; Friday–Saturday, 10 a.m.–4 p.m.;
    Sunday, noon–3 p.m.
Admission: Free
Wheelchair/Stroller Access: Yes

Known as the "birthplace of Seattle," Log House Museum is just a block from Alki Beach, and a few blocks from the historic marker at the beach memorializing the landing of the 1851 Denny Party at Duwamish Head. Initially the carriage house of the William Bernard family, the home is now under the guardianship of the Southwest Seattle Historical Society. In the early days, the ferry from downtown Seattle to West Seattle took eight minutes; nearby was an amusement park known as Luna Park—giving West Seattle the local slogan of "Coney Island of the West." The Log House Museum is an interesting collection of early Seattle memorabilia, especially to children studying our city's history. Kids are especially fascinated with an authentic display of wool swimsuits, which used to be loaned to youngsters and rented (for a dime) to adults coming to swim at Alki Beach. Parking is limited.

Seacrest Boat House   206-932-1050

Location: 1660 Harbor Ave. S.W.
Days/Hours: Monday–Friday, 5:30 a.m.–6 p.m.; Saturday and Sunday,
    4:30 a.m.–7 p.m.; closed Monday and Tuesday during the winter
Wheelchair/Stroller Access: Yes

You can putter around for about two hours on a tank of gas in one of their fourteen- or sixteen-foot Fiberglas boats. The six- or eight-horsepowered motor is strong enough to take you across Elliott Bay to a marina or the Fauntleroy ferry terminal. Boaters are discouraged from cruising up the Duwamish River where more than one embarrassed parent has had to be rescued after beaching a boat. Rentals run $15 an hour. You must be 18 or older to rent a boat at Seacrest, but adults are welcome to bring children along. Life jackets and cushions are provided.

Put teenage muscles to work by renting a Seacrest boat with oars—but no motor—for $25 per day. In summer, boats are available from 5 a.m. until at least 6 p.m., Sundays through Thursdays, and until 8 p.m. on Fridays and Saturdays. Life jackets are provided, but only for those twenty-five pounds or heavier. Smaller children may ride if they bring their own life jackets. Boating on Elliott Bay is exhilarating on a calm summer day, but avoid this outing if winds are gusty—the trip can turn dangerous. All boats are available on a first-come, first-served basis except during fishing derbies, when pay-in-advance reservations are required.

Walker Rock Garden   206-935-3036

Location: *5407 37th Ave. S.W.*
Days/Hours: *Open from late April to Labor Day; closed from Labor Day to early April*
Admission: *Free; donations appreciated*
Tours: *By appointment only. Call ahead; allow several days*

Milton and Florence Walker built their rock garden using imagination and available materials. Many of the materials used will surprise you, as will the beautiful view from the garden, overlooking the city. None of this is apparent from the street; behind the fence, the garden and its structures sparkle and twinkle with rocks, semiprecious stones, shells and cut glass. As you wander through the stone-studded walls, terraces, miniature mountains and rock towers, you'll come across surprises at every turn. Kids especially will be delighted with the fantasy they'll encounter—and hopefully they will take some flights of fancy home with them. *It is imperative to call first;* however, the Walkers do hold several open houses in spring which are usually announced in local papers.

Places to Eat

Husky Deli and Ice Cream   206-937-2810

Location: *4721 California S.W.*
Days/Hours: *Monday, 9 a.m.–7 p.m.; Tuesday–Friday, 9 a.m.–9 p.m.; Saturday, 9 a.m.–10 p.m.; Sunday, 9 a.m.–7 p.m.*
Wheelchair/Stroller Access: *Yes*

This take-out only sandwich deli and ice cream shop is so popular people have been known to drive all the way from the University District when they crave Husky's ice cream. There are more than a dozen flavors to choose from; all are homemade.

Pegasus Pizza   206-932-4849

Location: *2758 Alki S.W.*
Days/Hours: *Monday–Friday, 11:30 a.m.–11 p.m.; Saturday and Sunday, 11 a.m.–11 p.m.*
Wheelchair/Stroller Access: *Yes*

Pizza lovers who like a Greek flair to their pies should seek out this eatery, conveniently located across the street from Alki Park beach. Pegasus Pizza offers feta cheese, spinach, diced mushrooms, green peppers, mushrooms, olives, fresh garlic, and sunflower seed toppings, plus some traditional Italian varieties. Pizzas are available for take-out or dining in.

Spud Fish and Chips   *206-938-0606*

Location: 2666 Alki S.W. (Other locations at Green Lake in Seattle and Juanita Beach in Kirkland.)
Days/Hours: Daily, 11 a.m.–9 p.m.
Wheelchair/Stroller Access: First floor only

A Seattle favorite, this place makes some of the best fish and chips around. The fish and the chips are prepared in cholesterol-free oil, and the French fries are from fresh—not frozen—potatoes. Adults may order a single "fish with fries" or a heaping order of prawns, oysters, scallops, or clams. Kids may prefer the children's meal for less than $4. Most families like to sit at the second-floor window tables for a great view of the water. High chairs and booster seats available.

Resources

King County Library System: 425-462-9600 (the "answer line"); 206-684-4494 (TDD); **Web Site:** www.kcls.org

Books bring smiles at the King County Library. PHOTO COURTESY KING COUNTY LIBRARY SYSTEM

CHAPTER
3

Outside Seattle

• •

Seattle's residential areas originated in the 1880s, when trolleys made suburban life accessible. Today the Metro bus system accomplishes the same purpose. Over twenty small communities surround the downtown core. Attractive walking trails, picnic grounds, greenbelts, and parks, plus interesting shopping destinations are some of their best features.

North King County: Between Seattle and the Snohomish County line, three mostly residential communities predominate: Shoreline, Lake Forest Park, and Kenmore. At one time, these areas were so far removed from Seattle proper that most property was used only as summer or weekend homes for Seattle residents. It was easy for boaters to sail to Lake Washington's north end or along the Puget Sound shoreline and dock near the vacation homes. After World War II, the population here soared when veterans and their families settled in these communities.

East King County: Of all the areas in Washington state, the Eastside—Bellevue, Mercer Island, Issaquah, Kirkland, Redmond, and Woodinville —has probably changed the most dramatically in the past fifty years. Growing from strawberry fields and summer homes reachable from Seattle only by ferry to a major business and technology corridor, this area is host to internationally known companies such as Microsoft and Nintendo, as well as championing cultural and recreational activities of high caliber. And while Eastside residents hate to admit it, Bellevue Square is no longer a shopping destination just for locals; tourists and visitors from around the country are part of the scene now. Two freeway systems, I-90 and 520, can be charged with providing the access to accelerate the growth the area has experienced.

A costumed fur trapper at Marymoor Park's Heritage Festival. PHOTO COURTESY KING COUNTY PARKS

- Kirkland: This is a very eclectic water-side city with art galleries, restaurants, excellent recreational facilities, and some irresistible outdoor sculptures.

- Mercer Island: Once only a summer vacation destination, the I-90 corridor brought a whole new look to this residential community. People still tend to skate right by, but the island has a reputation for excellent schools and recreational programs.

- Redmond: An interesting association of suburbia and high tech, Redmond is home to Microsoft and Nintendo, along with recreational destinations such as the Sammamish River, a favorite for inner tubing and gentle rafting, a section of the Burke-Gilman Trail, and Marymoor Park, which hosts (among many other events) the annual Evergreen Classic, a major show-jumping event benefiting the Fred Hutchinson Cancer Center.

- Woodinville: An alluring little town that manages to cling to its rural roots even as encroaching suburbia and other signs of progress change the landscape. Many people come here for the elegance of Chateau Ste. Michelle or the magnetic charm of Molbak's.

- Bothell: Like Woodinville, Bothell has suffered from the economic turnaround resulting when river traffic between Lakes Washington and Sammamish, which had boosted the towns' growth, disappeared, due to completion of the ship canal, which lowered Lake Washington and left Sammamish too shallow for navigation. Bothell is less suburban in appearance, but nevertheless bustling and full of energy.

- Duvall and Carnation: The Carnation Milk Farm brought fame to the town in 1909 and is still a destination for families and tourists. But the countryside here is mainly agricultural, with some dairy and ranching activity.

- Issaquah: Don't blink or you'll miss another growth spurt here. The site of a coal find over a century ago, the settler's dreams of glory never materialized. Daniel Gilman planned to build a railroad (the Seattle, Lake Shore, and Eastern) to carry his coal to national markets, but it was never completed and the old depot still stands at the corner of Front and Sunset.

- Snoqualmie Valley: Farming and mining attracted the hardy people who settled here, but the spectacular Snoqualmie Falls is the main attraction today.

South King County: This part of Puget Sound is one of the industrialized arms of the region. Where coal mining once drove much of the economy, today The Boeing Company is the link to prosperity for many. The towns of Renton, Kent, Tukwila, and Federal Way reflect this. While there is extensive suburban development and many families call this home, the population growth has been so rapid that the cities are working very hard to provide the recreational and cultural programs that round out the quality of life. The towns of Enumclaw and Black Diamond, located on the way to Mount Rainier, are home to horse farms and those seeking a rural setting.

NORTH KING COUNTY
Places to Go

Highland Ice Arena   206-546-2431

Location: 18005 Aurora Ave. N., Shoreline
Days/Hours: Monday–Friday,10:30 a.m.–12:30 p.m., 3 p.m.–5:15 p.m.;
    Wednesday, 8 p.m.–10 p.m.; Friday, 7:30 p.m.–midnight; Saturday,
    10 a.m.–noon, 1:30 p.m.–4:45 p.m., 8 p.m.–midnight; Sunday, 10 a.m.–
    noon, 2 p.m.–5 p.m., 6:30 p.m.–9 p.m.
Admission: $4.50/adults; $4/students 6 to 12; free/children 4 and under.
    Checks not accepted. Some late evening sessions can be reserved for
    parties.
Wheelchair/Stroller Access: Yes

What a cooooool place for families to skate. The Sunday $9 family session from 2 p.m. to 5 p.m. is a favorite. For less experienced tots, consider classes available for kids 6 or younger. Skate rental, not included in the admission price, is $2.25.

Kenmore Air Harbor   425-486-1257

Location: In Kenmore, at the north end of Lake Washington
Web Site: www.kenmoreair.com
Days/Hours: Monday–Friday, 9 a.m.–5 p.m.
Tours: By request. Hours are flexible; no charge. Tours last about thirty
    minutes. Self-guided tours welcome any time.
Wheelchair/Stroller Access: Yes

Located just north of Tracy Owen Park (formerly Log Boom Park), Kenmore Air Harbor is a pretty exciting place to be when the float planes return from daily trips up north. In summer, they transport fisher-persons on expeditions, returning midafternoon with the plane's pontoons filled with fish. From early September through the winter and spring, they fly mainly to Victoria and the San Juans. Lots of visitors just hang around waiting to see a float plane come gliding in. Kenmore is the largest seaplane base in the United States; the most interesting part is their conversion program, in which they change regular aircraft to float planes. If you take a self-guided tour, don't hesitate to ask questions of the personnel. For special birthday ideas or out-of-town visitors, ask about their scenic flights.

Shoreline Historical Museum   206-542-7111

Location: 749 N. 175th St., Shoreline
Days/Hours: Tuesday–Saturday, 10 p.m.–4 p.m.; tours by appointment
   Monday–Saturday. No age minimum but 5 and older preferred; please
   bring one adult for every five children.
Admission: Free, but donations accepted and appreciated.
Wheelchair/Stroller Access: No

Local children discover the roots of their North King County community here. You can browse on a self-guided tour at this three-floor museum or reserve a forty-five-minute guided tour. Displays rotate regularly and curators make a point of including hands-on activities for children when possible.

Richmond Beach is filled with a host of natural treasures. PHOTO COURTESY SHORELINE PARKS DEPARTMENT

Richmond Beach Saltwater Park   206-296-2976

Location: At Richmond Beach Rd. and 20th Ave. N.W. From Aurora Ave. N.
and N.E. 185th St., turn west on N.E. 185th St. until it becomes
Richmond Beach Rd. At 20th Ave. N.W., turn south for three blocks to
park entrance.
Days/Hours: Daily, dawn to dusk
Wheelchair/Stroller Access: Yes

Local kids sometimes call this Puget Sound beach a "train park" because the noisy Burlington Northern cars rumble underneath a pedestrian overpass linking the parking lot to the beach. Friendly engineers
frequently wave at children peering down through the fenced walkway.
It can be both rocky and sandy here, fun for beachcombing and picnics. A
playground near the parking lot is designed for both toddlers and older
children, but lacks shade on warm days. On selected Saturdays, King
County Parks Department naturalists lead families on tide-pool walks.
In the summer, there are midweek concerts for children and evening sunset concerts for families. Call King County Parks for a current schedule.

Places to Eat

Great Harvest Bread Company (two locations in Seattle)

206-365-4778 (Lake Forest Park); 206-524-4873 (Sand Point)

Location: On the lower level of the Lake Forest Park Town Center at 17171
Bothell Way N.E.; 5408 Sand Point Way N.E.
Days/Hours: Monday–Friday, 6 a.m.–9 p.m.; Saturday–Sunday, 6 a.m.–
6 p.m.
Tours: Yes. Call for appointment, at least one week ahead.
Wheelchair/Stroller Access: Yes

Healthy, delicious oatmeal cookies are among the favorites at this
friendly bakery. Great Harvest is known for their hot fresh sample slices
of the day's specialty breads on the front counter, with plenty of butter to
go with them. Bakers knead the dough and pop loaves into the ovens
right behind the counter so kids can see everything happen. A window
inside the Lake Forest Park Town Center gives you a peak at the machines that stir and knead the dough. This is a popular stop for bicyclists
just off the Burke-Gilman Trail at Sheridan Beach.

Stores to Browse

Home Depot

*Locations: Bothell, Bellevue, Federal Way, Tacoma, Seattle (on Aurora),
    Everett, and Spokane*
Days/Hours: Saturday, 2 p.m. for workshop
Wheelchair/Stroller Access: Yes

For kids, the attraction to this mega-sized hardware store is the weekend Kids Workshop. Parents are encouraged—but not required—to attend. Kids can learn about tools and build a variety of small projects such as tool boxes, birdhouses, squirrel feeders, and foot stools. All "Saturday children" get a free child's carpenter apron to take home. Call ahead so materials can be reserved if your child wants to attend. This is a company-wide program. Home Depot will also design programs for Scout groups when possible.

Bellevue

Places to Go

Bellefield Office Park

Location: 1400 112th S.E.
Wheelchair/Stroller Access: Yes

This office-park complex borders on the Mercer Slough, which meanders through the complex around a manmade island in the middle. Boat ramps are available as is a three-mile path for jogging or strolling. Geese, ducks, and swans have populated the area and frequently cross the street. On weekends, you'll see lots of children in strollers with bags of bread bits; the fowl expect it!

Bellevue Art Museum   425-454-3322

Location: Third floor of Bellevue Square
*Days/Hours: Monday, Wednesday–Saturday, 10 a.m.–6 p.m.; Tuesday,
    10 a.m.–8 p.m.; Sunday, 11 a.m.–5 p.m.*
*Admission: $3/adults; $2/seniors and students 13 and older; free/children 12
    and younger. Tuesday admission is free to all.*
Wheelchair/Stroller Access: Yes

The Bellevue Art Museum makes a point of welcoming children each winter at their "Especially for Children" exhibit, which is always outstanding. Best suited to youngsters ages 6 to 12, the exhibits are designed for their level of interest, along with a number of hands-on activities that will give children a greater understanding of the visual arts. Its location inside Bellevue Square assures accessible parking. But there are other offerings during the year that will appeal to kids as well, so call ahead regarding rotating exhibits and guided tours.

Bellevue Botanical Garden

425-451-3755 (Bellevue Botanical Garden Society)

Location: 12001 Main St., in Wilburton Hill Park
Days/Hours: Daily, 7:30 a.m.–dusk. Visitors Center: daily, 10 a.m.–4 p.m.
Admission: Free, but donations encouraged
Wheelchair/Stroller Access: Yes, but certain areas are quite difficult to maneuver

No pets allowed here, but visitors abound. This is a thirty-six-acre complex of display and demonstration gardens; the most attention-getting is the massive perennial border featuring some spectacular year-round color and foliage, seen over the past three years on the covers of several national gardening magazines. There is also a wetlands area, a bog garden, an Asian garden, plus groundcovers, herbs, and more. Each year this garden has something new to explore. There's a half-mile loop trail for walkers; families often continue down the hill past the soccer field to a small play area with climbing equipment for youngsters. If you're really hardy, you can continue down the path, walk through the neighborhood (right on 128th Ave S.E., left on Fifth N.E.) and into Kelsey Creek Park to extend your hike. On a seasonal note: Don't miss the Holiday Lights display; it gets more impressive each year, and it's free. Hot beverages offered in the Visitors Center.

Bellevue Municipal Golf Course at Crossroads

425-453-4874

Location: 16000 N.E. 10th (it's tucked away just behind Crossroads Shopping Center)
Days/Hours: March 1 - mid-November: Monday–Friday, 9 a.m.–dusk; Saturday, 9 a.m.–5 p.m.; Sunday, 9 a.m.–6:30 p.m.
Admission: $5/adults; $4/children 17 and under

This three-par, nine-hole course is a mini-version of the full-size courses and a great place for families to practice together. Lots of trees and grass traps keep it authentic. Although skill level is a critical factor, you can get around in approximately two hours. A good beginning place for the Tiger Woods wanna-bes and youngsters with motivation.

Bellevue Nature Park

Location: 1905 118th S.E. Take I-405 to the Richards Road exit. Drive west to S.E. 118th; park is about a mile south of S.E. 118th.
Wheelchair/Stroller Access: Yes

Lake Washington receded when the Montlake Cut lowered the lake's level, leaving a huge peat bog that has become this park. Wear sturdy boots or old tennies and stay on the wide wood-chip paths; the peat can be as soft as butter. Hikers are asked to sign in and out of the park. In the center near the channel, the peat bog is six feet deep—a good reason to stay on the trails. In the swampy area look for water birch, the branches from which early pioneers made their brooms.

Bellevue Philharmonic   425-455-4171

Location: Subscription concerts at Westminster Chapel, 13646 N.E. 24th;
holiday concerts and special events at other locations
Hours/Days: Subscription concerts on Thursday and Friday at 7:30 p.m.; free
preconcert talks at 6:30 p.m. Friday is Family Night.
Admission: Kids 10 and under are free on Family Night when accompanied
by an adult.

Budding musicians can meet the real thing at the preconcert talks hosted by some of the musicians on Family Night. Attire is casual, and the conductor will introduce the evening's program with some remarks about the music that will help kids (and sometimes parents) understand what they'll be listening to with a more educated ear. Watch for information about their popular holiday and summer pops concerts, geared toward family audiences.

Bellevue Skate Park

Location: 14424 N.E. Bel-Red Rd.
Days/Hours: Tuesday–Friday, 3 p.m.–9 p.m.; Saturday, noon–9 p.m.;
Sunday, noon–8 p.m.
Admission: $2.

Those athletic wonders who love to maneuver their skateboards around obstacles, over ramps, and between cones will consider this center a challenge. Since skateboarding on most streets in King County is illegal, dozens of young people come here to practice and refine their skills. Hopefully these daredevils are safety-conscious and use helmets and knee and elbow pads on the course; if you don't have your own, they can be rented here for about $1.

Downtown Park

*Location: Downtown Bellevue, at the south end of Bellevue Square, between
N.E. 4th and N.E. 2nd*
Wheelchair/Stroller Access: Yes

On a warm summer day, the fountain at this park provides just
enough spray to keep kids cool. At the southwest corner, a play area with
swings, slides, and a climbing fort designed for toddlers and preschoolers
is very popular. Moms and strollers are frequent walkers around the
twelve-foot-wide canal; it's a social setting, especially popular in spring
and summer when the gardens are in bloom.

Geer Planetarium   425-641-2323

*Location: Bellevue Community College's Science Building, Room B-244,
3000 Landerholm Circle S.E.*
*Days/Hours: One autumn show and one spring show each year; dates vary,
so call ahead*
Admission: $2/person.
Wheelchair/Stroller Access: Yes

Stars millions of miles away seem very close at the Geer Planetarium.
Twice each year audiences are invited to study the night sky. Kids will
understand better the earth's small role in our giant galaxy after hearing
experts describe some of the constellations, planets, and black holes of outer
space. Call ahead to find out when shows are scheduled. Geer Planetarium
is the silver dome at the north end of the main cluster of buildings.

Kelsey Creek Park

425-452-6885 (information); 425-452-7688 (tours and parties)

*Location: 13204 S.E. Eighth Pl. Exit I-405 at S.E. 8th; head east, continue under
the freeway and through the light at Richards Road; follow S.E. 8th to 128th
Ave S.E.; turn left and go to 5th N.E.; turn right and drive into the park.*
*Days/Hours: Park: 9 a.m.–dusk. Farm area: 9 a.m.–4 p.m. Hours do change
seasonally, so call ahead.*
Wheelchair/Stroller Access: Yes on main park walkways. Difficult on hiker paths.

Spring is unquestionably the best time of year to visit this farm-in-a-
park because some of the animal population (goats, horses, rabbits, chickens, and pigs) may have just given birth to babies. Even the peacock shows
off to good advantage. It's a sprawling park with loads of running room,
easy hiking trails, and a delightful play area as well. The best time to visit
is between 10 a.m. and 2 p.m. when everyone is up and busy; if there are
milking cows and goats living here, plan to be come around 3:00 p.m.

Kelsey Creek also offers children's pottery parties, tours, and craft activities, and invites you to have your birthday party here. Check the Bellevue Parks and Recreation Department bulletins for special events.

Klub Kayak at Enatai Beach   425-637-8838

Location: Off I-90 at the Bellevue Way exit; turn at the first left, follow the arterial to a stop sign on 108th Ave. N.E., turn left again and head toward the water.
Days/Hours: Weekdays, noon–8 p.m.; weekends during summer, 9 a.m.–8 p.m.
Wheelchair/Stroller Access: Yes

Canoes and kayaks can be rented from this place during warm weather months. Single-seat kayaks are about $8 an hour; doubles are $12. Most families prefer the canoes that rent for $8 an hour. Life jackets are provided for those twenty-five pounds and heavier.

Mercer Slough Environmental Education Center
206-443-2925; 425-450-0207

Location: 1625 118th Ave. S.E.
Days/Hours: Daily for strolls; weekdays for scheduled school field trips; weekends for birthday parties
Admission: Free for strolls; about $105 for birthday parties for fifteen children (discounts available for Pacific Science members)
Wheelchair/Stroller Access: Limited

These are protected wetlands, great for family walking excursions. Programs here are run by the Pacific Science Center and birthday parties are a specialty. Naturalists lead up to fifteen guests for ninety minutes of outdoor activities and games, exploring creatures in the mud, water, and trees. Older children may handle microscopes to study the creatures that live in the ponds, and after the hike, the party guests are invited into a special room (for an hour) for cake and gifts. The Pacific Science Center provides the party invitations and a parting gift for each guest: a bug box with a magnifying lid. Special note: Boots are advised, as the walk can be muddy.

Pacific Northwest Arts Festival   425-454-4900

Location: Bellevue Square and the surrounding blocks of 100th Ave. N.E. and Bellevue Way between N.E. Fourth and 10th streets
Days/Hours: Always the last weekend in July, Friday–Sunday, about 9:30 a.m.–9:30 p.m.
Wheelchair/Stroller Access: Yes, but crowds can make it a tight fit

The festival is more than fifty years old now, and considered one of the most prestigious events of its kind in the entire country. As the most popular and best known event in downtown Bellevue, it's a visual arts extravaganza for all ages, with a special Kidsfair. The free event draws tens of thousands of visitors each summer. The younger set is invited to try their hands at the various art media set up on at least a dozen tables in Bellevue Place (diagonally across from Bellevue Square, on Bellevue Way and N.E. Eighth St.). Art projects feature fish rubbing, stained glass collages, tile designing, and more for children 3 years or older; most are free, but some have modest charges. Children may take their master-pieces home.

There are hundreds of the usual festival booths and exhibits on surrounding streets but the sought-after juried art will be found in the parking area behind Bellevue Square. If you're looking for something unique to buy, you'll not be disappointed.

Trails at many Bellevue parks can be negotiated by wheelchairs. Photo courtesy Bellevue Parks and Community Services Department

Paint Bar
425-637-9979

Location: 3rd floor, Bellevue Square (near Nordstrom)
Days/Hours: Monday–Saturday, 9:30 a.m.–9:30 p.m.; Sunday, 11 a.m.–6 p.m.
Wheelchair/Stroller Access: Yes

Children sit in high chairs or adult-sized chairs, painting pottery pieces they've purchased at this make-your-own art store. Paint and aprons are free. Plates are the perfect size for making a lasting handprint; pots are ideal gifts for a favorite teacher or a special relative. This store hosts birthday parties, too.

Playspace
425-644-4500

Location: At Crossroads Mall, 156th Ave. N.E. and N.E. Eighth St.
Days/Hours: Monday–Thursday, 9 a.m.–9 p.m.; Friday–Saturday, 9 a.m.–
    10:30 p.m.; Sunday, 10 a.m.–6 p.m.
Wheelchair/Stroller Access: Yes

Youngsters ages 3 to 12 may romp, tumble, and get physical at this supervised indoor playground (must be potty-trained!). On Fridays and Saturdays, check into Parents Night Out from 5:30 p.m. to 10:30 p.m. A Playspace pager will alert you if your child needs you to return to them for attention. During these sessions, kids have free time to play, watch PG-rated videos, create crafts, and eat dinner; this session is $18.50 per child. Otherwise, children can burn off energy while a parent or other adult stays on-site; this runs about $6 per day. If parents leave the site, the fee is about $8 for the first hour and roughly $1.50 for every fifteen minutes after that. It's vital that kids wear socks to play because they're asked to remove their shoes.

Robinswood Community Park
425-452-7850 *(for house rental)*

Location: 2340 148th Ave. S.E. Take I-90 and exit at Bellevue Community
    College/148th Ave. S.E. Drive north on 148th Ave. S.E.; turn right/east
    on S.E. 22nd St.; parking lot is on your right.
Days/Hours: Daily, year-round
Wheelchair/Stroller Access: Yes

Originally a log cabin homestead in 1882, Robinswood is now a multi-use park with thirteen acres of bridle trails and a public horse-show ring south of the park's meadow. North of the meadow there's a wonderful play area for smaller ones, with seesaws, climbing towers for both toddlers and older ones, and swings for different sizes. The wide asphalt paths are perfect for strollers, tricycles, and training wheels. You'll see lots of parents hauling bikes out of wagons and sports utility vehicles. There are benches and picnic tables for attentive parents, and the pond nearby is filled with water lilies and families of ducks. The older children head for the ball fields with bleachers, two lighted soccer fields, and tennis courts. A cabana, swimming pool, and main house are available for rental and are frequently used for private parties.

Rosalie Whyel Museum of Doll Art
425-455-1116

Location: 1116 108th Ave. N.E.
Web Site: www.dollart.com/dollart
Days/Hours: Monday–Saturday, 10 a.m.–5 p.m.; Sunday, 1 p.m.–5 p.m.
Admission: $6/adults; $5.50/seniors; $4/children 5 to 17; free/children 4 and younger.
Wheelchair/Stroller Access: Yes

This extraordinary museum is totally dedicated to dolls . . . dolls of all sizes, from many countries, from many cultures. More than 1,200 dolls, teddy bears, toys, and other favorites are on display with history and anecdotes to make them come alive. The cases are irresistible but don't forget the drawers below; they're filled with other fascinating items. A special gallery features rotating exhibits during the year. If arrangements can be made, this is a special place to have a birthday party. If you're an overnight guest at Bellevue's Hyatt Regency, you'll enjoy free admission. Call 425-462-1234 for more information.

A young visitor is entranced by a drawer full of dolls. Photo courtesy
Rosalie Whyel Museum of Doll Art

Sherwood Forest Park

Location: Sherwood Forest Elementary School, 16411 N.E. 24th
Days/Hours: After school and weekends, dawn to dusk
Wheelchair/Stroller Access: Yes

Designed for physically-challenged children, this innovative playground is really a favorite for all children. Look for sand and water tables, textured paths, a sensory maze, and embankment slides which are accessible to visitors with nearly all abilities.

Thistle Theater   206-524-3388 *(box office)*

Location: Moore Theater at Sacred Heart School, 9450 N.E. 14th, Bellevue
Days/Hours: Schedule varies; call for information
Admission: $7/adults; $5/children; free/children 2 and younger
Wheelchair/Stroller Access: Yes

Thistle Theater is a touring theater group; many of their performances take place in Bellevue and Burien. Appealing to children as young as 3, it's a delightful combination of a Japanese form of puppetry and acting. The musical tales range from children's classics to contemporary adventures. Watch for free performances at local schools and libraries.

Places to Eat

Burgermaster   425-827-9566

Location: 10606 N.E. Northrup Way
Days/Hours: Sunday–Thursday, 10 a.m.–1 a.m.; Friday–Saturday, 10 a.m.–
    2 a.m.
Wheelchair/Stroller Access: Yes

Burgermaster Drive-In takes you back to the good old days. Sometimes it's fun to eat in your car, van, or utility sports vehicle—and they make it very easy. Service is fast and good; menu specials for kids include the Kiddie Combo (small burger, fries, and a soft drink) for $2.49, or just a Kiddieburger for $1.79. Kids can have a small fish and chips (one piece or two), but don't miss the milkshakes. The usual flavors plus hot fudge, banana, orange, and pineapple (you'll have to ask, they're not on the menu), thick and yummy. And veggie burgers for those who want them. Everything is made to order, no hold-overs here. And if it isn't right, they'll fix it. You can walk in and order at the counter, if you prefer.

The New Jake O'Shaughnessey's   425-455-5559

Location: 401 Bellevue Way (at Bellevue Square, next to The Bon)
Days/Hours: Sunday–Thursday, 11:30 a.m.–9 p.m.; Friday–Saturday,
   11:30 a.m.–10 p.m. Reservations recommended.
Wheelchair/Stroller Access: Yes

Sometimes, for a family out-to-dinner night, you really want a nice place that's hospitable to kids. That's hard to find. But New Jake's is a good destination Their Just For Kids menu is for kids of any age but portioned for those 10 and under. Selections include clam chowder, burgers and fries, fish and chips, fettuccine, and grilled cheese. Beverages include milk, cocoa, and juices, plus the old favorites, Shirley Temples and Roy Rogers. Great desserts, too.

Noble Court   425-641-6011

Location: 1644 140th N.E.
Days/Hours: Monday–Thursday, 11 a.m.–3 p.m. for dim sum, 3 p.m.–9:30
   p.m. for dinner; Friday and Saturday, 10:30 a.m.–2 p.m. for dim sum,
   2 p.m.–9:30 p.m. for dinner; Sunday, 10 a.m.–3 p.m. for dim sum,
   5:30 p.m.–9:30 p.m. for dinner.
Wheelchair/Stroller Access: Yes

For dim sum on the Eastside, Noble Court offers the most varied menu, which is definitely on par with the downtown restaurants, but the prices are higher. Dishes start at around $2.00 and go up. Ample parking.

The Pancake Corral   425-454-8888

Location: 1606 Bellevue Way S.E.
Days/Hours: Monday–Friday, 5:45 a.m.–2:30 p.m.; Saturday and Sunday,
   6 a.m.–3 p.m.
Wheelchair/Stroller Access: Yes

No question about it, Bill Chace's Pancake Corral is a Bellevue fixture, and so are some of the regulars who make it a weekly habit. Its breakfast menu has changed little in thirty years; the pancakes are dependably good and filling, and the syrup comes heated. It's standing room only most weekends; allow for up to a thirty minute wait. Parking is limited during busy times. And they do like kids here.

Yeas Wok   425-644-5546

Location: 6969 Coal Creek Pkwy., Newcastle
Days/Hours: Tuesday, Thursday, and Sunday, 11 a.m.–9 p.m.; Friday–
Saturday, 11 a.m.–10:30 p.m.; closed Monday. Reservations for six or
more only.
Wheelchair/Stroller Access: Yes, but narrow spaces between tables are a
challenge

It's always fun to find a terrific restaurant tucked away in a rather
remote location. Yeas Wok has become so popular that it no longer seems
remote, but sometimes much of the crowd at the door is waiting for take-
out. Although the front of the restaurant looks small, there's a good-sized
back room that accommodates large family parties. It's popular because
the food is consistently good and the service friendly. High chairs and
boosters available.

Zoopa (also at Southcenter Mall, Northgate Mall, Bellevue
Square, and in Tacoma)   *206-776-2600; 206-440-8136 (Northgate)*

Location: 6003 244th St. S.W., between Mountlake Terrace and Lake Forest
Park
Days/Hours: Monday–Saturday, 11:30 a.m.–9:30 p.m.; Sunday, 11 a.m.–6 p.m.
Wheelchair/Stroller Access: Yes

Hard to say who likes this restaurant more—kids or parents. It was
designed with both in mind. Special trays with sections so foods don't touch
are available for children who want to dine from the children's snack bar
featuring raisins, fish-shaped crackers, favorite fruits, and more. Or they may
sample from the adult cafeteria-style bar with generous choices of salads,
baked potatoes, pasta, and soups. Adult meals are about $7, children 5 to 10
about $3.50, and tots 4 or younger eat for free. Paper place mats and crayons
make the visit more fun. Servers do the clean-up for you.

Stores to Browse

Crossroads Shopping Center   425-644-1111

Location: 15600 N.E. 8th St.
Days/Hours: Daily, 9:30 a.m.–9 p.m.
Wheelchair/Stroller Access: Yes

After struggling for years as an obscure Eastside location, Crossroads
has established itself as a unique and very interesting destination. For
families, there are some very particular reasons to come here. For little

ones under 7, the carousel (25¢ a go-round) is a major attraction; it's a short but delightful ride. For older children, the food court, the king-size chess board, and the Marketstage are equally magnetic. Called the East-side Public Market, the food court offers an amazing variety of choices from sixteen international restaurants, including Indian, Korean, Mediterranean, Chinese, and Japanese. The chess board is an ongoing game; it's usually a male contingent of players and onlookers, but kids into the game become easily engrossed and sometimes challenge the "old guys." On the stage, live music from jazz to folk on Friday and Saturday evenings is free; Thursdays is open mike; children's events happen on Sundays. It's an amazing mix of people and a great family experience. By now, the Kidpit, a play area, should be open again after their remodeling.

FAO Schwarz   425-646-9500

Location: 2070 Bellevue Square
Web Site: www.faoschwarz.com
Days/Hours: Monday–Saturday, 9:30 a.m.–9:30 p.m.; Sunday, 11 a.m.–
    6 p.m.
Wheelchair/Stroller Access: Yes

Step inside this extraordinary toy store, and you'll begin to believe that toys can talk! That's because the many items in the stuffed animal collection here—including a leaf-eating dinosaur and roaring lion—respond to visitors. Even the tree talks! At the back of the store, preschool and toddler toys are on display for children to test before parents buy them. The side room, filled with more Barbie things than most people can imagine, is sure to delight little girls. A giant water fountain bubbles hundreds of Barbie shoes around in a whirlpool.

Pets 'N Things   425-746-9782

Location: 14310 N.E. 20th
Days/Hours: Monday–Friday, 10 a.m.–7 p.m.; Saturday, 10 a.m.–6 p.m.;
    Sunday, 1 p.m.–5 p.m.
Wheelchair/Stroller Access: Yes

This is not your typical "cuddly creatures" pet shop. Owner Bob Mackin is a python breeder, and he usually has a family of snakes brooding at the back of the shop. You may also see a pocket mouse, a red-foot tortoise, African spiny mice, iguanas, exotic birds, lizards of all sizes, tarantulas, and scorpions.

Turn Off the TV *425-646-1070 (Bellevue); 206- 521-0564 (Seattle)*

Location: 256 Bellevue Square, Bellevue; 400 Pine St., #230, Westlake
   Center, Seattle
Web Site: www.turnoffthetv.com
Days/Hours: Bellevue Square: mall hours. Westlake Center: center hours
Wheelchair/Stroller Access: Yes

What would you do if the TV screen went black? Play games, of course, real games (not the computer version). There's an excellent assortment of mind teasers and games for all ages, none of which "requires— a remote control." You can play with the display models and test the merchandise before making your purchase; prices range from very affordable to pricey. They give game demonstrations when asked, and knowledgeable advice is free. Ask for a catalogue . . . great for browsing later. The Classic Roadster pedal car kit is pricey ($449.00), but a challenge for the right buyer.

Warner Brothers Studio Store *425-646-8738*

Location: 1050 Bellevue Square
Web Site: www.studiostores.com
Days/Hours: Monday–Saturday, 9:30 a.m.–9:30 p.m.; Sunday, 11 a.m.–
   6 p.m.
Wheelchair/Stroller Access: Yes

Kids will go loony over the Looney Tunes gang at this store. All the animated Warner Brothers characters—Bugs Bunny, Daffy Duck, the Tasmanian Devil, and more—are featured on clothes, toys, and other collectibles. At the store's rear there's a spaceship for children to crawl around in and other interactive games nearby.

Mercer Island

Places to Go

Children's Park

Location: Island Crest Way and 54th S.E. From I-90, take the Island Crest
   Way exit south to just beyond Island Park School at about 54th S.E.
Wheelchair/Stroller Access: Yes

Conceived and designed by the Mercer Island Preschool Association, the park's unique climbing equipment is specifically designed for young children, but everyone enjoys it. Two tennis courts adjacent and

small trails through shady woods make the park especially appealing and cool during the summer. A fence around the park keeps little ones from roaming; the older ones stay busy playing on the dinosaur, in the forts, and crawling around the oversized drain tiles. There are a few picnic tables; space is limited.

Clarke Beach Park

Location: 7700 block of E. Mercer Way (on the southeast part of Mercer Island)
Wheelchair/Stroller Access: Yes, on a paved walking path

This is a small but very pleasant park offering delightful privacy, donated to the city by the Clarke family. There are picnic areas and two swimming areas, one shallower for toddlers, and some marvelous views.

First Hill Lid

Location: W. Mercer Way and I-90

Creative park planners designed this site to hide from I-90 and they did it well. It features soccer, baseball, and other play fields, two playgrounds, a basketball court, tennis court, restrooms, and a picnic shelter. It's also a great place to enjoy views of Seattle, the Eastside, and Mount Rainier (Seattle's Lid Park is at 23rd Ave. S. and Yakima St.). Walkers and bikers frequent the area, too; you'll see many families biking together.

Luther Burbank Park   206-296-2966

Location: 2040 84th S.E. (north end)
Web Site: www.metrokc.gov/parks/
Wheelchair/Stroller Access: Yes

Originally a private estate, Luther Burbank Park now is one of the Eastside's favorite parks. It's a boating destination during warm weather, great for picnics or just hanging out. There are seventy-seven acres of lake front; three tennis courts; a fishing pier; a 2,000-person grass amphitheater well-used for summer concerts; and outstanding playgrounds with balance beams, climbing nets, and other climbing equipment for kids. For dog lovers, there's even an area for unleashed dogs to run. Skateboard enthusiasts cruise a downhill trail to the water's edge. Nearby moorage has room for eighty craft. Picnic tables with small barbecues overlook the swimming beach; groups wishing to use this area must make reservations with the King County Parks Department for weekends and holidays.

Youth Theater Northwest   206-232-2202

Location: S.E. 40th St. and 88th Ave. S.E.
Days/Hours: Box Office: Monday and Wednesday–Friday, noon–5 p.m.
Wheelchair/Stroller Access: Yes

Blending entertainment and education is one of the goals here, and they do it well. Children can have a firsthand part in theater while having a great time by getting immersed in backstage activity. They'll learn acting, construction, lighting, and other theater skills in weekly classes and special summer workshops. Five productions each season bring fairy tales (sometimes with a funny twist) and classic literature to life on stage. They particularly look for productions written by members of the group that they can adapt and produce. It's good theater for kids on both sides of the house. Call for schedules, ticket information, and audition announcements.

Places to Eat

Starbucks   206-230-8322

Location: 7814 S.E. 28th (just across from the QFC)
Days/Hours: Monday–Friday, 6:00 a.m.–9 p.m. (drive-through open at
*   5:30 a.m.); Saturday and Sunday, 6:30 a.m.–8 p.m.*
Wheelchair/Stroller Access: Yes

Of course it's a coffee house, but it's also the very first Starbucks drive-through, and a perfect stop-over for hot chocolate and snacks— delivered through your car window. Also for kids, fruit juices and carbonated beverages are available.

Store to Browse

Island Books   206-232-6920

Location: 3014 78th S.E.
Days/Hours: Monday–Wednesday and Friday–Saturday, 9:30 a.m.–6 p.m.;
*   Thursday, 9:30 a.m.–8 p.m.; Sunday, noon–5 p.m.*
Wheelchair/Stroller Access: Yes

One of the island's most faithful resources, Island Books was founded over twenty years ago and was formerly owned by Lola Deane, the very same person who was the inspiration for this book (and for whom the Children's Park is named). Not just an ordinary bookstore, their children's area is a veritable wonderland of books for all interests. They will special

order for you, but their real specialty is getting to know their customers (including the youngest readers) and their reading habits very well. Great browsing place.

Kirkland and Redmond

Places to Go

Farrell-McWhirter Park   425-556-2309; 556-2300

Location: 19545 Redmond Rd., off Novelty Hill Rd. from Avondale Road
Days/Hours: Daily, 6 a.m.–dusk; animals visible from 9 a.m.–5 p.m.
    Program times vary.
Wheelchair/Stroller Access: In most places

This seventy-acre farm-turned-park is like a snapshot from your imagination. The sprawling acreage encompasses a lookout on top of an old silo, a forest with wheelchair-accessible Charlotte's Trail, and a collection of farm animals that includes pigs, chickens, goats, and an albino cow named Ivory. Explore Mackey Creek Watershed Trail or picnic under one of the mammoth trees. Ask about pony riding classes and summer day camps here.

Juanita Bay Park   425-828-1217; 425-828-2237 (tour info)

Location: 2201 Market St., Kirkland
Days/Hours: Dawn to dusk
Tours: Free tours on the first Sunday of the month
Wheelchair/Stroller Access: Yes

There's lots of space for pushing strollers in this 113-acre park with trails, boardwalks, and observation areas. This is Kirkland's largest park and a unique urban habitat: Interpretive signs educate visitors to the animals that live and thrive in this wetland area. Nature tours are lead by volunteer rangers; groups leave from the Juanita Bay parking lot at 2201 Market St.

Kingsgate Ice Arena   425-823-1242

Location: 14325 124th Ave. N.E., Kirkland
Days/Hours: Open skating available April–August only; call ahead for hours
Wheelchair/Stroller Access: Limited

What a great place to be in the summertime! Open skate times and admission prices vary, so it's important to call ahead. From August to April, they offer figure skating lessons and hockey competition.

Marymoor Museum

425-885-3684

Location: In Marymoor Park, Redmond. From the Evergreen Point Bridge/
   Hwy. 520 or I-405, drive east to the Marymoor Park exit. Inside the park,
   follow signs to <S3>Marymoor Museum.
Days/Hours: Year-round: Tuesday–Thursday, 11 a.m.–4 p.m. Memorial
   Day–Labor Day: Saturday–Sunday, 1 p.m.–4 p.m. The rest of the year:
   Sunday, 1 p.m.–4 p.m.
Admission: Free; donations appreciated
Tours: One-hour tours for groups by appointment only
Wheelchair/Stroller Access: Yes

A longtime favorite on the Eastside, the Marymoor Museum occu-
pies the north half of the Clise Mansion. Five exhibit rooms showcase
Eastside history, including logging, farming, and mining displays, and
information about current silicon-chip-based industries. Call during the
summer or check local newspapers for special events for families. Some
rooms in the mansion are available for rentals; it's a nice place for a special occasion party.

Marymoor Park

425-296-2966

Location: 6064 W. Lake Sammamish Parkway N.E., Redmond (See Mary-
   moor Museum for driving directions)
Web Site: www.metrokc.gov/parks/
Days/Hours: Daily, 8 a.m.–dusk.
Wheelchair/Stroller Access: Yes

If you're looking for space, you've come to the right place. Marymoor features five hundred acres of picnic grounds, baseball and soccer
fields, swing sets, strolling places, and the Clise Mansion, home of the
Marymoor Museum. Dog trainers work their dogs here, but kids can also
play at the doggie playground. Model airplane fanciers will be flying
their toys in good weather. Marymoor is also the starting point for people
drifting down the Sammamish Slough in rafts or inner tubes. Four tennis
courts, a concession stand, and the jogging track are here, too. In another
section of the park, a large covered picnic area is frequently reserved for
family reunions and birthday parties. One of the park's most amazing
features is the Velodrome, one of a handful in the country; special bicycling activities take place here often. There are eighteen different stations
with facilities for wheelchairs and other equipment for the physically
challenged.

Daring visitors may want to try scaling the manmade climbing rock
south of the Velodrome. Thirty-five feet high and forty feet wide at the
base, this is one of the largest free-standing climbing structures in the

A covered wagon at Marymoor Park's Heritage Festival. PHOTO COURTESY OF KING COUNTY PARKS

country. A series of intersecting walls with fixed handholds gives climbers different routes to the top; there's also a route for physically-challenged climbers.

Watch for the annual Marymoor Heritage Festival in early July; thousands of visitors flock to a weekend of international foods, games, crafts, hands-on activities for kids, and more. Admission is $3, children 15 and younger are free, but parking runs about $5 per vehicle.

North Kirkland Park   *425-828-1105*

Location: 12421 103rd Ave. N.E., Kirkland
Days/Hours: Dawn–dusk
Wheelchair/Stroller Access: Yes

It's known as the "choo-choo train park" because its central climbing toy is a multi-car train with engine and caboose. Ladders, slides, windows, and other features on this preschooler-sized train provide hours of imaginative play. Grassy hills a few feet away are comfortable for sleeping babies and parents to relax. Shade trees planted a few years ago are beginning to provide relief from the summer sun.

Paint the Town   425-861-8388 (Redmond); 206-527-8554 (Seattle)

Location: 7529 164th Ave. N.E., Redmond Town Center (also in Seattle at University Village)
Days/Hours: Monday–Wednesday, 10 a.m.–8 p.m.; Thursday–Friday, 10 a.m.–9:30 p.m.; Saturday, 10 a.m.–7 p.m.; Sunday, 11 a.m.–6 p.m.
Wheelchair/Stroller Access: Yes

The magic here is becoming a do-it-yourself artist with all of the materials just waiting for you. There are over 200 unpainted ceramic pieces, priced from $5 to $40, from menorahs and Santa faces to tiny tea sets, plates, and picture frames. You select the piece, then design and paint it, with thirty colors on hand (from Salsa and Moody Blue to Leapin' Lizard and Rosey Posey). Kids can create personalized pieces for any occasion—perfect gifts for teachers, grandparents, or a friend's birthday. The $6 per hour fee includes the paint and brushes, plus the glazing and firing (they do that for you); your piece is ready for pick up in five to seven days. Great place for a birthday party; there's a party room in the back that accommodates up to twenty. They'll supply the activity, you bring the food. For parties and other groups, please reserve ahead.

Redmond Saturday Market   425-882-5151 (info)

Location: 7730 Leary Way, southeast of Cleveland St.
Days/Hours: May–early October: 8 a.m.–2 p.m.

From a small collection of local vendors, this market has grown to include numerous booths and some interesting artisans. It can make your Saturday very productive. Fresh fruit and vegetables always available; crafts vary from week to week.

Sammamish River Park

Location: N.E. 116th at the Sammamish River, Redmond
Wheelchair/Stroller Access: Yes

With sixty acres bordering the river, this park is a sports-oriented site that includes picnic facilities.

Sammamish River Trail

Wheelchair/Stroller Access: Yes

The flat surface of this ten-foot wide asphalt trail is a great place for young bicyclists to shed training wheels and give two-wheeling a try. It's a major favorite for bicyclists, joggers, skaters, and pedestrians. If the trail, which begins in Redmond, seems longer, it's because it now connects with the Burke-Gilman Trail. No motor vehicles or horses allowed, but horseback riders do frequent the riverbanks. Popular access points are near Redmond City Hall and off Leary Way in Redmond. Be forewarned—it is very popular.

Zones
425-746-9411

Location: 2207 N.E. Bel-Red Rd., in the Ethan Allen Building, Redmond.
Take Hwy. 520 east to Redmond; take the second exit (the 148th St. exit)
and turn right. At the first light (24th Ave.), turn left and go up the hill.
Turn right on N.E. Bellevue-Redmond Road; Zones is behind Ethan
Allen furniture store.
Days/Hours: Sunday–Thursday, 11 a.m.–10 p.m.; Friday and Saturday,
11 a.m.–midnight.
Wheelchair/Stroller Access: Yes

High-tech, state-of-the-art, and just plain fun video games are a major draw at this indoor amusement center. Small-scale versions of local landmarks—the Microsoft building and ferry boats—on the eighteen-hole indoor miniature golf course add some local interest. Though prices vary with the game or activity, mini-golf runs about $4 per player; call ahead for more details on prices. Rooms can be reserved for birthday parties and other entertainment events. Families with small children may prefer late afternoon and early evening visits here; the evening pace changes with the teen crowd.

Places to Eat

British Pantry
425-883-7511

Location: 8125 161st Ave. N.E., Redmond
Days/Hours: Sunday and Tuesday, 10 a.m.–5:30 p.m.; Wednesday–Saturday,
10 a.m.–9 p.m.
Wheelchair/Stroller Access: Yes

What a charming introduction to the elegant sociability of a tea party at this very English restaurant. There are two rooms, separate but shared; one is an authentic British bakery with tasty scones, shelves of English teas, candies, and other goodies, the other a lovely little tea room set with tea cozies and other appropriate accessories. Stop here for an afternoon respite or just to pick up some excellent baked goods. The waitstaff will divide an adult portion for children with small appetites. The owners tell us many of their customers are grandparents out with grandchildren for the day.

Great Harvest Bread Co.

425-883-6909 (Redmond); 425-643-8420 (Bellevue)

Locations: 17192 Redmond Way, Redmond; 3610-C 128th Ave. S.E., Bellevue (Loehmann Plaza)
Days/Hours: Monday–Friday, 6:30 a.m.–7 p.m.; Saturday, 6:30 a.m.–6:30 p.m.
Tours: Yes! For both stores: 10 a.m.–1 p.m.; tours are thirty minutes; groups and families welcome; adults must accompany children. Reservations are essential; make them two to four weeks ahead of time. For the Bellevue store (which is smaller), group size is eight to ten with adults; the age minimum is 5 (with at least two adults).
Wheelchair/Stroller Access: Yes

Same name, different owners. Great Harvest is a franchised company, and the Eastside bakeries are under different ownership than the Seattle stores. But you'll find the same wonderful whole wheat bakery products and great bread. And the same delicious bread sampling. They bake twenty different kinds of bread, plus cookies, muffins, and scones. On tours, you'll see the whole baking process from milling to sales, and, of course, get a treat at the end.

Store to Browse

Confetti Junction
425-861-0567

Location: 17181 Redmond Way and Hwy. 520. Take Hwy. 520 past Marymoor Park; exit at Redmond Way, turn left at the light. Confetti Junction is about half a mile ahead on Redmond Way.
Days/Hours: Monday–Friday, 9:30 a.m.–8 p.m.; Saturday, 9 a.m.–6 p.m.; Sunday, 11 a.m.–5 p.m.
Wheelchair/Stroller Access: Yes

If you can't find it here, it probably doesn't exist. This is the "mega" party supply store. Take the kids along to help; they might come up with a novel idea, and you can certainly use an extra pair of eyes here. Confetti Junction can provoke those imaginations, from candy eyeglasses to Dennis Rodman bubble gum, from piñatas to—well, try football, soccer, or Sylvester and Tweety cake icing decorations, or cowboy hat and dog bone cookie cutters. They rent Helium Express kits for blowing up your own balloons, or make the bouquets for you (up to $5.88/dozen). Costumes and favors exist here for every party theme imaginable.

Bothell and Woodinville

Places to Go

Bothell Landing Park

Location: In Bothell at Bothell Way and N.E. 80th Ave.
Wheelchair/Stroller Access: Yes

Three important historical buildings—a Swedish immigrant's cabin, the home of the town's doctor, and the Hannan House (now a historical museum)—have all been moved to Bothell Landing Park to commemorate the pioneer families who settled the area. You can sit on the sloped and terraced hillsides next to the river to listen to summer weekend evening concerts. Kids can play nearby on the climbing toys and swings.

Chateau Ste. Michelle   *425-488-4633 (tour information)*

Location: 14111 N.E. 145th, Woodinville. Take I-405 to exit 23 (Monroe-Wenatchee) and follow Hwy. 522 to the Woodinville-Redmond Rd. exit. In Woodinville, turn west at Route 202; cross the railroad tracks. Turn south on Route 202/Woodinville-Redmond Road. In about two miles the road curves toward the east and the winery is on the south side
Days/Hours: Daily, 10 a.m.–4:30 p.m.
Tours: Tours are forty-five minutes long; tours are available during the summer every half hour (winter tours are slated every hour during the week and every half hour on weekends).
Wheelchair/Stroller Access: Yes

One of Washington's best-known wineries, Chateau Ste. Michelle is modeled after a French country chateau and is a welcome stop for families bicycling on the Burke-Gilman/Sammamish River trails. Tours are interesting, geared more for adults than children. But youngsters in the tour group will enjoy grape juice samples at the finish while adults sample wine. Of high interest are the special events and concerts that take place on the grounds; watch the papers for announcements. There will be seating, but most families prefer to spread the blankets and enjoy a grassy vantage point. There's usually ample parking.

Columbia Winery
425-488-2776

Location: 14030 N.E. 145th St, Woodinville. From I-405, take the 124th St. exit (at Totem Lake). Turn right on 124th and follow it across the valley. At the Woodinville-Redmond traffic light, turn left. Continue to Hollywood Corners and turn left on 145th. Columbia Winery is on the road's north side.
Days/Hours: Tours by request on Saturday and Sunday, 10 a.m.–5 p.m.
Wheelchair/Stroller Access: Yes

Set in a blue Victorian manor, this winery offers tours by request on weekends. As at other wineries, children will be served nonalcoholic beverages at the end of the tour.

Gold Creek Trout Farm
425-483-1415

Location: 15844 148th N.E., Woodinville. Take I-405 to exit 23 to Hwy. 522/ Monroe-Wenatchee. Follow Hwy. 522 into Woodinville. Turn west at 175th and right at 140th. Drive about a mile before turning left on 148th. Go two more blocks.
Days/Hours: Daily, 10 a.m.–5 p.m.
Admission: Free; you pay only for the fish you catch.
Wheelchair/Stroller Access: Yes

No stories here about the one that got away; everyone catches something. Fisher-persons are charged by the size of their fish. Worms are used for bait. They do the cleaning and bagging for you; bring a cooler with ice to take your catch home. Appointments are recommended for large groups. This is a great birthday party option for kids 10 and under.

Spirit of Washington Dinner Train
425-227-7245; 800-876-RAIL

Location: Departs from 625 S. Fourth, Renton
Days/Hours: Daily, 6:30 p.m.; Saturday, noon; Sunday, 11:30 a.m.
Wheelchair/Stroller Access: Yes

Trains have a mystique all their own. This three and a half hour trip from Renton through Bellevue to Woodinville and back, has become quite popular with both adults and children. Kids 12 and younger dine free from November to April; other months the fare is $20 in regular cars, full price for those in the dome car. Adult prices range from $47 to $69; reservations are required for all. Along with some delightful scenery and good food, a forty-five-minute stop at the Columbia Winery adds to the ambiance of the experience.

A Places to Eat

Texas Smokehouse BBQ   425-486-1957

Location: 14455 Woodinville-Redmond Rd. N.E. (at Hollywood Corners).
From I-405, take the 124th N.E. exit; head east across the valley; turn left
at the Woodinville Redmond light and continue toward Woodinville.
Hollywood Corners is at the intersection of 145th Ave N.E.
Days/Hours: Monday–Thursday, 11 a.m.–8 p.m.; Friday and Saturday,
11 a.m.–9 p.m.; Sunday, noon–7 p.m.
Wheelchair/Stroller Access: Yes

This is great for dine-in or take-out. Kids' portions are half of adult
portions of anything on the menu, and it's an ample serving—no matter what you order. Favorites here are baby-back ribs, chicken, and
brisket. They will stop serving a half hour before closing for dine-in
guests; for take-out they take orders until closing. Their All You Can
Eat menu is irresistible: On Mondays, it's beef ribs, on Wednesday it's
"burnt ends" (of the brisket—a big favorite!), and Thursdays it's
chicken. Texas Smokehouse is habit-forming for lots of families; high
chairs available. Instead of napkins, you'll find rolls of paper towels
at the tables. Great idea.

Stores to Browse

Country Village   425-483-2250

Location: 23730 Bothell-Everett Hwy., Bothell. Take I-405 to exit 26 and
head south one mile.
Days/Hours: Monday–Saturday, 10 a.m.–6 p.m.; Sunday, 11 a.m.–5 p.m.
Wheelchair/Stroller Access: In most places, but some of the boardwalk has
stairs

Located just off the highway, tourists can browse for knickknacks
here, but kids do get a kick out of the Doll Palace General Hospital where
dolls under repair are "hospitalized." There are a few creative toy shops
in the complex, and a tiny parent-powered merry-go-round rests in the
center courtyard for toddlers. One of the best bets here is the Country
Cafe, with generous breakfasts and desserts. Biscuits are a specialty.

Molbak's Greenhouse and Nursery

425-483-5000, ext. 400 (direction line); 425-483-5000, ext. 349 (tours)

Location: 13625 N.E. 175th, Woodinville. *Take I-405 to the Monroe-Wenatchee exit. Follow State Route 522 to Woodinville and into town. Turn left at 175th. Drive two blocks and Molbak's is on your right.*
Days/Hours: Saturday–Thursday, 9 a.m.–6 p.m.; Friday, 9 a.m.–9 p.m.
Tours: Groups of ten or more only (chaperones not counted); age minimum is 6. Tour is usually one hour; Monday–Friday only.
Wheelchair/Stroller Access: Yes

Molbak's is a great destination for children any month of the year, but October and November are perhaps the most magical. In October, watch for Molbak's Floral Fairyland. The fun begins at the main entrance where you read "Once Upon a Time," then step into a storybook world. Six-foot-tall storyboards and handmade three-dimensional characters display scenes from classic fairy tales. Then the fairy tale comes to life right there in the greenhouse as plays are comically performed by professional actors. Look for ads in local newspapers for the schedule or call Molbak's for a brochure. In November, the Poinsettia Festival begins. Thousands of colorful "homegrown" poinsettias in many colors (not just red!) are blooming. You can also nibble on complimentary Danish pastry. Whenever you visit, don't miss the conservatory featuring tropical birds (it's near the espresso cart). Cameras are welcome. With so much to see and do here, it's easy to get kids excited and involved in gardening.

Woodinville Saturday Market

425-481-8300 (visitor information center)

Location: 13203 N.E. 175th St. (City Hall parking lot)
Days/Hours: Early April–the first Saturday in October: Saturday, 9 a.m.–4 p.m.

If you want to get away from the supermarket scramble, here's a nice collection of local produce, flowers, and arts and crafts. This market has been growing, and you'll often see different vendors on different weeks.

Duvall, Carnation, and Fall City

Places to Go

Balloon Depot   *425-881-9699*

Location: Most balloon trips originate at Remlinger Farms (see p 119)
Days/Hours: Only by appointment; make one several days in advance; daily
*   morning and evening flights, weather permitting*
Wheelchair/Stroller Access: No

Children need to be at least four feet tall (and preferably without
fear of heights) to venture into the loft of a hot air balloon. Usually four
to nine passengers comprise a group, kids included. The one-hour rides
will cost from $99 to $145 per person; there are no discounts for children. Sumner and Carnation are the departure points, and wind is a
major consideration. This is a very exciting excursion—the views (and
thrills) are different than any other experience. Great birthday gift for a
teenager.

Camlann Medieval Faire   *425-788-1353*

Location: 10320 Kelly Road N.E., Carnation
Hours/Days: August–Labor Day: Saturday–Sunday, 11:30 a.m.–6 p.m. Call
*   ahead.*
Admission: $5–$8; gate admission could include the evening banquet but
*   seating is limited.*
Wheelchair/Stroller Access: Yes

This fourteenth-century Olde English rural fair brings history to life
for a time. Even children too young to understand the history will be
entertained by the wandering minstrels, frolicking harlequins, historical
craft demonstrations by peasant-clad performers, and puppet and magic
shows. It's a whimsical environment, and the food is authentic, too. It's a
new experience for some (but old habit for others) to eat stew out of a
bowl with no spoon; be sure to sample the zesty grape juice called *ypocras*.

Carnation Research and Dairy Farm   425-788-1511

Location: 28901 N.E. Carnation Farm Rd., off Hwy. 203. Take I-90 to the
Preston-Fall City exit. Drive through Fall City to Carnation. Watch for
signs just outside Carnation.
Days/Hours: Varies annually; call for current information
Admission: Free
Tours: Yes. Group tours by appointment; self-guided according to their
schedule. Allow forty-five minutes.
Wheelchair/Stroller Access: Yes, but there are a lot of hills

Tour schedules for this working and research farm change often, so
it's important to call ahead before visiting. Once inside, kids will look at
milk with a new respect. Their eyes may pop at the statue of Possum
Sweetheart, a Carnation cow that produced 37,381 pounds of milk in 1920.
The tour features calves which can be touched, cows on assembly-line
milking machines, and carefully-tended gardens surrounding homes for
the cats and dogs used as taste-testers for Friskies brand pet food, a division of Carnation.

Fall City Farms   425-222-7930

Location: 3636 Neal Rd.
Hours/Days: Farm is open from July 1–November 1. July–September 30:
Thursday–Monday, 10 a.m.–6 p.m.; Sunday, 11 a.m.–6 p.m. October 1–
31: Monday–Saturday, 10 a.m.–dusk; Sunday, 11 a.m.–dusk. Varies
during late summer and autumn.
Tours: Yes. No age minimum. Tours customized to the group's interests.
Dam: For tours, $3.50/preschool (includes a pumpkin); $4.50/1st–3rd graders,
chaperones required. Tours are given in summer and fall months; spring
tours by request only.
Wheelchair/Stroller Access: No

Art and agriculture blend on this educational working farm. There's
no "entertainment" here—just the fun of learning what working on a
farm is all about. In August, children 6 to 13 are invited to attend art
classes where they learn to sketch sunflowers, squash, and the other things
they see on the farm tour. During the fall, visiting school classes (including preschoolers) ride the hay wagon to pick their own pumpkins. There's
time to press apples and taste your own apple cider, too. The "tools" on
this farm are the dogs, sheep, and hay wagon. Kids can roam the farm,
exploring wherever they'd like.

Remlinger Farms   425-333-4135

Location: One mile south of Carnation on Hwy. 203
Days/Hours: Mid-April–October: daily, 9 a.m.–7 p.m. Call ahead for special
    December hours.

What's really fun here is riding the train that loops through the farm
to pick a pumpkin in the fall or select a Christmas tree in the winter. It's
a real bonus for the hordes of kids who love to come to Remlinger. Ponies
masquerade as reindeer in December for visitors who want a ride. And a
wild maze built from hay challenges visitors of all ages. During the holiday season there'll be weekend entertainment inside one of the barns;
the audience sits on hay bales. Outside, kids are encouraged to feed the
barnyard animals (with special edibles provided). And, of course, the
general store, filled with fresh products, jams, and other specialties, is
part of the ambiance here.

Issaquah

Places to Go

Boehm's   425-392-6652

Location: 255 N.E. Gilman Blvd.
Days/Hours: November–Memorial Day: daily, 9 a.m.–6 p.m. The rest of the
    year: Monday–Thursday, 9 a.m.–6 p.m.; Friday–Sunday, 9 a.m.–7 p.m.
Admission: Free
Tours: For groups of at least fifteen visitors, forty-minute tours begin at 10:30
    a.m. and 1 p.m. every weekday but Wednesday and at 1 p.m. weekends.
    Reservations essential; best to make them at least a week in advance.
Wheelchair/Stroller Access: Yes

It's really a treat to visit this quaint Alpine chateau. Boehm's Chocolates is one of Issaquah's oldest and most charming attractions, and the
tours are fascinating. Candy makers here concoct more than 150 kinds of
European and American sweets. During the tour, you'll see the work areas with huge copper tubs and three-inch-thick marble slabs, and, of
course, enjoy some samples at the tour's end. If you happen to be there
when they're hand-forming the chocolates, you'll be intrigued by the
precision of the chocolatiers. Included in the tour is founder Julius
Boehm's authentic Swiss chalet—the first one built in the Pacific Northwest. The chalet is filled with his collection of European art and memen-
tos of a very unique and active life. Although he's been gone for some
years, the owners have kept the premises as they were when Julius lived.
When you sample this delicious candy you'll be hooked.

Cougar Mountain Zoological Park 425-391-5508

Location: 19525 S.E. 54th, Issaquah
Days/Hours: Zoo is open year-round. March–October: Wednesday–Sunday,
   10 a.m.–5 p.m. February and November: 10 a.m.–5 p.m. December 1-23:
   Reindeer Festival, Wednesday–Sunday, 5 p.m.–8 p.m.; January: Pre-
   arranged tours and birthday parties only.
Admission: Feb. 15–Nov. 15: $5.50/ages 16 and up; $4.50/seniors; $4/
   children 4–15; $2.50/children 2 and 3; free/children under two
Tours: Guided tours available by request.
Wheelchair/Stroller Access: Limited

Small but important, this fourteen-acre park is home to a number of
endangered or threatened species. In an intimate setting, children get a
chance to stop and "talk" with some brilliantly-colored exotic birds, or
perhaps an alpaca, emu, or cougar. In December, Santa's Reindeer Festival is authentic; reindeer live here, too. Birthday parties available with
special arrangements.

Geology Adventures 206-255-6635

Wheelchair/Stroller Access: No

Whether it's crystals in the Cascades, amethyst in California or glowing rocks and palm trees in Issaquah, Geology Adventures takes you
someplace out of the ordinary, off the beaten track. Bob Jackson is a ge-
ologist who loves to demystify science for children and adults, and offers opportunities for parents and children to learn and explore together.
Some trips are ideal for birthday parties. He also provides a number of
educational trips for schools, designing the field trip for the specific age
group. Call for the brochure.

High Country Outfitters/Camp Yahoo, Inc. 425-392-0111

Location: 3020 Issaquah-Pine Lake Rd., Suite 544
Days/Hours: Varies; call for schedule and required reservations
Wheelchair/Stroller Access: No, but horseback riding is available for people
   with some disabilities.

Summer trail rides, overnight, and extended pack trips are the focal
point of High Country in Cle Elum. Deep in the Wenatchee National Forest, Cle Elum means fresh air, sunshine, scenery, and solitude in the High
Cascades. It's a great way for families with children ages 8 and older to
test their skills and endurance while spending quality time together.
   Camp Wahoo, a summer horse camp in the wilderness, is for youth

Searching for rock crystals. PHOTO COURTESY GEOLOGY ADVENTURES

ages 9 to 16. Each camper is assigned a horse to care for and ride for the week. They learn to handle, saddle, and bridle a horse; advanced work is available for those with experience. Half-day, whole-day, and overnight pack trips are offered. Outdoor living skills, how to build a shelter, use a compass, read a map, build a cooking fire, and prepare meals on the trail are all part of this outdoor experience.

Issaquah Farmers Market   *425-392-2229*

Location: Community Center; 301 Rainier Blvd. S.
Days/Hours: Saturday, 9 a.m.–3 p.m.
Wheelchair/Stroller Access: Yes

Another grand opportunity for a Saturday outing that accomplishes several purposes: shopping and fun. It's a great way to teach your children how to select good produce and even plan some of the meals. What a concept for working parents!

Issaquah Salmon Days Festival   425-270-2532

Location: *Downtown Issaquah*
Days/Hours: *Usually the first weekend in October*
Wheelchair/Stroller Access: *Yes*

One of the fastest growing family events on the Eastside, Issaquah Salmon Days features hatchery tours, pony and train rides, plus a petting zoo and rock climbing wall. The downtown streets are lined with food vendors, and local naturalists celebrate volunteers' efforts to keep local waters clean so salmon can migrate upstream to spawn.

Lake Sammamish State Park   425-455-7010 *(reservations)*

Location: *Off I-90 take exit 15 or 17; turn north to Lake Sammamish.*
Web Site: *www.parks.wa.gov*
Wheelchair/Stroller Access: *Yes*

This marvelous park offers an expansive beach and swimming area and several play areas with climbing equipment made from rustic logs. A pagoda-covered eating area includes a central barbecue and running water. It's a popular spot for birthday parties, barbecues, reunions, and other large group events. There are three areas that can be reserved, which can accommodate groups of 100, 200, and 400; reservations in advance are required. Boating is a favorite activity here; you can rent a canoe or kayak from Klub Kayak. Single-seat kayaks are $8 an hour; doubles are $12. Most families prefer the canoes, which rent for $8 an hour; life jackets are provided. At Lake Sammamish, look for the rentals between 3 p.m. and 8 p.m. daily during summer months on Old Beach.

Village Theater   425-392-2202

Location: *120 Front St. N., from I-90 exit 17*
Days/Hours: *Box office: Tuesday–Saturday, 11 a.m.–7 p.m.*
Wheelchair/Stroller Access: *Yes*

While older children will probably most enjoy the productions at this excellent local theater, there is a viewing room at the back where families with young ones can sit together. Here the toddlers can move around and feel less confined, yet parents can enjoy some good stage fare, mostly comical and musical productions. Scenery, costuming, and production techniques are top-notch, especially for Broadway musicals. Schedules and prices vary, so it's best to call ahead. Season tickets go quickly, but there are singles to be had for individual performances. If you're new to this theater, ask ahead about parking.

Places to Eat

Cascade Garden   425-391-9597

Location: In Meadows Shopping Center at 1580 N.W. Gilman Blvd.
Days/Hours: Monday–Friday, 11 a.m.–2:30 p.m. for lunch, 4:30 p.m.–
9:45 p.m. for dinner; Saturday and Sunday, 5 p.m.–10:45 p.m.
Wheelchair/Stroller Access: Yes

A fun place to bring children for Chinese food! On Friday and Saturday nights, the chef will demonstrate how they make noodles.

Stores to Browse

Gilman Village   425-264-0594 *(office)*

Location: In downtown Issaquah. Take I-90 to exit 17 to Front St. Turn south
on Gilman Blvd. Turn right to cross the railroad tracks and turn left into
Gilman Village. You can also take the Renton/Lake Sammamish exit (exit
16); turn right at the light, go to the next light (Gilman Blvd.), and turn
left; continue east to Gilman Village (on your right).
Days/Hours: Monday–Saturday, 10 a.m.–6 p.m.; Sunday, 11 a.m.–5 p.m.
Some stores have extended hours.
Wheelchair/Stroller Access: Yes

Gilman Village is a collection of old houses moved from their original sites and refurbished to form a cluster of forty delightful specialty
shops and restaurants. Especially appealing in spring and summer, the
bright and festive look of flowers and outdoor accessories makes it a
relaxing shopping venture; but there's not a great deal for kids here, except some very good small restaurants. Call ahead for special events
geared for kids and families.

Kids with pets enjoy the goodies carried at Myken's (425-392-5672),
a specialty boutique for dog and cat owners.

Snoqualmie Valley
Places to Go

The Herbfarm   206-784-2222

Location: 32804 Issaquah-Fall City Rd., Fall City. Take I-90 to exit 22
(Preston-Fall City). Follow the road three miles; at the green bridge at
328th St., turn left, cross the bridge and drive another half-mile.
Web Site: www.theherbfarm.com
Days/Hours: April–September: daily, 10 a.m.–6 p.m. The rest of the year:
daily, 10 a.m.–5 p.m.
Wheelchair/Stroller Access: Yes

Although a terrible fire destroyed the restaurant in 1997, the rebuilding has challenged and inspired a new facility—a bed and breakfast opening in 1998, which will include the famous restaurant. The Herbfarm is a
magnet for gardeners; they sell over 160 varieties of succulents and 600
varieties of herbs, including fifteen kinds of mint. The display garden is
wonderful for the imagination. They have special events during the year
that are popular with families, especially the "Halloween Adventure."
During the year there are classes designed just for kids. Children are always drawn to the little aviary filled with cooing doves, and there are
animals to feed—llamas, ducks, geese, chickens, and goats (food provided).

Snoqualmie Falls

Location: Town of Snoqualmie
Wheelchair/Stroller Access: Yes

What a magnificent backdrop for your family and out-of-town visitor photographs. Some twenty-six miles east of Seattle, the falls plunge
268 feet into a sixty-five-foot deep pool; that's a hundred feet higher than
Niagara Falls. Tourists and locals are elbow-to-elbow at this gorgeous
waterfall. The roar of the spray, the gentle mists, and the fascination of
the falling water attracts thousands. It's especially dramatic when the
spring snow melts into the river, creating huge swells and currents. A
little known fact: This is the site of the first major electric plant in the
Northwest to use falling water as a source of power. Views of the Falls
from nearby Salish Lodge make dining here a treat, albeit pricey. A breakfast, lunch, or dinner table often requires early reservations.

Snoqualmie Falls Forest Theater   425-222-7044

Location: *Near Fall City at David Powell Rd. Take I-90 to exit 22. Follow
signs to Fall City for four miles. Turn right on David Powell Rd. and go
three miles to the gate*
Days/Hours: *Performances June–August; box office: Monday–Friday,
10 a.m.–5 p.m.*
Admission: *Prices vary, call ahead. Children 5 and under admitted free*
Wheelchair/Stroller Access: *Limited because of the dirt path*

For children, just getting to this outdoor amphitheater is half the fun.
Performances are during the summer months only. You'll hike down a
dirt trail through a pristine forest to the stage; the audience is seated on
the terraced hillside just above. The peaceful pounding of Snoqualmie
Falls and lush greenery on nearby mountains are the backdrop to the
stage. The group performs at least one youth production each year; most
shows are scheduled for Saturdays. Before or after the show, save time to
stroll through the quiet woods. Schedules and ticket prices vary, so call
ahead.

Snoqualmie Valley Historical Museum   425-888-3200

Location: *222 North Bend Blvd.; off I-90 take exit 31 (North Bend)*
Days/Hours: *April–October: Thursday–Sunday, 1 p.m.–5 p.m.*
Admission: *Free, but donations are appreciated*
Wheelchair/Stroller Access: *Yes*

Children can travel back in time to 1917 and see what mill-town life
was like in the Snoqualmie Valley. Sponsored by the Snoqualmie Valley
Historical Society, the museum features both permanent and changing
exhibits of Native American and pioneer life. You'll see models in authentic clothing from 1917–57 and a re-created kitchen and parlor. Out in
the farm shed, the equipment and tools date back nearly eighty years.
Special groups may make appointments to visit at nonscheduled times.
As at other local museums, it's the volunteers that build and maintain
these important reflections of our local history.

Snoqualmie Valley Railroad   425-746-4025; 425-888-3030

Location: In Snoqualmie at Route 202
Days/Hours: Summer weekends and holidays: 11 a.m.–4 p.m. Call for
information.
Admission: $6/adults; $5/seniors; $4/children 3–12; free/children 2 and
younger. Add a 5 percent tax for tickets purchased at the Snoqualmie
Depot.
Wheelchair/Stroller Access: No

Visitors climb aboard these vintage trains for a ten-mile journey
through scenic Snoqualmie Valley. You can board at North Bend or Snoqualmie for a one-way or a one-hour round-trip. Now on the National
Register of Historic Places, the Snoqualmie Depot was built in 1890 by
the Seattle, Lake Shore, and Eastern Railway. December's Santa Train is
very popular; tickets are often are sold out by October, so call early.

Snowflake Summit Tubing Center   206-236-7277, ext. 3377

Location: Off I-90 at exit 52
Days/Hours: Open late November–late March, as snow permits. Usual
schedule is: Friday, 11 a.m.–10 p.m.; Saturday, 8:30 a.m.–10 p.m.;
Sunday, 8:30 a.m.–8:30 p.m., although hours will vary during winter
holidays. The center may be open on weekdays in late December and early
January.
Admission: $8/per person; free/children 5 and under; $5/inner tube rentals
Wheelchair/Stroller Access: No

This center is probably the only one of its kind around. Now known
as Summit Central (formerly Ski Acres), this 400-foot snow hill has eight
chutes, is lighted for late evening runs, and even has a rope tow on the
hill's east side to pull tubers back to the top. Sleds and anything with
metal runners are not allowed, but you can bring plastic saucers or disks
if you prefer. It's a good idea to make sure your tube is sufficiently inflated before starting out. There is a pressure pump site, but cold weather
sometimes inhibits operation.

King County Hikes

Asahel Curtis Nature Walk   425-888-1421; 206-470-4060

Location: Snoqualmie Pass at I-90, exit 47

On the south side of I-90, just past Denny Creek, walk through a
quarter-mile of old fir, cedar, and hemlock. The Eastlake District of

Federated Garden Clubs has identified more than forty plants for novice botanists. The trail begins at the Asahel Curtis Picnic Area. Four of the twenty-eight picnic tables here are on the Snoqualmie River. There are fire pits to cook over. Some kids enjoy drawing water from the hand pump.

Denny Creek Campground   *425-888-1421; 206-470-4060*

Location: Snoqualmie Pass area

Located about seventeen miles east of North Bend along I-90, this campground is a base for several short hikes. In spring, the rushing water in this creek poses a hazard to children. In summer, shallow spots offer safe wading and water play. The Franklin Falls Trail, a little more than a mile off the Denny Creek Trail, leads to a cliff face where water falls more than seventy feet to a pool. It's a nice place to feel the spray and watch for rainbows.

High Point Trail   *425-888-1421; 206-470-4060*

Location: West Tiger Mountain

Paint Seattle's downtown skyline, Bellevue's sprawling landscape, and Issaquah's amazing growth on a picture postcard—these are the views you'll enjoy with a walk up Tiger Mountain. For children, it can be a new view of the world. To find the most traveled route up Tiger Mountain, leave I-90 at exit 20 (High Point Rd.). Turn right at the stop sign. At the frontage road, turn left and park on the shoulder. This is one of the area's most popular trails, so don't expect privacy.

Snoqualmie Tunnel   *425-888-1421; 206-470-4060*

Location: At I-90, exit 54 (Hyak)

This 2.3-mile-long abandoned railroad tunnel is the longest open to hikers in this country. The tunnel links the west and east sections of the John Wayne Iron Horse Trail, which begins at Rattlesnake Lake near North Bend. There are magnificent wild flowers growing at both ends of the tunnel in the spring and dazzling colors in the fall. Because it's under the solid rock of Snoqualmie Pass, the tunnel is unlighted, so be sure to bring a flashlight, good walking shoes, and a warm jacket, too. Some diehards attempt pushing strollers, but backpacks are the best way to get young ones through this tunnel.

Snoqualmie Pass Skiing

The Summit at Snoqualmie

206-236-1600; 206-232-8182 (reservations for child-care service)

Location: *Just off I-90 at exit 52*

One of the region's most popular downhill and cross-country skiing destinations, Snoqualmie Pass has consolidated its four areas—Alpental, Ski Acres, Snoqualmie, and Hyak—into Summit East, Central, and West, all part of The Summit at Snoqualmie. A single lift ticket is valid on all twenty-five chairlifts here. A new fixed-grip quad chairlift is a great new feature of the area, and fifteen more quadlifts are planned to be built before 2007.

Parents with young children will appreciate the child-care services provided at Ski Acres and Snoqualmie (phone listed above). Snowboarding continues to grow in popularity, too. Ask about guided hikes for young teenagers. Advanced skiers may want to explore the guided tours to the back country.

At nearby Snowflake Inner Tubing, you can flop onto an inflated tire tube and swoosh down the snow. At the bottom, the rope tow hoists tubers back to the top for another ride. This is one of the few inner tubing sites for kids to be found at Washington ski areas.

Lift ticket and inner tubing prices may change yearly; it's best to call ahead.

SOUTH KING COUNTY

Auburn, Renton, Kent, Tukwila, and Federal Way

Places to Go

Canterbury Faire   *253-859-3991*

Location: *Mill Creek Canyon Earthworks Park, 742 E. Titus St., Kent*
Hours/Days: *Usually a mid-August weekend; call ahead for schedule*
Admission: *Generally $1*
Wheelchair/Stroller Access: *Yes*

It seems like a slice of merry Olde England at this annual fair and a good weekend family experience. Creative children can try their hands at creating a coat of arms or weaving with a floor loom; these and other hands-on activities usually happen between noon and 5 p.m. Or you may prefer just milling among costumed lords and ladies, brave knights, and comical jesters, or having a spot of high tea served in the English Tea Garden. Shuttle buses carry passengers every half hour between the fair and Metro Park-and-Ride at Lincoln and Smith streets. Call ahead to check on seasonal changes.

Emerald Downs   253-288-7000

Location: East of Hwy. 167/Valley Freeway near Auburn. Take the 15th St. N.W. or 37th St. N.W. exits
Web Site: www.seattleonline.com
Admission: $3/general; free/children 10 and under
Days/Hours: Gates open at 11:30 a.m. on Sundays; post time is 1 p.m.; season runs early May–late September.
Wheelchair/Stroller Access: Yes

Even if you don't like the betting, there's a frequent Sunday afternoon slate of activities for children throughout the racing season. Pony rides, on-stage musicians, face painters, jugglers, mimes, and inflatable jumping toys are set up for youngsters on a grassy lawn at the northwest edge of the track; most activities are free. Picnic tables are available if you've brought your own food, or you can purchase ice cream and other snacks inside. Between races, families may wander down to the paddock where stewards bring the horses near the rails so children can see these sleek, muscular animals. General parking is free, but it can be a long hike for some children, so it's wise to ride the free shuttle buses. Reserved parking is $3.

Enchanted Village/Wild Waves Water Park

253-661-8000; 253-661-8001 (groups and birthday parties)

Location: 36201 Enchanted Parkway S. in Federal Way. Take exit 142B.
Web Site: www.wildwaves.com
Days/Hours: Memorial Day–Labor Day: 11 a.m.–7 p.m. Weekends during spring and fall: 10 a.m.–6 p.m. Call for specific dates.
Admission: Enchanted Village: $11/ adults; $7/seniors; $9/children under four feet tall. Village and Wild Waves (combined): $19.95/adults; $10/ seniors; $17.95/children. Includes unlimited rides; prices subject to change. Ask about season passes, group rates, and birthday parties.
Wheelchair/Stroller Access: Yes, at Enchanted Village; not at Wild Waves

With the wonders of a fantasyland and the exhilaration of a water park, these side-by-side attractions draw a variety of visitors. At Enchanted Village, activities are geared to younger children and there's a lot to do, so plan your time carefully. The colorful carousel, small train, and padded jumping area are favorites with the toddlers. Admission also includes on-stage entertainment featuring costumed animals.

Wild Waves is especially popular with preteens and teens. A river ride, slides, and fountains attract little ones; older kids go for the Raging River Ride, Cannonball Ride, and a giant wave pool. The highlight is the Wild Thing, zipping through a sixty-foot loop to a sixty-four-foot drop, calling itself the largest roller coaster in the northwestern U.S.

In the evening hours from late November through December, the Holiday Lights is a spectacular display of holiday characters throughout the park. Rides, trees, and other structures twinkle and sparkle, creating a very festive atmosphere.

Fat Bat   253-854-6783

Location: 1008 N. Central, Kent
Days/Hours: Monday–Friday, 2 p.m.–7:30 p.m.; Saturday and Sunday,
*   11 a.m.–5 p.m.*
Wheelchair/Stroller Access: Yes

Softball and baseball batting cages, nine holes of miniature golf, and an exhausting trampoline jumping game called SpaceBall make this a popular place for active preteens and teens. Games range from 75¢ for fifteen pitches to $2 per player for golf. SpaceBall is $3 for five minutes, but it may be the most tiring five minutes of a parent's life.

Gene Coulon Memorial Park

Location: In Renton at Lake Washington's south end. From I-405, take the
*   Sunset Hwy. exit. Follow to Puget Power Shuffleton Plant.*
Days/Hours: Daily, 6 a.m.–9 p.m.
Wheelchair/Stroller Access: Yes

Formerly known as Lake Washington Park, this is a delightful public beach with ample parking, a good boat launch site, and excellent picnic facilities, especially the covered pavilion with cooking areas. There are lots of ducks to feed, a complete first-aid station, bike racks, volleyball and tennis courts, shuffleboard, horseshoe pits, and concession stands. And the playground has small swings for small persons. A wooden bridge takes you to a small, grassy island with a sturdy climbing tower and fort donated by the Renton Lions. You may rent canoes, sailboards, and rowboats; picnic; listen to summer concerts; ride bikes; or take a stroll. The park prohibits kite flying because of nearby power lines. No animals or alcohol allowed. Lifeguards are on duty only during the summer.

Kids love the public beaches on Lake Washington. PHOTO COURTESY BELLEVUE PARKS AND COMMUNITY SERVICES DEPARTMENT

Pacific Rim Bonsai Collection

253-924-5206 (info); 253-924-3153 (group tour reservations):

Location: *33553 Weyerhaeuser Way S., Federal Way (next to Rhododendron Species Botanical Garden). From I-5, take exit 143 (Federal Way/320th St.) to the east side of the freeway onto Weyerhaeuser Way S. Follow signs to gardens.*
Days/Hours: *March–May: daily except Thursday, 10 a.m.–4 p.m. June–February: Sunday–Wednesday, 11 a.m.–4 p.m.*
Admission: *Free*
Wheelchair/Stroller Access: *Yes*

As you enter, be sure to pick up a brochure for the Bonsai Collection. Each specimen is identified with a history and description, which will enhance your understanding of this remarkable display. Children are usually quite amazed at the dwarf varieties, so perfect in their presentation. There are nearly sixty trees trimmed in this ancient art form; each is unusual for a different reason. The park was created in 1989 as Weyerhaeuser's tribute to the Washington State Centennial. To honor the company's trade relations, the plants on display come from Taiwan, Japan, China, Canada, and the United States. If you are interested in bonsai on a personal level, there are some internationally known experts right here in Washington. Tour guides are very knowledgeable and share volumes of information.

Pattison's West Skating

253-838-7442; 253-838-5788 (recorded information)

Location: *34222 Pacific Hwy. S., Federal Way, one mile south of Sea-Tac Mall*
Days/Hours: *Seasonal; call the recorded info line for current schedule*
Admission: *$3/with your own skates; $4/includes skate rental; $6/for in-line skates*
Wheelchair/Stroller Access: *Yes*

It's a large skating arena with a capacity for a thousand. Best to call ahead for detailed information; depending on the time of year, there might be special sessions for youngsters. It's very popular for school parties, service groups, and birthday parties. There's a snack bar on-site.

Rhododendron Species Botanical Garden   253-681-9377

Location: *33553 Weyerhaeuser Way S., Federal Way (right next to the Pacific Rim Bonsai Garden)*
Days/Hours: *March –May: daily except Thursday, 10 a.m.–4 p.m. June–February: Saturday–Wednesday, 11 a.m.–4 p.m.*
Admission: *$3.50/adults; $2.50/seniors and students; free/children 12 and under and school groups*

There's so much more than just rhododendrons here, although you'll find more than 500 species with 2,000 varieties displayed by the Rhododendron Species Foundation. The garden is on twenty-four acres donated by the Weyerhaeuser Company and is maintained magnificently. Did you know that the rhododendron is Washington's state flower? Other areas of the garden include a fern collection and an alpine garden, plus the woodland and azalea varieties. Don't overlook the plant sale area (some beautiful specimens here) or the gift shop, with a wonderful selection of floral-related items.

Renton Civic Theatre   253-226-5529

Location: 507 S. Third
Days/Hours: Box office: Monday–Wednesday, 10 a.m.–5 p.m.; Thursday–
   Saturday, noon–6 p.m.
Admission: $18/adults; $14/students and seniors.
Wheelchair/Stroller Access: Yes

With musicals and other family-oriented productions, this is a wonderful community theater for children. Many performances are ideal for children 7 years and older; past productions have included *The Secret Garden* and *Godspell*. The season runs September to June. You can purchase season tickets, but it's possible to find a good seat arriving at the box office thirty minutes before show time.

River Bend Mini Putt   253-859-4000

Location: 2020 W. Meeker, Kent. From Hwy. 167, take Hwy. 516/Willis St.
   exit. On Willis St., turn north on Washington Ave. and drive several
   blocks to Meeker. From I-5, head south; take the Kent-Des Moines exit,
   staying in the left lane. Turn left at the light, head down the hill to the
   light at Meeker; turn left; the mini-putt is there on your right.
Days/Hours: Mid-spring–Labor Day: Monday–Saturday, 8:15 a.m.–10 p.m.;
   Sunday, 8:15 am–9 p.m. The rest of the year: Monday–Saturday, about
   8 a.m.–9 p.m.; Sunday, 8 a.m.–6 p.m.
Admission: $4/adults; $3/children 12 and younger
Wheelchair/Stroller Access: Yes

This lighted eighteen-hole mini-putt course is next to a larger driving range. Miniature golf is a great family activity, especially for those with a short attention span or minimal golf skill or interest.

Springbrook Trout Farm   253-852-0360

Location: In Renton at 19225 Talbot Rd. Take I-405 to exit Hwy. 167 South.
   Take S.W. 43rd exit off Hwy. 167 to Valley General Hospital, which is
   one block east. Trout Farm is a mile south of the hospital.
Days/Hours: March–October: Monday–Saturday, 10 a.m.–dusk; Sunday,
   10 a.m.–6 p.m.
Wheelchair/Stroller Access: Yes, but ground can be soft in wet weather

It's a delightful woodsy setting, appealing to kids of all ages. Even toddlers can watch Dad pull one in—or even help. The cost depends on the size of the catch—it will range from 10 inches for $3.50 up to 19 inches for $9.50. They do birthday parties (three packages available) and educational tours (groups of ten or more) and provide picnic rentals for a minimum charge. There's also a small snack bar. Best of all, they clean and bag the fish; you can cook it for dinner or freeze it!

Stores to Browse

The Fish Gallery (three locations)

425-226-3215 (Renton); 425-641-9240 (Factoria); 253-852-9240 (Kent)

Location: *Renton Village, Renton; 3710 128th E., Factoria; Easthill Plaza, Kent*

Days/Hours: *Monday–Friday, 9 a.m.–9 p.m.; Saturday, 9 a.m.–6 p.m.; Sunday, 11 a.m.–6 p.m.*

Tours: *Group tours by request; morning hours preferred; reserve at least one week in advance.*

Wheelchair/Stroller Access: *Yes*

The tropical fish collection is extraordinary, but you'll also find some flamboyant parrots whose life spans are so great they'll likely outlive you. Pet choices here range from the traditional to the exotic; families are welcome to drop in and handle the animals or talk to the birds. The owners are happy to give group tours, but need plenty of warning and prefer morning hours.

Imaginarium (three locations)

206-439-8980 (Southcenter); 425-453-5288 (Bellevue); 425-771-7220 (Alderwood Mall)

Location: *Southcenter Mall, Tukwila; Bellevue Square, Bellevue; Alderwood Mall, Lynnwood*

Days/Hours: *Monday–Saturday,10 a.m.–9:30pm; Sunday, 11 a.m.–6 p.m.*

Wheelchair/Stroller Access: *Yes*

Tots feel very welcome here because of the special kid-size entrance just for them. Inside, you'll find an incredible array of toys to be tested and stuffed animals for hugging and purchase. In fact, signs on the toys read "Please Touch." The staff will help schools and day-care centers set up their libraries and manipulative materials

Black Diamond and Enumclaw

Places to Go

Black Diamond Historical Museum   360-886-1168

Location: In Black Diamond at Baker St. and Railroad Ave. From I-405 in
Renton, take the Enumclaw exit and follow Hwy. 169.
Days/Hours: Thursday, 9 a.m.–4 p.m.; Saturday and Sunday, noon–3 p.m.
Admission: Free, but donations accepted
Wheelchair/Stroller Access: Yes

There was a time when the railroad was the best transportation in
this area. This is an old train depot, restored and transformed into a museum with interesting tidbits about the region's old coal-mining communities. Look for the 1920s caboose at the museum's depot entrance. Next
door is the old Black Diamond Jail, built in 1910. Families may drop in to
visit; special groups should make arrangements. The small museum can
accommodate between fifty and seventy-five visitors.

The Sales Pavilion   360-825-3151

Location: In Enumclaw at 22712 S.E. 436th St. Take I-5 exit to Auburn.
Drive five miles on Hwy. 18 to the Auburn/Enumclaw exit. Turn east
and drive another twelve miles on Hwy. 164
Days/Hours: Doors open at 8 a.m., sales start at 10 a.m., the first Saturday
and Sunday of every month.
Admission: Free
Wheelchair/Stroller Access: Yes

If you think your children talk fast sometimes, take them to hear the
prattling of the auctioneers who sell pigs, sheep, goats, poultry, and horses
at the Sales Pavilion auctions. Much of the countryside near Enumclaw
and Black Diamond is farmland, so this is a center of activity year-round.
Auctions take place in a barn, and the atmosphere inside is ripe with
animal sounds and smells. The audience is seated in rows of old theater
seats, banked steeply and surrounding the stage. There's a snack bar and
some gift-type items nearby. In the lobby near the entrance to the auction, you'll often find vendors displaying Western-style hand-knit sweaters, hand-tooled leather goods, and more. This is a great, no-cost weekend
experience for families who appreciate new environments and enjoy
people-watching. Become part of the audience, sit back, and watch the
auction action.

Places to Eat

Black Diamond Bakery and Restaurant
360-886-2741 (bakery); 360-886-2235 (restaurant)

Location: 32805 Railroad Ave.
Days/Hours: **Bakery:** *Monday, 7 a.m.–4 p.m.; Tuesday–Saturday, 7 a.m.–*
5 p.m. **Restaurant:** *Monday–Friday, 7 a.m.–4 p.m.; Saturday and*
Sunday, 7 a.m.–5 p.m.
Tours: Yes, for groups of less than fifteen. Call ahead for arrangements
Wheelchair/Stroller Access: Yes

The bakery has grown up and includes a small coffee shop, as well. The restaurant is a perfect opportunity to sit down and enjoy something with—or on—their famous bread. On a clear day, the picture window, with a southern exposure, frames Mount Rainier—a most extraordinary dining experience! Some good advice on the wall for bakery visitors: "Don't count your calories; count your blessings!" That helps when you're tempted by their home-baked pies. The old brick ovens are still there and very much in use, turning out those delicious doughnuts for which skiers and hikers go out of their way.

Black Diamond Candy and Ice Cream Shoppe
360-886-0513

Location: 32805 Railroad Ave., Black Diamond (next door to the bakery)
Days/Hours: Monday–Friday, 10 a.m.–4 p.m.; Saturday and Sunday,
9 a.m.–5 p.m.
Wheelchair/Stroller Access: Yes

More than fifty kinds of candy here, with a good selection of sugar-free candy as well. Ice cream with three kinds of waffle cone: vanilla, chocolate, and sugar and spice. Owner Terry Thomas makes his own peanut brittle and taffy, and you can watch the process right there on Sunday mornings.

CJ's Bakery
360-886-0855

Location: 30800-A 3rd Ave., Black Diamond
Days/Hours: Monday–Friday, 4 a.m.–7 p.m.; Saturday and Sunday, 4 a.m.–
5 p.m.
Wheelchair/Stroller Access: Yes

If you're on your way to somewhere along Hwy. 169 (usually Enumclaw or Crystal Mountain), CJ's is right off the road. Scrumptious doughnuts and muffins delight (raspberry cream cheese and raspberry almond poppy seed look especially good), but the high point for kids is cookies—dinosaurs, rainbows, hot air balloons, and teddy bears. For birthday parties or special occasions, Jim (the owner) will "bake" your picture right on to the cake. It's a special process called "edible images," only 150 such machines exist in the U.S. currently, and you can use any photo you wish! If you need more of a snack, there are sandwiches and beverages as well.

Helpful Resources:

Chambers of Commerce:

Federal Way: 253-838-2605

Kent: 253-854-1770

Renton: 425-226-4560

King County Park Districts:

Marymoor/Eastside District: 206-296-2966

Northshore/Shoreline District: 206-296-2976

South District: 206-296-4232

Mercer Island Parks and Recreation Department: 206-236-3545

Bellevue Parks and Recreation Department: 425-455-6885; 425-462-6046

Snoqualmie Pass Visitor Information Center: 206-434-6111 (Thursday–Sunday only)

Other Resources:

East King County Convention and Visitors Bureau: 800-252-1926

King County Library System: 425-462-9600 (the "answer line"); 206-684-4494 (TDD)

Snoqualmie Pass Visitor Information Center: 425-434-6111 (Thursday–Sunday only; Backcountry and Avalanche Center)

* Lake Washington beaches with daily summer lifeguards: Lake Washington's Juanita Beach in north Kirkland; Mercer Island's Luther Burbank Park; Issaquah Plateau's Pine Lake Park; Lake Wilderness east of Kent and Five Mile Lake Park near Federal Way.

* www.metro.kc.gov provides links to bus and ferry schedules

Meeting a favorite ballplayer is always a thrill. Photo by Michael R. Sage courtesy the Tacoma Rainiers

CHAPTER
4

Southwest Washington

• •

In many ways, Tacoma is the gateway to the southwest part of our state. As you travel southward, you have the option of interesting inland towns or the elegant coastline and coastal beaches. Some of Washington's most important history came from the economies of the lumber industry, inherent in towns like Shelton, Longview, Raymond, and Kelso. As the economics of these cities change, families find other interesting aspects of the area to explore.

- **Tacoma:** Tacoma, nicknamed the "City of Destiny," is the second largest city in Washington and the major city in the southwest portion of our state. While the citizens still work to define that destiny, Tacoma has developed an ambiance all its own. The Tacoma Dome hosts world-class sporting events, top-drawer entertainers, and some of Puget Sound's most popular annual festivals. The historic Pantages Theater was restored in 1983 and is a showcase for many different stage productions. Tacoma's Metropolitan Park District has developed one of the state's finest parks and recreational systems; Point Defiance Park is a part of that system.

- **Olympia:** Here lies the heart of the state's eminent political system. Olympia is the state capital, residing on a thirty-five-acre campus that is jumping when in session (usually the first four months of the year) and more subdued in the off-season. Elected officials represent a great mix of the rural and metropolitan, sophisticated and naive, and, to the public's credit, diversity in ethnicity. There is much history in this city; some of the old homes here reflect some grand traditions past.

- **Lewis and Cowlitz Counties:** Lewis County is named for famed explorer Meriwether Lewis. Cowlitz County is home to the mountain that blew its top. In May of 1980 Mount St. Helens drew international attention when it exploded, sending 8.8 billion cubic yards of ash, ice, rock, and dirt 75,000 feet into the air. The mushroom cloud was seen through most of the state; 57 people died and 300 homes were demolished. People are still talking about it, and hundreds of families drive through the area each year. Thousands of acres of trees were demolished, but Weyerhaeuser, which operates the forestry center with the state Department of Transportation, has reforested much of the land. The Mount St. Helens National Volcanic Monument is accessible from two directions: from the west via I-5, exit 49 at Castle Rock; drive five miles to the Visitors Center at Silver Lake; from the north, take Hwy. 131 south from Randle, via Morton and Randle to Windy Ridge on the crater's east side.

- **Clark County:** Clark County can boast of numerous parks for recreational enjoyment. Along the shores of the Columbia River you'll find a working model of Fort Vancouver, one of the first settlements in the Oregon Territory. A number of popular hikes to Mount St. Helens are accessible through Clark County.

SOUTH PUGET SOUND

Tacoma and Greater Pierce County

Places to Go

Children's Museum of Tacoma   253-627-6031 *(information)*

Location: 936 Broadway
Days/Hours: Tuesday–Saturday, 10 a.m.–5 p.m.; Sunday, noon–5 p.m.;
    Friday, 5 p.m.–9 p.m. is free. Closed Mondays and major holidays.
Wheelchair/Stroller Access: Yes. There is a ramp between 9th and 11th at
    Court St.
Admission: $3.75/ages 3 and older; $2.75/grandparents; free/children under 2
Groups: Welcome Tuesday–Saturday, 9:30 a.m., 11:15 a.m., and 1 p.m. $2.75/
    per person; minimum of ten people. Wednesday and Friday at 9:30 a.m.
    for preschoolers only. One adult per five children, please; up to thirteen
    chaperones per group admitted free. Allow one and a half hours per visit.

This is a museum for children, with new offerings, and ongoing activities (held in the Annex) that are free with museum admission. Of special interest: "Omokunle" or "house full of children," a replica of a

Nigerian Village (limited run). Look for the Personal Collections Exhibit, too (presenting multi-generational and multi-cultural opportunities), and the Kids' Gallery with art for, by, and about kids. There are overnight programs, too, for youth groups and families, usually on Saturday. Children should be 5 to 11 years old. Call for complete information.

Fort Lewis Military Museum   253-967-7206

Location: At I-5 exit 120; Fort Lewis main gate is just west of the freeway
Days/Hours: Wednesday, Sunday, noon –4 p.m.; closed federal holidays
Admission: Free
Tours: One-hour guided tours available for school groups; fifteen to thirty-five people maximum; call ahead for reservations.
Wheelchair/Stroller Access: Yes

Tanks, Jeeps, rockets, missiles, and armored cars are on display here, plus three galleries with nearly 2,000 Northwest military exhibits. Artifacts, uniforms, and weapons from the mid-1950s to the present day are part of the presentation, including Stormin' Norman Schwartzkopf's Jeep.

Les Davis Pier

Located right on Ruston Way, it offers public fishing and ample parking, with a bait and tackle shop, and a fish and chips stand nearby.

Marine Park

Location: Ruston Way

Very popular in the summer time with families and singles. There are grassy areas with benches and picnic tables. Fabulous views of mountains and water traffic.

Nature Center at Snake Lake   253-591-6439

Location: 1919 S. Tyler St.
Web Site: www.tacomaparks.com
Days/Hours: Monday–Friday, 8 a.m.–5 p.m.; Saturday, 10 a.m.–4 p.m.
Admission: Free
Tours: Guided tours for groups of twelve to sixty; call ahead.
Wheelchair/Stroller Access: Yes

Snake Lake has long been one of Tacoma's special places. This fifty-four-acre wildlife preserve has thirty-five educational stops along three miles of wooded paths. Visitors are asked not to feed the waterfowl, which exist here in their natural setting. In the Interpretive Center there's a wetlands diorama, a small beaver lodge for small ones to crawl through, and many hands-on exhibits that are entertaining as well as educational. Get on their mailing list for some exciting classes and workshops.

Northwest Trek   *253-847-1901; 360-832-6117; 800-433-TREK*

Location: 11610 Trek Drive E., Eatonville. Take I-5 exit 127 east to Hwy. 512. Turn on South Hill Mall/Eatonville exit to Hwy. 161.
Web Site: www.nwtrek.org
Days/Hours: March–October: daily, 9:30 a.m.-closing. November–February and selected holidays: Friday–Sunday, 9:30 a.m.–closing. Tram tours on the hour from 10 a.m. until closing (depending on season). Hours subject to change without notice.
Admission: $8.25/adults; $7.75/seniors 62 and up; $5.75/children 5–17; $3.75/children 3–4; free/children 3 and under. Discount rates for groups of fifteen or more with advance reservations.
Wheelchair/Stroller Access: Yes

Northwest Trek's 600 acres of natural wetlands, forests, and grasslands are home to hundreds of animals, including grizzlies, black bears, big-horn mountain sheep, shaggy goats, beaver, wolverines, and much

Getting acquainted with a friend. PHOTO COURTESY NORTHWEST TREK

more. They thrive in a very authentic environment; the Trek Tram carries you through the park to view them foraging for food, building homes, and at play. Start with the fourteen-minute show at the Forest Theater, and save time for the hands-on exhibits in the Cheney Discovery Center. Spring is a special time here, with babies everywhere. This can be an all-day destination; a picnic area, restaurant, and covered outdoor eating space offer you choices. Call ahead to learn about their special events or camping in your own tent on Trek grounds. Ample parking.

Parkland Putters   253-588-2977

Location: 10636 Sales Road, Parkland. Take I-5 to exit 127 (Hwy. 512) to the
    Steele St. exit. Turn at the first right.
Days/Hours: April–Labor Day: Sunday–Thursday, 10 a.m.–11 p.m.; Friday–
    Saturday, 10 a.m.–11 p.m. After Labor Day through October: Friday–
    Saturday, 10 a.m.–11 p.m. Closed through February; opens in March for
    weekends only.
Admission: $4.50/ages 13 and up; $3.50/children 12 and under
Wheelchair/Stroller Access: One of the four courses is suited for wheel-
    chairs; strollers can be maneuvered on all four.

There are four eighteen-hole courses testing your skills here; they vary in difficulty, but you will be rewarded. Sinking a hole-in-one on the eighteenth hole earns a trophy; top scores earn blue and red ribbons and the honor of having your name read over the loudspeaker. The courses are well-lit and nicely landscaped, with a snack bar nearby.

Pioneer Farm   360-832-6300

Location: 7716 Ohop Valley Rd., Eatonville
Days/Hours: Open March 1–Thanksgiving. Public tours are one and a half
    hours, from 11:15 a.m. –4:00 p.m.
Admission: $5.50/adults; $4.50/seniors and children 3-18; free/children under
    2. Groups must have 20 or more: $4/per person or $80/group minimum.
    One adult per 10 children; group visits available March–November.
Wheelchair/Stroller Access: Yes

This is the hands-on place to get a taste of the Pacific Northwest in the 1880s. From milking cows and churning butter to hand-washing clothes, you'll get an authentic view of how the early settlers lived. The ninety-minute tour includes visits to a trading post, barn, blacksmith shop, a vintage log cabin, and more. Another opportunity here is the Native American Seasons Tour focusing on the life of the Salish Indians, offered June 1 through August, on Fridays, Saturdays, and Sundays only. This tour has access for strollers but not wheelchairs.

Point Defiance Park   253-305-1000

Location: N. 54th at Pearl St. *Take I-5 to exit 132; follow to Hwy. 16; take*
the 6th Ave. exit and turn left. Continue to Pearl St., turn left, and follow
this into the park.
Web Site: www.tacomaparks.com
Days/Hours: Daily, dawn to dusk
Wheelchair/Stroller Access: Yes

Tacoma and its Metropolitan Park District are known for an outstanding park system, and this is the jewel in their crown. We've offered the
various areas in separate blocks so you can plan your trip accordingly.
Also available: educational overnight programs that give families and
youth groups a chance to see what happens in the park at night! Best for
those 5 to 12 years old; rates are $35 to $40.

Point Defiance Zoo and Aquarium   253-591-5337

Location: Near park's east entrance
Days/Hours: January–March: 10 a.m.–4 p.m. April–May: 10 a.m.–5 p.m.
Memorial Day–Labor Day: 10 a.m.–7 p.m. September: 10 a.m.–5 p.m.
October–December: 10 a.m.–4 p.m.
Admission: $7/ages 14 and older; $6.55/seniors 62 and older; $5.30/children
4–3; free/children 3 and under
Wheelchair/Stroller Access: Yes

If you like zoos, you'll love this one! This combined facility offers something for everyone in the family, from the outdoor elephant exhibit to the
indoor shark tank. There are two aquariums in one here: North Pacific and
Discovery Reef. North Pacific is home to cold water fish and invertebrates,
many found here in Puget Sound. Discovery Reef is definitely more tropical, with brilliantly colored fish, young shark, and eels. Kids can see as
much as they want against the floor-to-ceiling windows. At Rocky Shores,
the bigger guys are busy—sea otters, walruses, beluga whales, and harbor
seals are at home here. In the zoo complex, you'll see polar bears, monkeys, apes, and more. A zoo tradition for many here is the Zoolights holiday display from around Thanksgiving through New Year's, when a
half-million lights decorate the grounds, buildings, trees, and walkways.
You'll recognize Northwest landmarks and zoo animals in the glitter and
sparkle. Admission is usually $3.25 in advance (at the zoo before 4 p.m. or
at Metropolitan Community Centers) and $3.95 at the gate.

Point Defiance Park/Boathouse Marina   253-591-2068

Location: Park's northeast corner near the Vashon Island ferry terminal

*Days/Hours: Summer: daily, 5 a.m.–8 p.m. September–March: daily, 5 a.m.–
6 p.m.*
Wheelchair/Stroller Access: Yes

Commencement Bay affords good fishing here. Rent a small boat
with or without a motor, buy bait in the tackle shop, or check out the
boats moored nearby at Old Town Dock. The ferry to Vashon Island docks
here, also.

Point Defiance Park/Camp 6 Logging Museum
253-752-0047

Location: Park's southwest corner
Web Site: www.tacomaparks.com
*Days/Hours: Museum: Wednesday–Friday, 10 a.m.–5 p.m., Saturday and
Sunday, 10 a.m.–7 p.m. Logging trains: Saturday and Sunday, every
thirty minutes from noon–6 p.m. The outside exhibits of the museum are
open every day.*
*Admission: $2/ages 12–64; $1/seniors 65–99; $1/children 3–12; free/children
under 3 and seniors over 99*
Wheelchair/Stroller Access: Yes

Keeping the old logging days alive, the museum is modeled after an
authentic logging camp, and steam-powered locomotives and equipment
from the 1880s–1940s are on display. The train is great fun; it operates
spring and summer weekends and selected holiday afternoons. Mark
your calendar for the Santa Claus train ride through the park (first weekends in December).

Point Defiance Park/Fort Nisqually
253-591-5339

Location: Park's southwest corner
Web Site: www.tacomaparks.com
*Days/Hours: Memorial Day–Labor Day: daily, 11 a.m.–6 p.m. October–
March: Wednesday–Sunday, 11 a.m.–4 p.m. April, May, and September:
daily, 11 a.m.–5 p.m.*
*Admission: Weekends in April, May, September, and October, daily in June,
July, and August: $1.50/adults, 75¢/children 5–12. Free during the week
(only museum is open then).*
*Wheelchair/Stroller Access: Yes, but grass and wood paths make it slow
going.*

Summer visits are the most fun here; interpreters are on hand, dressed
in costumes, and full of information and anecdotes. The Hudson Bay Company fur trading and farming post south of Tacoma was lively 160 years
ago; it's been reconstructed here at Fort Nisqually, with great attention to

detail and authenticity. The outhouse is especially interesting! Take your imagination with you—the blacksmith shop is aromatic. The Factor's House (also houses a gift shop now) symbolizes a delightful lifestyle even then. Now there's a stove in the Trading Store, so lectures are offered during winter months. The majority of customers at the original fort were Native Americans, so bartering and trading were the norm. Ask about their fall candlelight tours; they're a magical experience and sell out early.

Point Defiance Park/Never Never Land   253-591-5845

Location: Park's southwest corner
Web Site: www.tacomaparks.com
Days/Hours: June–August: 11 a.m.–6 p.m.
Admission: $2.25/adults; $1.75/teens 13–17 and seniors; $1.25/children 3–12; free/children 2 and under
Wheelchair/Stroller Access: Yes, but wood-chip paths are rough

What a great place for little ones! Mother Goose's messenger, Humpty Dumpty, greets you from atop the arch as you enter this ten-acre haven for nursery rhyme characters. There are nearly three dozen exhibits based on favorite stories; lots of visual help here for your short memory. Warning: Potty facilities are in short supply.

Port of Tacoma Observation Tower   253-383-5841

Location: From I-5, take exit 126; head north on Port of Tacoma Rd.; go left on E. 11th St., which veers right onto Sitcum Rd.
Days/Hours: Open twenty-four hours
Wheelchair/Stroller Access: No

It's a free view of the Olympic Mountains, especially gorgeous at sunset, when you climb the three flights of stairs to the top of the tower (cameras encouraged). You'll watch marine traffic of all kinds moving in and out of the port. There's a free telescope as well.

Ruston Way

Location: From I-5 south to Tacoma, take a City Center exit, and follow signs to Ruston Way.

Ruston Way runs along Commencement Bay and overlooks the Port of Tacoma. There are patches of beachfront up and down the parkway, with benches and grass for water gazing, strolling, picnicking, and even swimming. A two-mile pathway dedicated to bikers, walkers, and skaters becomes a sidewalk intermittently. There's a fragrance here you find only near saltwater byways. Trains go rolling by periodically; bike and blade rentals available. Mount Rainier is in full view on a good day. This is a picturesque part of Tacoma.

Tacoma Art Museum   253-272-4258

Location: 1123 Pacific Ave.
Days/Hours: Tuesday, Wednesday, Friday, Saturday, 10 a.m.–5 p.m.;
   Thursday, 10 a.m.–7 p.m.; Sunday, noon–5 p.m.; closed Monday
Admission: $4/adults; $3/seniors and students; free/children 12 and under.
   Third Thursday of every month is free to all; members free year-round.
Wheelchair/Stroller Access: Yes

Along with the adult displays are exhibits paralleling the subjects, but designed for kids to enjoy. Well-known Northwest artists are featured here, as well as national and international names. Children can pose for portraits and test their own artistic skills with watercolors; one section of the museum is devoted to art by local children.

Sidewalks along Ruston Way are great for rollerblading. Photo courtesy Metropolitan Park District of Tacoma

Tacoma Rainiers   800-281-3834

Location: Cheney Stadium
Days/Hours: Early April through Labor Day
Wheelchair/Stroller Access: Yes

As the AAA affiliate / farm club of the Seattle Mariners, the Tacoma Rainiers draw a vocal and enthusiastic crowd throughout their season. It's a great place to get autographs of soon-to-be big leaguers or see some of the big guys come down from the majors to play for a while. Autograph time is best about one hour before the game, during batting practice. Groups (and Little League teams) can reserve blocks of seats by calling ahead.

Wapato Park at Wapato Lake   253-305-1070

Location: S. 68th St. at Sheridan Ave., South Tacoma
Web Site: www.tacomaparks.com
Days/Hours: Daylight hours
Wheelchair/Stroller Access: Yes

Wapato Lake is a great place for kids to fish because only those 13 or younger may dip their lines into the waters. The State Department of Fisheries regularly stocks this freshwater lake with wily trout. Adults and older children can rent paddleboats and canoes here or stroll the great paths around nice picnic areas. Lifeguards are on hand to watch summer swimmers.

Washington State History Museum   888-238-4373

Location: 1911 Pacific Ave. Take exit 133 off I-5; take the E. 26th St. exit;
*   turn left on E. 26th St. and head three blocks to Pacific Ave. Turn right,*
*   continue five blocks. The museum is on the right.*
Days/Hours: Labor Day–Memorial Day: Tuesday–Saturday, 10 a.m.–5 p.m.;
*   Thursday, 10 a.m.–8 p.m.; Sunday, 11 a.m.–5 p.m.; closed Monday.*
*   Memorial Day–Labor Day Monday–Saturday, 9 a.m.–5 p.m.; Thursday,*
*   9 a.m.–8 p.m.; Sunday, 11 a.m.–5 p.m.*
Wheelchair/Stroller Access: Yes

If their slogans are accurate, "history with an attitude" and "first-person present-tense exhibits," you'll enjoy this museum even more because it's about where you live (if you're a Washingtonian, of course). If not, you'll learn heaps about this wonderful state and enjoy your visit more. They present Washington state historically, culturally, and even philosophically, using well their 106,000 square feet of space. For kids, the largest model railroad in the state is here. The museum covers events electronically, using visual, audio, and interactive aides. Motion sensors in mannequins trigger characters to "talk" about state history, including some of the tragedies that were endured. There's also a replica of a covered wagon, perfect for climbing on and pretending. The gift shop and cafÉ are nice amenities; there are indoor and outdoor theaters, dioramas, and videos. Plan to spend several hours there; it's worth it.

Western Washington State Fair— The Puyallup Fair
253-841-5045

Location: Puyallup Fairgrounds; 110 9th S.W. From I-5, take exit 127 (Hwy. 512) east to Puyallup.
Web Site: www.seattleonline.com
Days/Hours: Daily for seventeen days; 8 a.m.–11 p.m., usually starting the first Friday after Labor Day.
Admission: Varies; grandstand tickets are separate; kids under 5 are free.
Wheelchair/Stroller Access: Yes. Strollers and wheelchairs available for rent.

Exhibits open at 10 a.m., but the first thing to do is buy your bag of scones. Rides open at noon weekdays, earlier on weekends. If this is your first visit to the fair, allow the whole day—it's a total experience! From the food to the exhibits to the grandstand shows, it's a must. Onion burgers are one of the favorites here. At least one day is devoted to discounted kiddy carnival rides. Parking can be difficult on crowded days. Wear good walking shoes and bring an appetite. Weather is no hindrance.

W. W. Seymour Botanical Conservatory
253-591-5330

Location: Wright Park; 316 S. G St., Tacoma. From I-5, take exit 133 to City Center; follow signs for 705 N.; take the Stadium Way exit; turn right on Stadium Way, left on 4th St.; follow to G St. into Wright Park.
Web Site: www.tacomaparks.com
Days/Hours: Daily except for Thanksgiving and Christmas. Conservatory: 10 a.m.–4:30 p.m. Plant and gift shop: 11 a.m.–4 p.m.
Wheelchair/Stroller Access: Yes, although the aisles may be narrow in places.
Admission: Free
Tours: Yes; $1.50 per person; groups up to twenty-five. Call ahead for information and reservations.

This lovely Victorian-style building, built in 1908, is now listed on the state and national historic registers. It features a twelve-sided central dome and over 4,000 panes of glass. Not to mention 200 species of exotic

A quiet pool in Point Defiance Park. PHOTO COURTESY METROPOLITAN PARK DISTRICT OF TACOMA

tropical plants in the permanent displays, an amazing lemon tree with fruit the size of grapefruit, and seasonal displays that sometimes change monthly so there is always something new to see. The holiday floral displays are especially enticing. Look for the goldfish and the waterfall; kids can run off some energy in the park as well.

Places to Eat

Antique Sandwich Company   253-752-4069

Location: 5102 N. Pearl
Days/Hours: Monday–Saturday, 7 a.m.–7 p.m.; Sunday, 8 a.m.–7 p.m.
Wheelchair/Stroller Access: Yes

Here's a favorite of ours; they've grown up with this book. There are nineteen sandwiches (whole and half) to choose from (pb and j still a favorite!); homemade pies created right there are now on the menu. Good drink selection—and a great play place for the kids. Toy baskets are full of irresistibles. If you wonder what's going on in town, glance at the posters that line the counter. Don't miss the lovely old ceramic chandelier. Restrooms are up the loooong staircase. Fresh fruit milkshakes are a specialty.

C. I. Shenanigan's   253-752-8811

Location: 3017 Ruston Way
Days/Hours: Daily for lunch and dinner
Wheelchair/Stroller Access: Yes

Ideally located, overlooking Commencement Bay, you can eat on the deck at umbrella tables in summer. The seagulls paddle back and forth, biding their time, waiting for the inevitable tidbit. For kids, a Little League menu has some specials under $6.

Flakey Jake's   253-565-5911

Location: 6409 Sixth Ave.
Days/Hours: Sunday–Thursday, 11 a.m.–10 p.m.; Friday and Saturday, 11 a.m.–11 p.m.
Wheelchair/Stroller Access: Yes

A design-your-own burger place where you put your own delicious combination together from a well-stocked condiment bar. The menu features four kids' meals; all come with French fries.

The Lobster Shop   253-759-2165

Location: 4015 Ruston Way
Days/Hours: Daily from 4:30 p.m.; dinner only
Wheelchair/Stroller Access: Yes

Looks like a very adult dining spot, but they have three items for kids: fish and chips, pasta, and chicken strips.

ART FOR VIEWING: On public display next to the Lobster Shop is a Headsaw and Carriage. It's sixty-one tons, stands two stories tall, and was salvaged from the Dickman Lumber Company, the last mill along the old Tacoma waterfront.

Point Defiance Park/Boathouse Grill
Restaurant   253-756-7336

*Location: 5910 N. Waterfront Dr., at the park's northeast corner at Boat-
house Marina, just west of the ferry dock.*
*Days/Hours: Sunday–Thursday, 7 a.m.–9 p.m.; Friday and Saturday,
7 a.m.–10 p.m. Weekdays, breakfast till 11 a.m., lunch from 11 a.m.
Saturday and Sunday, breakfast till 12:30 p.m. Kids' menu available; top
price $3.50.*
Wheelchair/Stroller Access: Yes

The amazing view from this restaurant is six-sided, taking in the
Olympic Mountains, Mount Rainier, Commencement Bay, and more. The
style is casual; the menu offers everything from steak to fish and chips.
Or you can order take-out for eating on the nearby beach.

Stores to Browse

The Children's Bookstore   253-565-3039

Location: 6615 S. 12th, at 12th and Mildred streets.
*Days/Hours: Monday–Friday, 10 a.m.–8 p.m.; Saturday, 10 a.m.–6 p.m.;
Sunday, noon–4 p.m. Closed Sundays from June 1–August 31.*
Wheelchair/Stroller Access: Yes, but watch for some narrow aisles

There are more than 23,000 titles for youngsters from which to choose,
and a play area for little ones while adults are browsing. Good discounts
for school groups and other organizations, plus a Birthday Club and frequent customer discounts.

Freighthouse Square   253-272-6178

Location: 25th Ave. and E. D St., one block north of the Tacoma Dome
*Days/Hours: Monday–Saturday, 10 a.m.–7 p.m., Sunday, noon–5 p.m.;
closed Thanksgiving, Christmas, New Year's, Easter, and July 4*
Wheelchair/Stroller Access: Yes

It's called Freighthouse Square because it's the Milwaukee/St. Paul
Railroad freighthouse rejuvenated. There are many small shops with lots
to interest kids, from fudge to inflatables and places to pick up a snack.
It's easy to pop over and browse a while if you're going to the Tacoma
Dome.

Mount Rainier National Park

Fortunately our trademark is—currently—a dormant volcano. It is also the highest volcanic peak in the Cascade Mountains. Of course, there's no guarantee it will remain dormant; predictions include a possible eruption several hundred years from now. Hikers, climbers, and tourists ignore the predictions and flock to the mountain by the thousands. Many are looking for old-growth forest, to be found at Ohanapecosh at the park's southeast corner. Here some of the Douglas fir, western hemlock, and red cedar are 500 to 1,000 years old. A walk through the Grove of the Patriarchs will give you an appreciation of the grandeur here.

Crystal Mountain Resort
360-663-2265

Location: Just off Hwy. 410 on Crystal Mountain Blvd. Take I-5 exit 142A; follow Hwy. 164 through Enumclaw to Hwy. 410; drive thirty-three miles east to the Crystal Mountain turnoff (just before entering Mount Rainier National Park). Yakima Route (closed during the winter): follow Hwy. 410 from Yakima west, over Chinook Pass; turn onto Crystal Mountain Blvd. just after leaving the national park.
Web Site: www.crystalmt.com
Days/Hours: Lifts closed September 7 till the snow starts (hopefully mid-November)
Wheelchair/Stroller Access: Yes, in summer; winter snow makes it difficult. Summer Rates: $10/adults; $60/summer pass; $7/seniors 65 and older; free/ children 6 and under. 4 p.m. pass: $8/adults; $6/seniors. All-day tickets: $7/children 8–17. Winter rates: Vary; call for info.

Washingtonians know Crystal as an exceptional winter destination for skiing, but Crystal is great in summer time as well, especially in June when the wild strawberries are out. The chairs run to the top of the mountain; you'll think you can practically reach out and touch Mount Rainier (you're only twelve miles away). It's an exquisite view, a perfect place to bring visitors. The Summit House at the top offers dining from 10 a.m. to 5 p.m. daily in summer months. For overnight accommodations, try the Silver Skis year-round, 360-663-2558, or Alpine Inn, 360-663-2262. Summer activities include hiking and horseback riding; trail maps available at Crystal Mountain Resort.

Longmire Museum at Mineral Springs
Resort
360-569-2211

Location: Take Hwy. 706 to Longmire
Days/Hours: Daily, 9 a.m.–4 p.m.
Wheelchair/Stroller Access: Yes
Admission: Free

There are no tours here; the emphasis is on the exhibits and displays on the biology, geology, and history of the area. A restaurant here is open daily.

Mount Rainier Scenic Railroad
360-569-2588

Location: In Elbe. Take I-5 exit to Hwy. 512. Turn on the Mount Rainier exit
to Pacific Ave./Hwy. 7. Turn right and follow for thirty-three miles.
Days/Hours: June 15–Labor Day: daily, 11 a.m., 1:15 p.m., and 3:30 p.m.
Memorial Day–September: weekends.
Wheelchair/Stroller Access: No, but assistance provided to those with
disabilities
Admission: $9.50/adults; $8.50/seniors 60 and older; $7.50/children 12–17;
$6.50/children 2–11; free/children under 2. With over a hundred people,
you'll receive a 15 percent discount. Telephone reservations accepted for
groups of twenty-five or more.

Riding a train is one of those unexplainable, simply terrific experiences—and this one is no exception. For ninety minutes you'll rumble across bridges, through lush forests to Mineral Lake and back again. With lively music to keep things humming, the ride passes too quickly. There's also a premier forty-mile, four-hour excursion that includes a five-course prime rib dinner; prepaid reservations required.

Ski Touring Center, Longmire
360-569-2411

Location: Mount Rainier National Park
Web Site: www.nps.gov/parks.html]
Days/Hours: Mid-December–April: daily
Wheelchair/Stroller Access: Wheelchair access at shop only.

Snowshoes may be rented here. If you're planning to do some sledding or inner tubing, you'll have to bring your own equipment.

Places to Stay and Eat

Paradise Inn   *360-569-2275 (for reservations)*

Location: Mount Rainier National Park
Days/Hours: May 15–early October
Wheelchair/Stroller Access: Limited

If you're planning a trip to the "Mountain," you might want to stay overnight. The inn is a rustic lodge built in 1917, with massive stone fireplaces, exposed beam ceilings, and log furniture. Rooms for families with small children can accommodate up to five.

Sweet Peaks Bakery and Ski Mountaineering

360-569-2720

Location: 38104 Hwy. 706 E. in Ashford
Days/Hours: Daily, 6 a.m.–9 p.m.
Wheelchair/Stroller Access: Yes, except for one small step outside to the
    main floor of the bakery and shop.

If huckleberry pie or a fresh cinnamon roll is irresistible, especially after a rugged day on the slopes, stop here to indulge. Steaming hot espresso makes the perfect treat. You can also rent or buy ski and mountain equipment here as well.

Wild Berry Restaurant   *360-569-2628*

Location: 37721 Hwy. 706 E., Ashford
Days/Hours: April–September: 11 a.m.–8:30 p.m. Winter months: 11 a.m.–
    7 or 8 p.m. (depends on how busy they are).
Wheelchair/Stroller Access: Yes

More good food for hungry skiers, hikers, and travelers. Wild blackberry pie, made fresh daily. Mountain trout a specialty here. Children's menu has good selections, including ham, roast beef, turkey, grilled cheese, and pb and j sandwiches. Comfortable family dining; high chairs available.

Olympia
Places to Go

Bigelow House Museum   360-753-1215

Location: 918 Glass Ave. N.E.
Days/Hours: Saturday–Sunday, 1 p.m.–3 p.m.; third Thursday of the month,
   9 a.m.–3 p.m.; Thursday–Friday by appointment (group tours)
Admission: $3/adults 18 and older; $1/children under 18
Wheelchair/Stroller Access: Yes

Fortunately the Bigelow family saved things—for nearly 140 years. So visitors today can enjoy authentic antique furnishings—including books, paintings, photographs, tools, and household items—still in remarkable condition. The first floor of the house is the museum; family members still reside upstairs. To their credit, the original Daniel Bigelow and his wife Ann were ardent supporters of important movements such as education and suffrage for women. Susan B. Anthony is reputed to have visited them; the chair in which she sat is on display.

Capitol Tours   360-664-2700 (Visitor Services and Reservations);
                        360-586-8687 (Capitol Visitors Services)

Location: Olympia State Capitol. Take I-5 to exit 105; follow signs west
Days/Hours: Daily, 10 a.m.–4 p.m., except holidays
Tours: Free; they leave on the hour. Reservations preferred for groups of fifteen
   or more.
Age Minimum: None, but children must be at least 10 to attempt the 262-
   step climb to the top of the Dome.
Wheelchair/Stroller Access: Yes

It's sometimes a bit of a shock to see what the legislative process *really* involves, but there's no better place to do it than our own state capitol. Typical legislative sessions are January through early spring. Kids love to run up and down the marble steps and challenge the building's echo. On the guided tours you'll walk through the Senate and House chambers and, if they're in session, you can pause in the balconies to observe the process. The twenty-eight-story building features lamps, sconces, and chandeliers designed by Louis Tiffany, and railings, doorknobs, and (looking up) ceilings with the state seal. The red-and-blue-clad teenagers are House and Senate pages sponsored by their local lawmakers. If you have a high school student interested in becoming a page have him or her call your district representative or senator and ask for a week-long assignment.

TV-W: This station broadcasts everything at the Capitol, and offers free tours. Call the number above for arrangements.

Governor's Mansion   360-586-8687

Location: Walking distance north of the Capitol
Days/Hours: Tours on Wednesdays only, every fifteen minutes from 1 p.m.–
2:45 p.m. Reservations required; call or visit the Capitol Visitors Center.
The exception is December, when tours are offered all day to view the
holiday decorations (reservations begin in May for this!).
Wheelchair/Stroller Access: No

Private quarters are off-limits here, but you'll tour through the library, sitting room, dining room, and ballroom. Our current governor lives here with his family; they occasionally feel like it's a fishbowl! The furniture and accessories added over the years by former governors are part of the history. No, you won't see any bats.

Balloons in an Olympia park are always an attraction. Photo ©Marge and Ted Mueller

Hands-On Museum of Olympia   *360-956-0818*

Location: 108 Franklin N.E. (between Fourth Ave. and State St.)
Web Site: www.win.com/~deltapac/hocm.html
Admission: $3.50/per person; free/under 2
Wheelchair/Stroller Access: Yes

Environmentalism is the key here. The museum's exhibits are designed for children ages 1 to 10, and they're encouraged to really get involved. Kids can count tree rings, examine leaves through a microscope, make bark rubbings in the Science Shelter, or perhaps use the professional lighting and sound equipment and costumes to create a theater performance. They can even climb up the forest ranger's lookout tower or camp in a tent by a lake with backpacks–using their imaginations, of course. Overnight slumber parties can be arranged for $20 per guest; this includes dinner, a snack, art and science activities, storytelling during the evening, and breakfast the next morning. Free parking available in spaces one to five in the lot on the State St. side of the museum.

Millersylvania Memorial State Park/
Deep Lake   *360-753-1519*

Location: Ten miles south of Olympia and three miles east of I-5 at exit 95 on
    Tilley Road S.W.
Web Site: www.parks.wa.gov
Days/Hours: Daily, dawn–dusk; overnight camping year-round
Wheelchair/Stroller Access: In most places

One end of the park has cabins with bunks, a swimming beach, and well-groomed fields for outdoor recreational activities. It's a very popular spot for outdoor camps. At the other end, tent and RV campers inhabit the area. A sandy beach, a dock for fishing, and benches are available. Deep Lake Resort nearby (within walking distance) offers paddleboats and bikes for rent, or you can play a round of miniature golf.

Olympia Brewery/Pabst   *360-754-5000*

Location: In Tumwater. Take I-5 exit 103; go east several blocks.
Days/Hours: Tours offered Tuesday–Saturday, 9:30 a.m., 11:30 a.m., 1:30
    p.m., 3:30 p.m. Closed Sunday, Monday, and holidays.
Wheelchair/Stroller Access: Yes

The lighted sign reads "Olympia," but Pabst is the beer maker now. The tour moves through the brew house where the beer is flavored, to the cellars where it ages, then to the packing room where the beverage is funneled into cans and bottles. The place is spotless; visitors usually comment on this amazing fact. Samples at the end include beer for adults, Pepsi for the kids.

Olympia Farmers Market   360-352-9096

Location: 700 N. Capitol Way
Days/Hours: April: Saturday and Sunday. May–September: Thursday–
    Sunday. October: Friday–Sunday. November 1–December 21: Saturday
    and Sunday.
Wheelchair/Stroller Access: Yes

Located on the waterfront, you can shop for almost anything here and enjoy some gorgeous views as well. Lots of free parking.

State Capitol Museum   360-753-2580

Location: 211 West 21st Ave., eight blocks south of the capitol campus
Days/Hours: Tuesday–Friday, 10 a.m.–4 p.m.; Saturday and Sunday, noon–4
    p.m.; closed on all public holidays
Admission: $2/adults; $1.75/seniors; $1/children 7–18; free/children 6 and
    under; $5/families
Tours: Yes; guided tours only, reservation required. Groups up to fifty; no age
    minimum. For school groups: $1/student. Each student receives a free
    pass to return for another visit.
Wheelchair/Stroller Access: Yes, via an elevator

You'll learn much about Washington state history here, but the emphasis is definitely on Olympia as the state capital. If you're planning to spend the day in Olympia, be sure to include the governor's mansion and a tour of the capitol campus.

Taylor United   360-426-6178

Location: S.E. 130 Lynch Rd. Take I-5 exit 104 onto Hwy. 101 to Taylor
    Farm, three miles south of Shelton (in Mason County, northeast of
    Thurston County).
Days/Hours: Monday–Friday, 8 a.m.–5 p.m.; Saturday, 9 a.m.–4 p.m.; closed
    Sunday. Appointment required for tours.
Wheelchair/Stroller Access: Yes

The tour is free and fun. Here workers shuck thousands of oysters daily. After watching a while, you'll admire their nimble fingers and quick, sure gestures. The oysters then go into jars and containers. Outside, the empty shells become small mountains! The tour includes a fifteen-minute video about oysters and their clam cousins. Warning: Floors can be slippery. Shoes with good traction advised.

Tumwater Falls Park   360-943-2550

Location: Just north of the Olympia Brewery. Southbound on I-5: take exit
  103; go straight on 2nd Ave. through the stop sign; turn left onto Custer
  Way and cross the bridge; take the first right (Boston St.); turn left onto
  Deschutes Way and left again onto C St.
Days/Hours: Usually daily, 8 a.m.–4:30 p.m., but hours will change seasonally.
Wheelchair/Stroller Access: In some areas. There is a steep gravel trail
  leading to the park with no barriers between it and the Deschutes River.

This is a privately-owned park in a beautiful natural setting. The
concrete gunboats and pirate ships planted in the sand are magnetic to
children. Once down there, you'll discover more playground apparatus
at adjacent Tumwater Historical Park. There is a half-mile of walking
trails and good restrooms. In spawning season a fish ladder and holding
ponds are also attractions. The geese and ducks here are primed for handouts, so be prepared.

Washington State Capitol Grounds
and Conservatory   360-586-8687 *(information)*

Location: Capitol Way and 14th St.
Days/Hours: Conservatory is open weekdays, 9 a.m.–3 p.m.
Admission: Free
Wheelchair/Stroller Access: Yes

There is much to see on the grounds of our state capitol, including a
sunken garden filled with perennials and roses and a glass conservatory
containing tropical and subtropical plants. The horticultural staff is quite
creative on holidays; look for a splendid Fourth of July display. There are
restrooms available.

Wolf Haven International   800-448-9653; 360-264-4695

Location: 3111 Offut Lake Rd., Tenino. Take I-5 to exit 99 (93rd Ave.—just
  south of Olympia) and head east. Follow the brown and white signs; Wolf
  Haven is seven miles southeast of the freeway.
Days/Hours: Summer tours every hour on the hour: daily, 10 a.m.–5 p.m.;
  closed on Tuesday, Thanksgiving, and Christmas. Howl-Ins: May–
  September: Friday and Saturday, 6:30 p.m.–9 p.m. Reservations required.
  Winter: Tours daily except Tuesdays, 10 a.m.–4 p.m.
Admission: Howl-Ins: $6/adults; $4/children 5–12; free/children under 5.

*Daily **Tours:** $5/adults; $2.50/children 5–12; free/under 5. Ask about special mini-tours for kids. Group discounts available.*
Wheelchair/Stroller Access: *Not good.*

There are no big, bad wolves here, just animals that are revered and respected. More than three dozen wolves, coyotes, and foxes are living in this sanctuary. This is not a hands-on experience, rather hands-off, but the guides are well-versed in stories and anecdotes about the wolves' relationships and behavior. The Friday and Saturday Howl-Ins have become a very popular event in the Puget Sound area. Visitors sit on bleachers around a campfire, while storytellers weave legends about wolves, and youth from the audience beat drums or dance wearing animal headdresses. After the stories, the audience is invited to howl to the nearby wolves—and yes, they do howl back. It's an awesome experience. Special note: You can "adopt a wolf" or join the pack; ask about "Picnic for the Pack," a July event, which includes "all the food you can wolf down" (their bad pun, not ours).

Yashiro Japanese Garden

360-753-8380 (Parks and Recreation Department)

Location: *Ninth and Plum streets*
Days/Hours: *10 a.m.–dusk*
Admission: *Free*
Tours: *Call the Parks and Recreation Dept for guided tours*
Wheelchair/Stroller Access: *Yes*

Planned and created to honor Yashiro, Olympia's sister city in Japan, this garden bespeaks tranquillity. An ideal time to visit this delightful little park to enjoy a quiet stroll and pristine landscape is in spring, when the flowering cherry trees are in bloom. This is a good example of the "hill and pond" style of classic Japanese gardens. The serenity of the garden is heightened by the calming influence of the waterfall. Japanese lanterns lend texture to the scene.

Stores to Browse

Buck's Fifth Avenue

360-352-9301

Location: *209 Fifth Ave. E.*
Days/Hours: *Tuesday–Saturday, 10:15 a.m.–5:15 p.m.*
Wheelchair/Stroller Access: *Yes*

There are some wonderfully different things going on here. Several shops coexist under one roof, in a sense. All Spices offers many things you can't buy elsewhere in Olympia. The Flea Market caters to kids and their pets. Children can come here to make dog collars, bake dog biscuits, learn how to grow essentials such as catnip—or take home a cookbook for your cat to indulge your favorite feline. Upstairs at Pins and Needles, children's sewing lessons are offered, and the Tree House offers lessons for youngsters in photography, art, and calligraphy. Owner Ann Buck is versatile and innovative; you'll always find something quite different when you visit.

LEWIS AND COWLITZ COUNTIES

Places to Go

Chehalis-Centralia Railroad   360-748-9593

Location: In Centralia on Main St. near the Dairy Queen; in Chehalis just south of Main St. near Dairy Bar.
Days/Hours: Memorial Day–Labor Day: weekends, 1 p.m.–5 p.m.
Admission: $7/adults; $5/children 4–16
Wheelchair/Stroller Access: Yes for strollers; limited for wheelchairs

You can ride this vintage ninety-ton locomotive for the twelve-mile round-trip between Chehalis and Centralia and get a flavor of the long ago rail crews bringing logs to the mill. There's something magical about a train, no matter where it goes. They also offer a dinner train now for $39.95 per person.

Coldwater Ridge Visitors Center   360-274-2131

Location: On Hwy. 504. Take I-5 exit 49 at Castle Rock and drive forty-three miles east
Web Site: www.fs.fed.us/gpnf
Days/Hours: April–September: daily, 9 a.m.–6 p.m. October–March: 9 a.m.– 5 p.m.
Wheelchair/Stroller Access: Yes, including some trails

The Mount St. Helens crater is less than eight miles away, and the view from the highway is amazing, including some spectacular spans. At the route's end, the Visitors Center has a hands-on geology lesson for both children and adults. It's literally the "after" part of a remarkable story, for here the wildlife and wildflowers have refurbished the blast zone, bringing new life and vibrant color to a dead area. If you want to do some walking or mini-hiking, the Winds of Change Trail is a paved path with some moderate grades; it leaves from the Visitors Center and offers crater views.

Johnson Ridge Observatory is at mile marker 5.2 on Hwy. 504, and has the same hours as above. Here they focus on the geological aspects of the mountain; it is closed during winter.

Mount St. Helens Monument: Due to the Fee Act, these fees are stable until at least 1999. **Admission:** Three-day pass: $8/adults 16 and older; $4/seniors 62 and older; free/children under 16.

Mount St. Helens Forest Learning Center   *360-414-3439*

Location: About thirty-four miles east of I-5 at exit 49 on the N. Fork Ridge of Spirit Lake Memorial Hwy. 504
Days/Hours: May–October: daily, 10 a.m.–6 p.m. Office is open daily, 8 a.m.–5 p.m.
Admission: Free
Wheelchair/Stroller Access: Yes

Inside the center, the focus is forestry. A miniature working railroad, reminiscent of the ones that used to work around the mountain, a one-seat helicopter youngsters can sit in, and videos in the "Destruction Chamber" depicting the May 18, 1980, eruption, and telescopes for viewing the Toutle Valley—this is part of the story before the mountain blew. Today, of course, most of the land has been reforested by Weyerhaeuser, which operates the forestry center with the State Department of Transportation. Outside, the children's playground is definitely thematic: a "crater" to climb inside of and a "mudflow" to slide down. A small picnic area is nearby; hiking trails made of recycled rubber tires are easy to walk on.

Silver Lake/Mount St. Helens Visitors Center
360-274-2100; 360-274-2102 (TDD)

Location: Five miles east of I-5 at exit 49 at Mount St. Helens
Days/Hours: Daily, 9 a.m.–5 p.m. except Thanksgiving, Christmas, and New Year's
Admission: $8/adults; $4/seniors 62 and older; free/children 15 and under
Wheelchair/Stroller Access: Yes

Your fees are good for all sites, including the monument and those dealing with the biological and geological aspects of the eruption. Each center is theme-related.

Windy Ridge

*Location: A drive-up lookout overlooking the crater on the monument's east
side of Hwy. 131*
Days/Hours: Daylight hours year-round except when there is heavy snowfall
Wheelchair/Stroller Access: Yes, but it's rustic

On a clear day, park here to enjoy the view near the crater. Good for
camera buffs, but there are no facilities nearby.

Places to Eat

Burgerville USA   360-736-5212

Location: 818 Harrison Ave., Centralia
*Days/Hours: Daily, 10 a.m.–11 p.m., except Fridays from June–August,
when they are open till midnight*
Wheelchair/Stroller Access: Yes

This southwest Washington burger chain has outlets in the Vancouver area as well. They're popular for their sundaes and milkshakes, especially the green shamrock shakes on St. Patrick's Day. Another attraction
is their fenced-in outdoor playground for toddlers and young children,
including a slide, merry-go-round, and bouncing rides. Kids also receive
a free eight-page activity and coloring book.

Izzy's   360-578-1626

Location: Three Rivers Mall, 1001 Grade St., Kelso
*Days/Hours: Sunday–Thursday, 10 a.m.–9 p.m.; Friday–Saturday, 10 a.m.–
10 p.m. The buffet: Sunday–Thursday, 11 a.m.–8 p.m.; Friday–Saturday,
11 a.m.–9 p.m.*
*Cost: 45¢ for each year up to 12; free/2 and under. Charge for adults is
different.*
Wheelchair/Stroller Access: Yes

It's a pizza chain with affordable prices (what a concept!). The "great
pizza feed and salad bar" equals one trip through the salad bar plus all-
you-can-eat pizza and cinnamon rolls.

CLARK COUNTY

Places to Go

Ape Caves
None at site; 360-247-3900 (caves and monument)

Location: *From I-5 take exit 21 at Woodland; drive twenty-seven miles east to Cougar, then eight miles beyond. Turn left on 83 Road, go two miles to 8303 Road. Ape Cave is a mile ahead on the right. On the map, the Ape Caves are in Skamania County, but the best access is through Clark and Cowlitz counties.*

Web Site: *www.swwcn.org/gpnf*

Days/Hours: *Daily year-round. Parking lot: dawn–9 p.m. in winter. Lantern rental is $2; available daily, 10 a.m.–5 p.m., during summer; last rental is at 4:00 p.m. and must be returned by 5:30 p.m.*

Tours: *Daily from 10:30 a.m.–3:30 p.m., every hour on the half-hour. Guided tours last thirty minutes; self-guided tours also.*

Admission: *$8/adults (3-day pass); $4/seniors 62 and older; free/children 15 and younger*

Wheelchair/Stroller Access: *No*

This is the longest intact lava tube in the continental United States, and no—there are no apes here. The tube was named for some adventurers who called themselves the St. Helens Apes. Actually two caves neighboring Mount St. Helens, the mountain itself was created by St. Helens' eruption 1900 years ago. Today the four thousand foot lower cave is the best choice for exploring. But please note the following: It's a tight fit (not the best place for the claustrophobic); it's chilly and dark year-round so warm sweaters or jackets advised; the floor is sharp in places; hardhats, flashlights, or lanterns definitely recommended (see lantern rental above). Guided tours are really helpful here; youngsters under 5 might find this tough going.

Carter Park

Location: *Columbia and 33rd streets, Vancouver*

You could call this a "petite" park, nestled on a half-acre in this downtown Vancouver neighborhood, but the crawl-through toys, merry-go-round, slides, and high-to-the-sky swings are magnets for families with children 8 and under.

Fort Vancouver National Historic Site   360-696-7655

Location: 1501 E. Evergreen Blvd., Vancouver
Web Site: www.vancouverusa.com
Days/Hours: Daily, 9 a.m.–5 p.m.
Admission: Free mid-September–mid-May; $2/person, spring and summer
   months; $4/family groups; free/children 16 and under
Tours: For groups of fifteen or more. Reservations must be made by phone or
   mail; call the number above at ext. 14 for tour information.
Wheelchair/Stroller Access: Yes at the Visitors Center, limited at the fort

There's a great deal to see and do here, so allow ample time for your visit. For kids it's a very cool fort from the 1840s, including the bastion tower where they can watch for intruders. Best to begin with the fifteen-minute video at the Visitors Center; the encampment is just a walk down the hill (or a ninety-second drive to Fifth St.). Tours are short (thirty minutes) and dedicated to the working exhibits, but very enlightening. It's always nice to go away with more information that you started with! Kids really enjoy watching a pioneer baker baking bread or a blacksmith working on horseshoes. Ask about their October event—historical re-enactments by candlelight by costumed guides—when the fort is open after dark for just two days. Sounds enticing!

Hazel Dell Golf-O-Rama
360-694-4719; 360-694-3421 (The Steakburger restaurant)

Location: 7120 N.E. Hwy. 99 (Vancouver's Hazel Dell Community). Take I-
   5 to exit 4 at N.E. 78th St.
Days/Hours: Summer: Friday and Saturday, 9 a.m.–11:30 p.m.; Sunday–
   Thursday, 9 a.m.–10:30 p.m. Winter daily, 10 a.m.–9 p.m.
Admission: Eighteen holes: $3/ages 12 and up; $2/children 11 and under.
   Thirty-six holes: $4.75/ages 12 and up; $3/children 11 and under.
Wheelchair/Stroller Access: Yes

Sinking a hole-in-one on the eighteenth hole wins you a prize here. There are two well-lit eighteen-hole courses to play on, and The Steakburger restaurant to console the troops if you don't play as well as you thought you should!

Lewisville Park

Location: 26411 N.E. Lewisville Hwy. (north of Battle Ground)
Days/Hours: Daily, dawn–dusk
Wheelchair/Stroller Access: Yes

This park is so spread out it may feel as if it is several parks. As Clark County's oldest park, there are 154 acres with a great variety of opportunities for families to spend the day. Nearly all areas have picnic shelters; some have a wealth of children's play equipment, baseball fields, swimming, and more. The park is especially popular in the warm summer months for swimming and inner tubing, especially over the mild rapids of the Lewis River. Old-growth trees here provide delightful shade. Minimal charge for parking.

Marine Park

Location: S.E. Marine Park Way, south of Hwy. 14, near Vancouver's Blandford Dr. intersection

Vancouver's largest park is stretched along the north edge of the Columbia River. Its ninety acres of trails are ideal for bikes and in-line skating, and there is delightful playground equipment for younger ones. Tables and restrooms are on hand for picnics, but there is a modest parking charge.

Pendleton Woolen Mills   800-568-2480

Location: Off Hwy. 14 along the Columbia River, Washougal
Days/Hours: Open weekdays year-round for mill tours except for two weeks in mid-August. Tours take place at 9 a.m., 10 a.m., 11 a.m., and 1:30 p.m., lasting forty-five minutes long. The store is open Saturdays.
Wheelchair/Stroller Access: No strollers; wheelchairs permitted

Seeing how they process raw wool into the final products here is fascinating. Once it leaves the sheep's back, visitors will see the wool spun, colored, and eventually finished in large rolls. The Pendleton name is synonymous with warm, sturdy wool clothing, especially sweaters and blankets. Of course you can buy Pendleton items in the adjacent gift shop.

Pomeroy House/Living History Farm   360-686-3537

Location: 20902 N.E. Lucia Falls Rd. in Yacolt; thirty miles northeast of Vancouver.
Web Site: www.pacified.com/~pomeroy/all^fam
Days/Hours: Tea Room: Wednesday–Saturday, 11:30 a.m.–3 p.m. (except major holidays). Gift shop (under the Tea Room): Monday–Saturday, 10 a.m.–5 p.m.; Sunday, 1 p.m.–5 p.m.
Admission: For displays: $3.50/adults; $2/children 3–11, free/children 2 and under
Wheelchair/Stroller Access: Possible but difficult

Always amazing is how intriguing it is to look backward at the way things used to be. Children can try their hands here at grinding coffee, churning butter, spinning and weaving wool. It requires a little muscle but they can also use a cross-cut saw, make rope, and pump water. Younger ones can feed the chickens. Look for cider pressing, hayrides, and harvest fun on fall weekends. For a different atmosphere, sip tea and enjoy the special Tea Plate in the Tea Room. A typical serving includes finger sandwiches, scones, soup, fruit, sorbet, and dessert for around $7.

Tears of Joy Theater   360-695-3050; 800-332-8692

Location: 400 W. Evergreen Blvd., Columbia Arts Center, downtown Vancouver
Days/Hours: Season runs November–April; call ahead for performance
    schedules
Admission: $9/children 2–16; $12/adults and seniors; $8/three-show
    subscribers (youth or adults)
Wheelchair/Stroller Access: Yes

This award-winning puppetry troupe is at home in Vancouver, but travels to Portland to perform as well. Using shadow, stick, and hand puppets, they tell their multicultural stories to children of all ages. You'll usually find the parents as enraptured as their offspring; somehow puppets seem to have a life of their own.

Water Resources Education Center   360-696-8478

Location: 4600 Columbian Way, Vancouver. From I-5 north or southbound,
    take the Camas Hwy. 14 exit; within a quarter of a mile, take exit 1 south.
    Travel under the railroad berm; at the traffic signal, turn east onto
    Columbia Way. Travel to the end of the road; turn north at the traffic
    circle and follow the drive around the fountain to the center parking lot.
Days/Hours: Monday–Saturday, 9 a.m.–noon. School visits by reservation:
    October–June: Tuesday–Thursday, 9 a.m.–1 p.m.
Wheelchair/Stroller Access: Yes

They've worked hard to make this central water station an interesting and challenging place for kids. There are nature walks along the Columbia River, Saturday morning story times for 2 to 7 year olds, hands-on water and science activities on Thursdays and Saturdays, and art classes led by naturalists using leaf prints and fish printing. During your visit, the kids can test their strength lifting and pushing a make-believe water pump and taste treated water. Of interest to families: the annual Sturgeon Festival in late June.

Places to Eat

Uncle Milt's Pipe Organ and Pizza   *360-695-6895*

Location: *2410 Grand Blvd., in Vancouver (near Fourth Plain)*
Days/Hours: *Sunday–Thursday, 11 a.m.–10 p.m.; Friday and Saturday,
11 a.m.–11 p.m.*
Wheelchair/Stroller Access: *Yes, on the main floor (there is one step outside
from the curb into the restaurant)*

It's not just the vintage pipe organ that gets things going here. Their special pizza offers are intriguing, too; call ahead to see what's on that day—or evening. The organ music begins at 1:00 p.m. on weekends, 6:00 p.m. on weekdays. Bubbles burst forth, to make things more lively! There's a game room, old movies, and kiddy rides as well. Vegetarians may prefer the salad bar.

Helpful Phone Numbers

Chambers of Commerce:
    Battle Ground: 360-687-1510
    Camas-Washougal: 360-834-2472
    Gig Harbor/Peninsula: 253-582-6865
    Lakewood Area: 253-582-9400
    Longview: 360-423-8400
    Puyallup: 253-845-6755
    Tumwater: 360-357-5153

Visitor Information Services:
    Olympia: 360-753-8262
    Eatonville: 360-832-4000
    Lewis County: 360-736-7132
    Mount Rainier Disabled Visitor: 360-569-2211, ext. 2304
    Mount Rainier TDD: 360-569-2177
    State Capitol: 360-586-3460
    Tacoma: 253-272-7801
    Tacoma/Pierce County Visitor and Convention Bureau:
        800-272-2662, ext. 1-B
    Vancouver/Clark County: 800-377-7084

Other

    Metropolitan Park District: 253-305-1000

Enjoying the beach at Westhaven State Park near Grays Harbor. Photo ©Marge and Ted Mueller

CHAPTER
5

Olympic Peninsula, Hood Canal, and Ocean Beaches

• •

Many visitors are surprised that much of the Olympic Peninsula is a rain forest, with up to 175 inches of precipitation annually. No wonder there are majestic trees and monster mosses. Even in summer, it's smart to bring a raincoat. But the rain doesn't slow anyone down! National Park Service naturalists host programs for both children and adults at Mora, Kalaloch, Hoh, and Heart o' the Hills. Other places to visit are Port Gamble, Port Townsend, and Port Angeles; each has its individual attractions.

- **North and North Central Beaches:** Washington's coast is rugged and often misty. Beachcombing is fun but challenging. The shoreline is not nearly as permissive as neighboring Oregon's, but the "catch" can be rewarding. Driftwood, rocks polished by the tides, and other finds become treasures. Lake Quinault and Kalaloch Lodges provide a stopping and resting place for vacationers. There are also some good places to spot bald eagles. The thirty-mile stretch between Moclips and Ocean Shores is razor-clam paradise, with a gentle coastline and sandy beaches. Be sure to check with authorities about the legal clam-digging seasons. Sand castles, tide pools, and kite flying—all inviting activities for families who love to play on the beach.

- **South Beaches:** Grays Harbor, Aberdeen, Hoquiam: These waters are home to fishing charter boats, and oyster and crab catch-ers. From Grays Harbor to the mouth of the Columbia River, fishing is a high priority. Timber was once the primary industry, but has declined precipitously in the past decade. Today, Westport is a great attraction for its recreational fishing. A major attraction down here is the migration of the gray whales, as they move north along the Washington coast from Mexico, usually between late February and April. Long Beach is on state Hwy. 103, about four miles north of U.S. Hwy. 101 and seventy-three miles south of Aberdeen. It's a long day trip, and overnight accommodations are in short supply. Call the Visitors Bureau (see the end of the chapter) for recommendations.

OLYMPIC PENINSULA AND HOOD CANAL

Port Townsend

Places to Go

Fort Worden State Park   360-385-4730

Location: One mile north of Port Townsend
Web Site: www.parks.wa.gov
Days/Hours: Daylight hours for day visitors; overnight camping and rental home accommodations year-round.
Wheelchair/Stroller Access: Yes, in most places

Gun mounts and bunkers are just waiting for make-believe battles and war plans. Flashlights are an appropriate accessory here, for playing inside the armaments. The beach outside is part of the park and a wonderful destination for exploring and sand architecture. But there's lots of running around and biking space, too. If you're interested in Fort Worden history, visit the Commanding Officers' Quarters Museum, open daily from 1 p.m. to 5 p.m., or the 248 Coastal Artillery Museum, open Wednesday to Sunday, noon to 5 p.m. There are eighteen turn-of-the-century officers' quarters, furnished in an ornate Victorian style, which are available for overnight rental. These are quite popular, so allow two to four months advance planning. Call the number above. Warning: They don't accept credit cards.

Olympic Music Festival   206-527-8839

Location: Olympia Peninsula; ten miles west of the Hood Canal Bridge, near Quilcene
Days/Hours: June–September: Saturday–Sunday, 2 p.m.

Admission: $11–$24; special prices for children. Free/children under 6. Season passes and group rates available. Advance reservations strongly recommended.
Wheelchair/Stroller Access: Yes

The Olympic Music Festival's "Concerts in the Barn" series is a summer highlight for many families. The chance to sit on bales of hay or just relax on the grass outside the barn is unique, and the music is exceptional. You'll hear masterpieces in chamber music performed by top-notch musicians in a turn-of-the-century barn. Inside you can sit on padded church pews or the hay bales; acoustics are really quite good. Families usually bring picnic lunches, but be sure to arrive early enough to eat, picnic, and stroll around, and pet the very friendly farm animals. Concessions sell sandwiches, espresso, and other beverages; gourmet lunch boxes can be ordered in advance (call the number listed above), and picnic tables are provided.

A World War I bunker at Fort Worden State Park invites exploration.
PHOTO ©MARGE AND TED MUELLER

Port Townsend Marine Science Center   360-385-5582

Location: In Fort Worden State Park, at the end of the dock
Web Site: www.northolympic.com/museums/html
Days/Hours: June 15–Labor Day: Tuesday–Sunday, noon –6 p.m. September
   10–October and April–June 14: Tuesday–Sunday, noon–4 p.m.
Admission: $2/adults; $2/students; free/preschoolers
Wheelchair/Stroller Access: Yes

There's a live underwater video camera here that captures action under the pier. Kids find it fascinating and so do parents. Indoors, there are touch tanks with underwater sea creatures. "Touch" means do just that—poke your fingers in to see what the creatures feel like. They offer interpretive programs daily, and day and overnight camps dedicated to hands-on marine science.

Places to Eat and Stay

Elevated Ice Cream Co.   360-385-1156

Location: 627 Water St., Port Townsend
Days/Hours: May–September: daily, 9:30 a.m.–10 p.m. October–April: daily,
   11 a.m.–10 p.m.
Wheelchair/Stroller Access: Yes

From a tiny shop so small it fit into an unused Victorian elevator car, this wonderful ice-cream boutique has "elevated" itself to a popular place that can accommodate the many visitors looking for delicious homemade ice cream. They've added a candy shop (which shouldn't disappoint anyone!) and pastries, plus Italian ices, sherbet, and frozen yogurt. Many of their flavors are made with local Sequim strawberries or Olympic Peninsula raspberries. There are child-size scoops and adult scoops—take your choice!

Port Ludlow Resort

   360-437-2222 (resort); 800-732-1239 (reservations;
   front desk open twenty-four hours)

Location: 9483 Oak Bay Rd.
Web Site: www.northolympic.com/portludlow/
Days/Hours: Overnight accommodations available year-round
Wheelchair/Stroller Access: Yes, by ferry; on-site, some units are accessible

Most folks prefer to cruise up to the marina, which holds three hundred comfortably. Otherwise, the ferry is the usual mode of transportation (some will go by small plane). Lots to do here: golf, tennis and bicycling, strolling, maybe just relaxing. There are guest rooms or one- to four-bedroom suites with kitchens and fireplaces. Children under 12 are free in their parents' room. In summer, the Club Lud program offers recreational activities for guests age 4 to 12.

Sequim

Places to Go

Dungeness Spit National Wildlife Refuge   360-683-5847

Location: Off Sequim Ave. and Marine Dr., north of U.S. 101
Days/Hours: Summer months: daily, 6 a.m.–10 p.m. The remainder of the
   year: dawn to dusk.
Admission: $2/per family. Seniors with an annual pass admitted free.
Wheelchair/Stroller Access: Very difficult

This rugged, windswept spit reaches for over five miles into the Strait of Juan de Fuca. The longest sand spit in the United States, its beauty lies in the stark yet fertile beach and cliffs. There's much to see here—a peaceful bay, sandy and rocky beaches, tide flats, and a short but steep half mile trail to reach the bluff. There's great bird-watching and clam digging (always check first with the Refuge or Clallam Bay Recreation Area rangers regarding conditions). It's a twelve-mile round-trip hike out to the New Dungeness Lighthouse at the end of the spit; volunteers from the U.S. Lighthouse Association lead daily tours between 10 a.m. and 4 p.m. For lighthouse information, call 360-460-3259.

Olympic Game Farm   800-778-4295; 360-683-4295

Location: 1423 Ward Rd., just outside town
Web Site: www.northolympic.com/gamefarm
Days/Hours: Driving tour: mid-May–mid-September: daily, 9 a.m.–6 p.m.
   The remainder of the year: 9 a.m.–3 p.m. Walking tour: mid-May–mid-
   September: 9 a.m.–3 p.m.; closed remainder of year.
Admission: Driving tour: $6/ages 13–60; $5/children 5–12 and seniors 60
   and older; free/children 4 and under. Walking tour: $7/ages 13–60; $6/
   children 5–12 and seniors 60 and older. Combo package: $9.50/ages 13–
   60; $7.50/children 5–12 and seniors 60 and older.
Wheelchair/Stroller Access: Not on walking tour

There are fifty-six species of animals here, and you can view most all of them, especially on the driving tour, which takes about forty-five minutes. There are wolves, bison (big bison!), bears, and even Siberian tigers, plus a myriad of other wildlife on this ninety-acre preserve. Many of the animals have been used in films and television; the one-hour walking tour includes a visit to the movie set, fish ponds, and aquarium. As part of the driving tour, you can purchase loaves of bread at the front gate. Note the strict warnings about remaining in your car. From a special observation tower you can watch the cave- and den-dwellers. There's a free petting farm, and in summer months, lots of babies are tagging along behind their moms. Also in summer, a "you fish" pond is open on Saturday and Sunday from 10 a.m. to 4 p.m. Kids get a tremendous kick out of seeing the animals "up close and personal," but the condition of the outdoor environment here gets very mixed reviews.

Places to Eat

Hiway 101 Diner   *360-683-3388*

Location: Downtown Sequim, on U.S. 101
Days/Hours: Daily, 6 a.m.–9 p.m.
Wheelchair/Stroller Access: Yes

Yes, it's noisy, but that's part of the fun here. The period decor pulls you in and the food is pretty good, with hamburgers and Chicago-style pizza as the specialties. There's a CD player tucked into the rear of a 1956 Thunderbird, good for some very nostalgic music. Kids may not appreciate the tunes, but parents will.

Oak Table Cafe   *360-683-2179*

Location: 292 W. Bell St., Sequim
Days/Hours: Daily; 7 a.m.–3 p.m.
Wheelchair/Stroller Access: Yes

We wouldn't make a visit to Sequim without including this in our itinerary. The apple pancakes for breakfast are worth the trip; actually a mega-pancake, it begs to be shared, but it's absolutely delicious. The rest of the breakfast menu is good, too, and portions are more than generous. Home-style meals are the draw here; they do lunch and dinner equally well. This is definitely a family destination. On weekends, go early or expect a moderate wait.

The Three Crabs   *360-683-4264*

Location: 11 Three Crabs Rd., in Sequim
Days/Hours: Daily, 11:30 a.m.–10 p.m., except Sunday, when they close at
*   9 p.m.*
Wheelchair/Stroller Access: Yes

Considered one of the outstanding dining spots in the area, The Three Crabs specializes, of course, in fresh seafood, and Dungeness crab is always a good choice. On the children's menu, the fish or clam basket, grilled cheese, or a cheeseburger tops the list of favorites.

The Crab Sack is the retail store across the street. They're open from Sunday to Thursday, 11:30 a.m. to 9 p.m., and on Friday and Saturday from 11:30 a.m. to 10 p.m.

Port Angeles

Places to Go

Arthur D. Feiro Marine Laboratory   360-417-6254

Location: On the Port Angeles City Pier, near Hollywood Beach off Railroad Ave.
Web Site: www.northolympic.com/museums/html
Days/Hours: Mid-June–September: daily, 10 a.m.–6 p.m. The remainder of the year: weekends, noon–4 p.m.
Admission: $2/adults; $1/children 6–12 and seniors; free/children 5 and under with parent
Wheelchair/Stroller Access: Yes

This is an ideal place for children to learn about the marine creatures of the Washington coast—and never get wet! They have recently undergone remodeling, so check them out for yourself. It's well worth it.

Hurricane Ridge   360-928-3380 *(Ranger Station);*
360-452-4501 *(Olympic National Parks);*
800-550-3858 *(Olympic Bus Line)*

Location: Seventeen miles south of Port Angeles
Web Site: www.nps.gov/parks.html; www.nps.gov.parks.olym
Admission: $10 to drive up; $13 for a bus tour
Days/Hours: Daily, depending on snow access; open twenty-four hours during summer, daylight hours other months.
Wheelchair/Stroller Access: In some places

A seventeen-mile drive up the Ridge takes less than thirty minutes; the view is worth all of that and more. Explorers on an expedition there in 1855 took a week. There are more than two dozen day hikes in the Olympic National Park; several are very forgiving for less experienced hikers. Hurricane Trail has a half-mile of paving; Meadow Loop Trail is half paved, but has some steep hills, and both are accessible to wheelchairs and strollers. Black-tailed deer and other wildlife share the woods with you. If you make it to the top, you'll see the Strait of Juan de Fuca and the surrounding Olympic Mountain peaks—the view (and the climb) takes your breath away.

The bus tour on weekends is an easier way to get to the top; the buses leave every half-hour from the west end of the Peninsula College parking lot at East Lauridsen Blvd. and Ennis St.

In winter, cross-country skiing, snow-shoeing, and inner tubing are big attractions. From mid-December through March you can rent snowshoes at the Hurricane Ridge Shelter. The National Park Service leads guided trail walks on weekends. However you get down the hill, you'll have to take yourself back up. There are no rope tows. The Lodge is open year-round; in summer there's a restaurant.

Olympic Park Institute   *800-775-3720; 360-928-3720*

Location: 111 Barnes Point Rd., Port Angeles
Web Site: www.olympus.net
Days/Hours: May–September: two- and five-day camps. Children must be 5 and older.
Admission: Program range is from $15/day programs to $150 for weekends ($85/youth, $140/adults, includes meals and lodging).
Wheelchair/Stroller Access: No

This is an education center that really mixes it up. They have a complete catalog of activities available to families; samples are "Plants, Plankton, and Phun," and "Birds, Bats, and Bugs." Course fees will vary. Participants taking overnight programs will stay at the Rosemary Inn on Lake Crescent; meals included.

Sol Duc Hot Springs   *360-327-3583*

Location: On U.S. 101, a few miles past Lake Crescent; take Sol Duc Road twelve miles to its end
Web Site: www.northolympic.com/solduc/
Days/Hours: Mineral pools: mid-May–October: daily, 9 a.m.–9 p.m.
Admission: $6.50/adults; $5.50/seniors 52 and older; free/children 4 and under; $5/twilight rates, 7–9 p.m.
Wheelchair/Stroller Access: Yes

The bubbling mineral water of this natural hot springs can be as hot as 122 degrees, but by the time it reaches the three pools here, it cools to 100 to 107 degrees. There is a shallower, cooler pool for youngsters, and a large chlorinated swimming pool for everyone. For families, eighty-four campsites or thirty-two furnished cabins are available.

Places to Eat

Frugals   360-452-4320

Location: 1520 E. Front St., Port Angeles
Days/Hours: Summer months: daily, 10:30 a.m.–11 p.m. Hours variable
during the rest of the year.
Wheelchair/Stroller Access: Not relevant; no inside dining

A drive-up burger bar, they've won local and regional polls for the best "cheap eats," and they serve monster-sized buns and burgers. It's a very convenient family stop.

NORTH AND NORTH CENTRAL BEACHES
Neah Bay, Ocean Shores
Places to Go

BJ's Family Fun Center

360-289-2702 (the center); 360-289-0752 (Peppermint Parlor, next door)

Location: Point Brown Ave., across from Ocean Shores City Hall
Days/Hours: Summer–Labor Day: daily, 10 a.m.–10 p.m. Labor Day–
summer: weekends and two weekdays, 10 a.m.–9 p.m.
Admission: $3/bumper cars; $3.50/boats and go-karts; $4/slick track (this is an
oval track for go-karts that is watered). Discount for groups of twenty-five.
Wheelchair/Stroller Access: Only for game-viewing

Kids must be at least 3 years old and within a designated height range to join the ranks of hot-rodders here.

Makah Cultural and Research Center   360-645-2711

Location: In Neah Bay, seventy-five miles west of Port Angeles
Days/Hours: June–September: daily, 10 a.m.–5 p.m. Closed Mondays and
Tuesdays the rest of the year.
Admission: $4/adults; $3/students and seniors; free/children under 5 and
Makah Tribal members
Wheelchair/Stroller Access: Yes

The Makah Indians on Neah Bay can trace their ancestry back to 1000 B.C. History tells us that a mudslide buried some Makah houses at a village called Ozette over 500 years ago, and in 1970, after years of soil erosion, artifacts from that village began to appear, telling the Makah story. Those artifacts and more items recovered from an eleven-year excavation are on display at this museum. There are replicas of whaling and sealing canoes, and a full-size longhouse.

Nan-Sea Stables   360-289-0194

Location: At beach entrance off Chance-a-La-Mer Road at Ocean Shores
Days/Hours: Summer: daily, 10 a.m.-5:30 p.m. Winter: daily, 10 a.m.–4 p.m.
Admission: Prices vary: $15/thirty minutes; $20/one hour; $34/sunset ride;
  $28/for four. Discounts available for groups of eight or more.
Wheelchair/Stroller Access: Not equipped for disabled riders

Trotting along the beach on horseback is an adventure you have to feel, rather than describe. The sensations are heightened if the sun is setting. Later, when you're not sore, it's a delicious memory. If you're an experienced horseperson, you may ride at your leisure here; if you're a novice, staff will escort you. For the sunset rides, those over 6 years may ride on their own; younger children will ride with an adult.

Red's Off-Course Mini Golf   360-289-4190

Location: Copalis Beach along Copalis River
Days/Hours: Daily, 10 a.m.–8 p.m.
Wheelchair/Stroller Access: Yes

Another great experience for a vacationing family. You can work your way around eighteen holes in no time.

Places to Eat and Stay

Kalaloch Lodge   360-962-2271

Location: Olympic National Park, on U.S. 101, thirty-five miles south of
  Forks
Web Site: www.travel-in-wa.com (under "very special places")
Days/Hours: Overnight accommodations year-round
Wheelchair/Stroller Access: Yes, at the lodge; also, two of forty cabins are
  accessible

On a bluff overlooking the Pacific Ocean, Kalaloch Lodge offers a relaxing retreat from the city. Many families make this an annual vacation, no matter how brief. There are forty cabins, some with kitchenettes, for overnight accommodations, and the lodge as well. Children 5 and younger stay free, and the lodge's dining room features a children's menu and high chairs. It's a Mecca for beachcombing; winter specials are more economical, and winter storms provide an ambiance all their own.

Lake Quinault Lodge

800-562-6672 (Washington state); 360-288-2571 (out of state)

Location: Southwest of Port Angeles on U.S. 101 at mile post 125; turn onto South Shore Road.
Web Site: www.travel-in-wa.com (under "very special places")
Days/Hours: Overnight accommodations year-round
Wheelchair/Stroller Access: Yes

If ever there was a place to get away from it all, this is it. No television or telephones at this seventy-year old lodge. For entertainment there's canoes, seacycles, rowboats, badminton, and croquet, reading in front of a hospitable brick fireplace, hiking trails that take you all the way to the rain forest, and walking around the grounds. Swimming in a heated pool is a favorite activity here. The lodge dining room serves breakfast, lunch, and dinner daily; homemade cheesecake and stuffed trout are specialties. Room rates will vary, children 5 and under stay free, and cribs and rooms with fireplaces are an option.

Horses can by rented for a brisk ride along the beach. PHOTO ©MARGE AND TED MUELLER

Mariah's
800-562-4836

Location: At the Polynesian Resort on the south end of Ocean Shores Blvd.
Days/Hours: Summer: weekdays, 4 p.m.–9:30 p.m.; weekends, 4 p.m.–
*   10 p.m.; Sunday Brunch, 8 a.m.–1 p.m. Winter: weekdays, 4 p.m.–9 p.m.*
Wheelchair/Stroller Access: Yes

The children's menu here is $2.99 for main items; this includes chicken strips, corn dogs, hamburgers, or fish; all have French fries on the side. Booster and high chairs available for small ones, darts and big screen TV for the older kids.

Stores to Browse

Kite Shops: One of the special delights around Ocean Shores is kite flying. To take the kids out onto the beach to indulge in this great family sport, you can buy or rent from any of the three shops listed below.

Cloud Nine Kite Shop
360-289-2221

Location: Just outside north gates of Ocean Shores entrance
Days/Hours: Summer: Friday–Saturday, 10 a.m.–7 p.m. March–October:
*   weekdays, 10 a.m.–6 p.m. November–February: selected weekends.*
Wheelchair/Stroller Access: Yes

Cutting Edge Kites
360-289-0667

Location: Nantucket Mall on Ocean Shores Blvd.
Web Site: www.techline.com/~cutngedg
Days/Hours: Open daily year-round. April-September: weekdays, 9 a.m.–
*   7 p.m.; Friday–Saturday, 9 a.m.–9 p.m.; Sunday, 9 a.m.–6 p.m. October–*
*   March: Monday–Saturday, 10 a.m.–6 p.m. 10 a.m.-6 p.m.; Sunday,*
*   10 a.m.–5 p.m.*
Wheelchair/Stroller Access: Yes

Flippers
360-289-4676

Location: Chance-a-La-Mer Road near Ocean Shore Blvd.
Days/Hours: June–September: daily, 10 a.m.–6 p.m.
Wheelchair/Stroller Access: Yes

SOUTH BEACHES

Grays Harbor, Aberdeen, Hoquiam, and Long Beach

Places to Go

Funland   360-642-2223

Location: 200 Pacific Hwy. S. in Long Beach
Days/Hours: May–August, daily, 9 a.m.–10 p.m. September–April: 10 a.m.–
   10 p.m.
Wheelchair/Stroller Access: Yes

The fact that this place has been around since pinball was the only
game in town doesn't make it any less popular. Funland offers both old
favorites and new attractions in the world of video games. This amusement arcade is one of the hot spots in town. Winners get tickets that can
be redeemed for stuffed animals and other souvenir prizes.

Grays Harbor Historic Seaport and
Lady Washington   360-532-8611

Location: Heron St. in Aberdeen, where the Wishkah and Chehalis rivers
   meet.
Web Site: www.travel-in-wa.com
Days/Hours: Varies; please call ahead
Tours: $4/adults; $2/seniors and students; $1/children 11 and younger; thirty
   minutes in length
Cruises: $25/adults; $20/seniors and youth 12 and under; three hours long, in
   Grays Harbor only. Reservations required.
Wheelchair/Stroller Access: Special wheelchair lift available, not useful for
   strollers

This majestic eighteenth-century ship is docked here most of the year,
but does visit other seaports. For those students studying Washington
state history, this is a visual experience: shipboard life as Capt. Robert
Gray, commander of the exploration of the Columbia River and Grays
Harbor, knew it. Wheelchairs can be lifted aboard by crane, but there are
no ramps on board.

Hoquiam's Castle   360-533-2005

Location: 515 Chenault Ave., Hoquiam
Web Site: www.travel-in-wa.com
Days/Hours: Daily, 10 a.m.–5 p.m., except closed in December
Admission: $4/adults; $1/children 6–16; free/children 5 and younger
Tours: Guided tours available
Wheelchair/Stroller Access: No

Hoquiam's Castle celebrated its 100th year anniversary in 1997. This century-old estate was built by a turn-of-the-century lumber baron, and the antiques reflect the elegance and luxury of the lifestyle at that time. The name "Hoquiam" is derived from an Native American word meaning "hungry for wood," and indeed this part of Washington state was heavily forested at that time.

Long Beach Go-Carts   360-642-2904

Location: Pacific and 10th streets in Long Beach
Days/Hours: Summer: daily, 9 a.m.–5 p.m. or whenever everyone leaves
     (they will close at midnight). Winter 10 a.m.–whenever (depends on the
     weather).
Admission: $3.50/three minutes
Wheelchair/Stroller Access: Okay for viewing

It's a pretty large go-cart track as tracks go. They even offer a senior track for those 12 and older and a junior track for 5 to 11 year olds. It's a fast blast around, taking all of three minutes.

Long Beach Kite Museum and Hall of Fame 360-642-4020

Location: Corner of Third and Blvd., Long Beach
Days/Hours: Daily, 11 a.m.–5 p.m.
Admission: $4/families of four or more; $1.50/adults; $1/children 15 or
     younger and seniors
Wheelchair/Stroller Access: Yes

Exhibits change regularly here, and you can always count on seeing award-winning kites. They have special days for children, which include clowns, face-painting, and hand-crafted kites. A special children's kite display is in the museum.

Kite-flying festivals are a grand spectacle at Long Beach. PHOTO ©MARGE AND TED MUELLER

Nahcotta Tidelands Interpretive Site

Location: Sandridge Road and 268th, in Nahcotta

Is the red tide really red? What happens when a crab loses its claws? A five-panel interpretive display tells the story of Willapa Bay and its lusty oyster community. It is fascinating to learn how this natural setting (assisted by local concern) continues to be a healthy and productive economic center.

Oyster U-Pick

Location: 270th and Sandridge Rd. *in Nahcotta (next to the Nahcotta Post*
  Office), about twelve miles from Long Beach
Days/Hours: Seasonal but open year-round
Wheelchair/Stroller Access: Not really. If the ground is dry, you can roll to
  the water's edge, but it requires caution.

Larry Warrenberg is your host, and he welcomes families. The bay
tide here is one hour later than the tide book; you'll have a three-hour
window with one and a half hours on either side. Cost is $5 for a five-
gallon pick. Suggested equipment: coolers for transporting the little gems,
good fitting knee-high boots, rubber gloves, and screwdrivers (to pry the
oysters off the stakes they grow on). The u-pick flats are muddy and to
quote Larry, they'll "suck the boots right off you!" if your footwear doesn't
fit well. Rain gear may be needed, but not usually in summer. Larry offers a free campground for cyclists and kayakers only. If you haven't tasted
fresh oysters from Willapa Bay, you have a delicious experience waiting
for you.

Pacific Salmon Charters   *360-642-3466; 800-831-2695*

Location: Port of Ilwaco
Days/Hours: January–October; call ahead for current times and dates
Wheelchair/Stroller Access: Three boats are equipped for wheelchairs.

While they offer charters for fishing (salmon or sturgeon, regular
bottom fish and deep-water fishing as well), you can also enjoy a two-
hour scenic cruise on one of the boats during the summer. Deep-sea fishing is quite strenuous; they prefer youngsters over 10. Some of the larger
fishing boats are designed to hold passengers as well, which is a great
way to break in to this sport. The rise and fall of ocean swells is a totally
new feeling for landlubbers.

Sandsations   *800-451-2542*

Location: On the beach at Long Beach
Days/Hours: Last weekend of July
Wheelchair/Stroller Access: Tough on the sand, but viewing is great from
  the boardwalk.

This annual sand-building competition gets a little wilder each year,
but that's the fun of it. Families can team together for competition entries
($15-35) or children can create on their own ($1 per child). The creativity

starts at 8 a.m. on Saturday; judging is on Saturday only and takes place from noon to 1 p.m. Prizes are awarded for all the events. After the competition, the sand architects team up to build a giant castle to compete with out-of-state challengers. There's a dance on Friday night, and a volleyball tournament takes place during the sand-building contest. Sandsations is a great excuse to come down to Long Beach; it's a fun town for families.

Twin Harbors State Park   360-268-9717

Location: Three miles south of Westport on Hwy. 105
Web Site: www.parks.wa.gov
Days/Hours: Overnight camping year-round; 320 campsites available
Wheelchair/Stroller Access: Yes

The saltwater shoreline offers razor clams in season, beachcombing, and lookout sites for gray whales migrating north (usually February and March). On the park's north beach are designated areas for horseback riding. The Shifting Sands Nature Trail is interesting for its plants and wildlife; pick a up brochure that will help you to see what's important here. The one-mile trail does have tall beach grass that can sometimes be confusing; best not to let children wander here alone.

Washington State International
Kite-Flying Festival   800-451-2542

Location: On the beach near the Long Beach boardwalk
Days/Hours: Third week of August
Wheelchair/Stroller Access: Mostly on the boardwalk; sand is hard packed
*   in places but difficult to negotiate*

Kite flying is a major sport in this part of Washington; in 1997 the sixteenth annual World Kite Festival was celebrated here. It's usually held mid-August, and the town becomes packed, so if you're planning to come down for it, make your reservations well in advance. At the festival, kites float to music, sail majestically on wind currents, and even light up the night. The competition is open to novices and masters alike; there are special children's and seniors' days.

Westport Maritime Museum   *360-268-0078*

Location: 2201 Westhaven Dr., Westport
Days/Hours: Summer: daily, noon–4 p.m. Some changes for winter months.
Admission: $2/adults; $1/children 12 and under; $5/families
Wheelchair/Stroller Access: No

This former Coast Guard station has become a museum dedicated to showcasing the immense gray whales that live off our Washington coast. Outside the museum, some very large, thick whale bones are your introduction to the stories inside. How these mammals were once hunted by fishermen is recounted in the exhibits; a children's room features some interesting shell exhibits.

Store to Browse

Jack's Country Store   *360-665-4988 or 4999*

Location: Ocean Park
Days/Hours: Winter: daily; 8 a.m.–8 p.m. Summer: daily, 8 a.m.–9 p.m.
Wheelchair/Stroller Access: Yes

The general market in the front is disarming, but keep going—there's much to see here. Pass through the doorway into the dry goods and hardware sections, and it's a different world: the world the way it used to be with old display cases and shelves to the ceiling full of items you didn't know existed any more. From kerosene lamps to the pocket knife collection, more nuts and bolts than you can image, this is the old country store.

Helpful Phone Numbers:

Chambers of Commerce:
    Elma: 360-482-2212
    Forks: 800-44-FORKS
    Grays Harbor: 800-321-1924
    Long Beach: 360-642-2400
    Montesano: 360-249-5522
    Ocean Shores: 360-289-2451
    Port Townsend: 360-385-2722
    Raymond: 360-942-5419
    Sequim/Dungeness Valley: 800-737-8462
    Westport/Grayland: 800-345-6223

Other:

Grays Harbor Tourism: 800-621-9625
Hoh Visitor Center (west side): 360-374-6925
Hoodsport Ranger Station (east side): 360-877-5254
Makah Tribal Council: 360-645-2201
National Park Service/U.S. Forest Outdoor Information Center (Seattle): 206-470-4060
North Olympic Peninsula Visitor and Convention Bureau: 800-942-4042
Olympic National Park Visitor Center (north side): 360-452-0330
Port Angeles Visitors Center: 360-452-2363
Long Beach Peninsula Visitors Bureau: 800-451-2542

Making acquaintance at Hovander Homestead Park. Photo courtesy
Bellingham/Whatcom County Convention and Visitors Bureau

CHAPTER
6

North Puget Sound and the San Juan Islands

• •

North Puget Sound, the Kitsap Peninsula, and the San Juan Islands comprise some of Washington's most marvelous getaways, especially for one-day trips. Often—especially in summer—it makes more sense to drive around through Tacoma, rather than fighting the water traffic—but the trip is worth it. The Kitsap Peninsula is across the Sound from Seattle, thirty miles south on I-5 to Tacoma, eighteen miles northwest on Hwy. 16 to Port Orchard and Bremerton. There's lots of shoreline, but much is owned privately. Visiting Bainbridge and Whidbey Islands is a delightful day trip for kids. And the Skagit Valley is haven for bikers, gardeners, and weekenders.

North Puget Sound has some unique attractions. Anacortes is a sleepy town come alive. More than just a gateway to the San Juans, it has a personality all its own and a certain whimsy, too. Watch all over town for the fabulous cut-out murals that artist Bill Mitchell has created. On almost every building there is a reminder of people and events from Anacortes's early history. They'll take you by surprise, but you'll be charmed by them. And pick up a copy of The Clamdigger, a local paper that includes all kinds of helpful hints, information, and some good coupons! You can definitely find a copy at the Visitors Center at 819 Commercial. La Conner is a popular day's destination, especially around tulip time, and leaving Bellingham, coming down Chuckanut Drive is another heart-stopping experience at times.

NORTH PUGET SOUND

Bremerton

Places to Go

Bremerton Naval Museum   360-479-7447

Location: 130 Washington Ave.
*Days/Hours: Memorial Day–Labor Day: Monday–Saturday, 10 a.m.–5 p.m.;
     Sunday, 1 p.m.–5 p.m.*
Admission: Free; tours are self-guided
Wheelchair/Stroller Access: Yes

This is the place for all things nautical and people who are fascinated with them. The USS Washington and USS Puget Sound are docked here as well. You'll find ship models, naval weapons, and military historical artifacts to satisfy the most avid of naval buffs, and you'll probably be amazed at how much naval operations have changed over the past century.

Kitsap Harbor Tours   360-377-8924

Location: Departs from the boardwalk on the Bremerton waterfront
Days/Hours: Tour ships: May–October: every hour from 11 a.m.–4 p.m.
Admission: $8.50/adults; $7.50/seniors; $5.50/children 5–12
Wheelchair/Stroller Access: Yes

There is some breathtaking scenery on these Bremerton-area cruises. On a clear evening Mount Rainier, the Olympic Mountains, and Seattle's beautiful skyline are visible and astounding. Tillicum Village is included in their itinerary (see Chapter One).

One of the cruises will take you around the harbor on a nostalgic look at some World War II ships. Aircraft carriers USS *Nimitz* and USS *Midway* and battleship USS *New Jersey* are on this narrated tour. The destroyer USS *Turner Joy* is docked here year-round.

Silverdale

Places to Go

Anna Smith Children's Park

*Location: At the intersection of Tracyton Blvd. and Fairgrounds Rd., between
     Bremerton and Silverdale*

Days/Hours: Daily, 9 a.m.–9 p.m.
Wheelchair/Stroller Access: Yes

For families who like to feed ducks, this is an ideal place to stop for a while. A quiet park with a charming duck pond at the center, there are fragrant and colorful flower beds to stroll through. This beautifully landscaped area is linked to the saltwater below by a steep trail.

Bangor Naval Submarine Base   360-396-4843

Location: Off Hwy. 305, north of Silverdale, near Keyport
Web Site: www.nsb.navy.mil
Days/Hours: Monday–Friday, 8:45 a.m.–3:30 p.m., for general public tours;
    Saturday, 10 a.m.–3 p.m., for Boy Scouts only.
Admission: Free
Tours: Yes; age minimum of 11. Only written requests considered.
Wheelchair/Stroller Access: No

Another must for the naval-inclined mind. Pick up your entry pass at the main gate before entering. The tour is by bus, because officials are concerned about disrupting routine activity here, but the shuttle buses carry up to thirty-five passengers. There are several tours available of varying lengths, from three hours to seven hours. The base itself is 7,000 acres; the business here is training people for submarine work. There's a great deal of information offered on the tour, particularly about the eight Trident nuclear missile subs in the Navy's fleet. Groups taking the longer tour may arrange to eat lunch in the galley; cost is about $2 per person. It's fascinating, even if you can't get out and wander on your own.

Naval Undersea Museum   360-396-4148

Location: In Keyport, between Poulsbo and Silverdale. From Hwy. 3, take
    State Hwy. 308; go east for three miles; follow the signs.
Web Site: www.kpt.nuwc.navy.mil/
Days/Hours: October–May: daily except Tuesday, 10 a.m.–4 p.m. June–
    September: daily, 10 a.m.–4 p.m.
Admission: Free
Tours: Yes. Guided tours by appointment
Wheelchair/Stroller Access: Yes

Visiting this extraordinary, $10 million museum is a little like being immersed in Jules Verne's 20,000 Leagues Under the Sea. Not only is the tour free, it's highly educational and entertaining. There are displays of underwater vessels to explore, plus habitats designed to teach about the diverse underwater life in our environment. Mini-subs and deep submergence vehicles are on exhibit for viewing only, but there are many other fascinating exhibits dealing with related subjects such as the physical properties below the water's surface; the interdependency of geology, weather conditions, and undersea life; and weaponry, including mines and torpedoes, some of which date back to the Revolutionary War. Parking is free; cameras are welcome.

Places to Eat

Red Robin
360-698-4822

Location: 10455 Silverdale Way
Days/Hours: Monday-Saturday, 11 a.m.–midnight; Sunday, 9 a.m.–
midnight.
Wheelchair/Stroller Access: Yes

The Robin is a favorite among local families, with over a dozen burger selections, plus some jumbo salads and side dishes. Another favorite here is the sweet, nonalcoholic fruit and ice cream "mocktails," popular with the younger set. High chairs and boosters available.

Bainbridge Island

Places to Go

Bainbridge Island Historical Museum 206-842-2773, ext. 3663

Location: 7650 N.E. High School Road
Days/Hours: Wednesday–Sunday, 1 p.m.–4 p.m.; and by appointment
Wheelchair/Stroller Access: Yes

This small but interesting collection of local photos and artifacts is housed in a one-room schoolhouse at Strawberry Hill Park. If you're interested in Bainbridge history, you'll learn a lot about the early days here.

Bloedel Reserve
206-842-7631

Location: 7571 N.E. Dolphin Dr., Bainbridge Island
Days/Hours: Wednesday–Sunday, 10 a.m.–4 p.m.
Admission: $6/adults; $4/seniors 65 and older and children 5–12; free/
children under 5
Wheelchair/Stroller Access: Limited. It's difficult to maneuver the walking
paths in places.

Described by a garden writer as "an artful woodland tapestry," Bloedel is worthy of a day's visit, at the least. By reservation only because they only "invite" a limited number of people per visit, the reserve is always a gift of privacy and reflection. There are two miles of trails which take you through "garden rooms," broad meadows, narrow ravines, woods, and glens, and a chance to explore the Bloedel home, with its magnificent Sound view and elegant furnishings. Be sure to see the Japanese Garden, the Moss Garden, the Reflection Pool, and the Glen. There is something every season—you'll never be disappointed. Children can enjoy this panorama thoroughly; there is much to explore on their level. Note: No dogs allowed, in or out of the car.

Fay Bainbridge State Park   206-842-3931

Location: 15446 Sunrise Dr. N.E.; from the ferry, take Hwy. 304 north to the traffic light at Day Rd.; turn right. The road dead-ends at Sunrise; turn left and follow the signs.
Web Site: www.parks.wa.gov
Days/Hours: Daily, 8 a.m.–dusk, year-round for day use; for camping, park closes in November for the winter and re-opens on April 10
Admission: $8–$11/camp sites
Wheelchair/Stroller Access: Yes

This is a beautiful, seventeen-acre park with a waterfront view of downtown Seattle and a challenging driftwood beach.

Suquamish Museum   360-598-3311, ext. 422; 206-464-5456

Location: 15838 Sandy Hook Rd., off Hwy. 305, between Poulsbo and Winslow
Admission: $2.50/adults; $2/seniors; $1/children 12 and under
Days/Hours: October–April: Wednesday-Sunday, 11 a.m.–4 p.m. May 1– September 30: daily, 10 a.m.–5 p.m.
Wheelchair/Stroller Access: Yes

The lifestyle and lives of the Suquamish people, past and present, are the focus of the museum, noted for its authenticity. The Suquamish have worked very hard at preserving their heritage and their history. Part of the museum is a longhouse replica and inside the fifteen-minute video, Come Forth Laughing, features tribal elders and their stories of growing up on the 8,000-acre Port Madison Reservation. The intricate basketry of the Suquamish is on display, as is a hand-carved canoe. If you go to the cemetery at St. Peter's Church nearby, you will find the headstone marking the grave of Chief Sealth (Seattle)—appropriately designed with painted canoes.

Places to Eat

The Streamliner Diner   206-842-8595

Location: 397 Winslow Way, Winslow
Days/Hours: Monday–Friday, 7 a.m.–3 p.m.; weekends, 8 a.m.–2:30 p.m.
Wheelchair/Stroller Access: Yes

Even if you're on Bainbridge Island for just the day, this diner should be on your itinerary. It's a longtime favorite with both visitors and islanders; everyone comes back and back and back for their country-style breakfasts and generous sandwiches on homemade bread.

Poulsbo

Places to Go

Marine Science Center   365-779-5549

Location: On Front St., across from the New Day Fishery
Days/Hours: Tuesday–Saturday, 10 a.m.–4 p.m.; Sunday and Monday, noon–4 p.m.
Admission: $4/adults 18 and older; $3/seniors and children 13–17; $2/children 12 and under; free/children under 2
Wheelchair/Stroller Access: Yes

Here young marine biologists can examine plankton under microscopes, then watch their experiments on a nearby video monitor. Most of the exhibits here are touch tanks, allowing youngsters to get a hands-on feel for the underwater creatures. The jellyfish and octopus are especially popular!

Places to Eat

Sluy's Bakery   360-697-BAKE (2253)

Location: 18924 Front St. N.E.
Web Site: www.poulsbo.net/sluysbakery
Days/Hours: Sunday–Thursday, 5 a.m.–6:30 p.m.; Friday and Saturday, 5 a.m.–6 p.m.
Wheelchair/Stroller Access: Yes

Starting as a local favorite, Sluy's fame has spread, and Poulsbo bread has become a regional staple, available in many stores throughout the state. A tasty multi-grain generously-sliced bread with a nutty flavor, it's popular for toast and sandwiches. But pastries are another specialty here, especially the Danishes and the scones. Great stopping point for coffee and a sweet treat; if weather permits, take your reward over to Waterfront Park and enjoy.

SNOHOMISH COUNTY
Edmonds
Places to Go

Funtasia   *425-775-GAME (general info); 425-775-2174 (direct line)*

Location: 7212 220th St. S.W.
Days/Hours: Summer: Friday–Saturday, 10 a.m.-1 a.m. The rest of the year: Sunday–Thursday, 10 a.m.–11 p.m.; Friday–Saturday, 10 a.m.–1 p.m.
Admission: None; fee is charged per game. Fun Pass or Super Pass cost $5–$12, depending on age.
Wheelchair/Stroller Access: Yes

It's a veritable amusement center for kids; the main attractions are bumper cars, Indy go-karts, an outdoor batting cage, eighteen-hole miniature golf course, Lazer Tag, and Fun Fortress. During the day, many of the rides and activities are restricted to persons at least forty-two inches tall, so of course you'll see lots of 5 to 12 year olds. Children must be at least 6 years old to hit softballs and 8 years old to bat baseballs in the cages, but they can select various pitching speeds. The evening crowd becomes teens and young adults. You can reserve a party table for birthdays.

Sierra Park   *None*

Location: At 191st St. S.W. and S.W. 80th Ave.
Days/Hours: Daily, dawn to dusk
Wheelchair/Stroller Access: Yes

Located in north Edmonds, Sierra Park is designed with sight-impaired children and adults in mind, although it is enjoyed by everyone. There are interpretive markers with Braille which describe the natural surroundings along the trail. The paved path is smooth and fairly flat, a big plus for those in wheelchairs or pushing strollers.

Places to Eat

brusseau's   425-774-4166

Location: N.E. corner of Fifth and Dayton streets in downtown Edmonds
Days/Hours: Weekdays, 7 a.m.–4 p.m. (after February, till 5 p.m.); Satur-
    day–Sunday, 8 a.m.–5 p.m.
Wheelchair/Stroller Access: Yes

Long considered a local favorite even though it's under new man-
agement, brusseau's is a bakery and sidewalk café with some unique
recipes and delicious specialties. They roast their own turkey and feature
homemade soups, not to mention some irresistible unmentionables beckoning to you from the bakery case. Good stopping place for either breakfast or lunch. Booster chairs available; they will adjust portions to a child's
appetite.

Maltby Cafe   425-483-3123

Location: 8809 Maltby Rd., Maltby (in Snohomish). Take 405 north, exit on
    Hwy. 522 East (Woodinville). Stay on the main road to the Maltby
    intersection (Bothell-Monroe Rd). Turn left at the light and bear left at
    the Y.
Days/Hours: Daily, 7 a.m.–3 p.m.
Wheelchair/Stroller Access: Yes

This is a place you go to eat. Breakfast is served all day on the weekends and until 11:30 a.m. on weekdays. Lunch from 11:30 a.m. to 3 p.m.
Go hungry—it's worth it. Huge cinnamon rolls and delicious buttermilk
biscuits; everything is fresh and there's Starbucks coffee to top it off. Usually a wait (maybe twenty minutes), but it goes quickly. The kids' menu
has crayons to go with the smaller portions and prices; lunch includes
grilled cheese, turkey sandwiches, or junior pb and j sandwiches. Adult
portions are generous but you can share, with no extra charge (they don't
do half portions). High chairs and boosters, but no changing table. Of
interest nearby: Flower World.

NORTH SNOHOMISH COUNTY

Snohomish

Places to Go

Blackman Museum   360- 568-5235

Location: 118 Ave. B, Snohomish
Days/Hours: Wednesday–Sunday, noon–4 p.m.
Admission: $1/adults; 50¢/seniors and children under 12

This is a really a genteel old mansion built in 1878. It has been re-stored by the local historical society and furnished with antiques. Note this admission information: You're an adult in Snohomish if you're over 12. Novel idea.

Harvey's Airfield   360-568-1541

Location: 9900 Airport Way, Snohomish
Days/Hours: Field is open daily year-round.
Wheelchair/Stroller Access: Yes

There are a number of attractions here. The restaurant overlooks the airfield, has a kid's menu, and does birthday parties. The playground outside, plus outdoor dining, is great in good weather. While you dine, you can watch the skydivers as well as planes taking off and landing. But for those bitten by the flying bug, there's magic here. Harvey's houses up to 300 planes, all privately owned, many of special interest. They offer Scenic Airplane Flights for three ($62/half hour, $124/one hour); Helicopter Flights for two ($150.00); Discovery Flights for one ($35.00) where you get to take part. For youths 12 to 17, the Summer Youth Camp is a good intro to the world of flying; it's a week-long summer experience that includes two hours of flying (cost varies). Call about Harvey's Corn Roast Fly-In, usually mid-September. An all-day affair, all the corn you can eat, with balloon rides, aerobatics contests, aircraft displays, and much more.

Pioneer Village and Museum

No phone at the village; call the Blackman Museum at 360-568-5235, they will also arrange group tours

Location: *Second and Pine streets in Snohomish; parking is behind the Pilchuck Shopping Center.*
Days/Hours: *Mid-May–August: daily, noon–4 p.m.*
Admission: *$1/adults; 50¢/seniors and students*
Wheelchair/Stroller Access: *Possible, but be prepared for some rough grass.*

The air is rich with the history of the Snohomish of a hundred years ago at the Pioneer Village, a collection of cabins and other buildings from earlier days. Now restored and authentically furnished by the Historical Society, it's easy to imagine what life was like. The Kikendall Log Cabin, originally on the Pilchuck River, dates back to 1875. You'll find Cook's General Store, the blacksmith's shop, and even an outhouse out back.

Snohomish Family Theater

360-568-5333

Location: *1003 First, Snohomish*
Days/Hours: *Daily, year-round*
Wheelchair/Stroller Access: *Yes*

They run films here rated PG-13. Average admission is $3.25, and there are two screens from which to choose. On holidays they do film packages; a real favorite is Halloween Movie Madness. Gift certificates here make a nice birthday option.

Places to Eat

Cabbage Patch Restaurant and Inn

360-568-9091

Location: *111 Ave. A, Snohomish*
Days/Hours: *Sunday–Thursday, 9 a.m.–10 p.m.; Friday–Saturday, 7 a.m.– 11 p.m.*
Wheelchair/Stroller Access: *No*

At one of Snohomish's best known, long-standing attractions, especially for delicious desserts, dinner is half price for kids under 12 (except for steak orders). For breakfast, a smaller portion is the Bear Pancake with one egg. You can share portions with no extra charge; high chairs and boosters available. It's a large menu, lots of variety. The large room at the back is for families and can accommodate up to twenty-five; close the door and let the kids relax.

Snohomish Valley Ice Cream   *360-568-1133*

Location: 902 First St., Snohomish
Days/Hours: Summer: Monday–Saturday, 10 a.m.–9 p.m.; Sunday, 11 a.m.–
 8 p.m. Winter: Monday–Saturday, 10 a.m.–5 p.m.; Sunday, 11 a.m.–5 p.m.
Wheelchair/Stroller Access: Yes

Milkshakes are special here. Real ingredients, made the old way in a metal cup on a long-arm blender. They make their own waffle cones and do half sandwiches with pb and j on request. Plus sodas, floats, and sundaes. Candy and popcorn, too.

Store to Browse

Weed's Variety   *360-568-5161*

Location: First St. in Snohomish
Days/Hours: Monday–Saturday, 9:30 a.m.–5:30 p.m.; Sunday 11 a.m.–
 5 p.m. Open year-round except for holidays.
Wheelchair/Stroller Access: Yes

If you're strolling First St., here's a well-remembered version of the variety store. Worth just ducking in for a look around.

Lynnwood

Places to Go

Roll-a-Way Skate Center   *425-778-4446; 425-778-8738*

Location: 6210 200th S.W.
Days/Hours: Public Sessions: Wednesday–Friday, 4 p.m.–6 p.m.; Friday–
 Saturday, 7 p.m.–11 p.m.; Saturday–Sunday, 1 p.m.–3:30 p.m., 3 p.m.–
 5:30 p.m.; Sunday, 7 p.m.–9 p.m.
Wheelchair/Stroller Access: In the viewing area

Skate rental is included in the price of admission, $2.50, during the day, $5 on weekend evenings.

Sno-King Ice Arena   425-775-7512

Location: 19803 68th Ave. W.
*Days/Hours: Public Skating: daily, 11 a.m.–1 p.m.; also, Tuesday–Thursday,
7 p.m.–8:50 p.m.; Saturday, 3:30 p.m.–5:50 p.m., 9 p.m.–1 a.m.; Sunday,
3 p.m.–5 p.m.*
Admission: $7 including skate rental; $4.75 if you bring your own skates
Wheelchair/Stroller Access: Yes, for viewing

Skating has always been a great family-togetherness experiment, and
for some it becomes an ongoing resource for entertainment, exercise, and
even a stress-reliever. Great place for kids' birthday parties, too. Sno-
King offers a package that includes skate rental and admission, ice-cream,
and a soft drink; you bring the cake and everything else. The party takes
place in the public area (no separate party room), but with all the com-
motion, no one ever seems to mind. It's fun if your ankles hold up.

Places to Eat

Chuck E. Cheese   425-771-1195

Location: 3717 196th St. S.W.
Web Site: www.chuckecheese.com
*Days/Hours: Sunday–Thursday, 11 a.m.–9 p.m.; Friday and Saturday,
11 a.m.–10 p.m.*
Admission: None
Wheelchair/Stroller Access: Yes

Mechanical animal characters sing, dance, and play musical instru-
ments on stage while the audience munches on pizza, salads, and soft
drinks. Most of the audience is composed of families celebrating birthdays or groups with postgame victories. Other activities include air
hockey, ski-ball, basketball hoop-shoot games, and mechanized rides for
toddlers (weighing less than thirty pounds); tokens are the "coin of the
realm" here; purchase them when you arrive. Be prepared for noise and
lots of it.

Mukilteo

Places to Go

Games Family Fun Center   360-353-6800

Location: 3616 South Rd. *(behind Children's World Learning Center on
Mukilteo Speedway)*
*Days/Hours: Sunday–Thursday, 10 a.m.–10 p.m.; Friday and Saturday, 10
a.m.–midnight*

Admission: $3.75/adults; $2.75/children 12 and under; free/children 3 and under
Wheelchair/Stroller Access: Yes

The games here are geared for children age 8 and older, and it's a good destination on a rainy day. Lots of choices here, from softball and baseball batting cages to pool, video games, and eighteen-hole miniature golf.

Places to Eat

Ivar's   425-742-6180 (Mukilteo restaurant)

Location: Three locations in Snohomish County: Ivar's Mukilteo Landing and Seafood Bar at 710 Front St. in Mukilteo; Ivar's Seafood Bar at 1520 41st St., Everett; and Ivar's Seafood Bar at 9910 Edmonds Way, Edmonds.
Days/Hours: Mukilteo: Monday–Thursday, 10 a.m.–11 p.m.; Friday, 10 a.m.–midnight; Saturday, 8 a.m.–10 p.m.; Sunday, 8 a.m.–9 p.m.
Wheelchair/Stroller Access: Yes

The Mukilteo restaurant is next to the ferry terminal, with a view of boats coming and going. The seafood bars have a "kid's catch" of fish and chips. Their clam chowder is filling and quite popular.

Marysville
Places to Go

Big D's Batting Cage and Mini Golf   360-659-4086

Location: 1070 Columbia Ave. in Marysville (behind Gold's Gym)
Days/Hours: Monday-Friday, noon–8 p.m.; Saturday, 10 a.m.–8 p.m.; Sunday, 11 a.m.–7 p.m.
Admission: No admission fee; charges for individual activities
Wheelchair/Stroller Access: Yes

Little Leaguers and other baseball advocates can sharpen their skills here quite nicely. With a ball coming at them every ten to twenty seconds, they have to concentrate! You can select the speed of pitch; the charge is twenty-two baseballs for $1. Reserve a cage in advance at $14 for thirty minutes or $25 for an hour. The mini-golf is $2.50 for 12 and younger, over 12 costs $3. Special note: They will close during a thunder and lightning storm.

Everett

Places to Go

Biringer Farms   425-259-0255

Location: 37th Ave. N.E. off Hwy. 529. Heading north on I-5 to exit 195,
   turn left and continue two miles to Hwy. 529; cross the Snohomish River
   Bridge; take the second right to 37th Ave. N.W. Follow a bumpy dirt road
   in to the farm.
Days/Hours: Seasonal; call for info
Admission: Just for the pumpkin tours; usually $3–$4.50
Wheelchair/Stroller Access: Yes

Biringer's attracts families for a number of reasons, not the least
of which is their U-Pick berry fields. Strawberries and raspberries are
irresistible in the summer months. Halloween is a wonderful time out
here, with the "boo barn," the hay maze, and pumpkins galore to
choose from.

Boeing Plant   206-544-1264;
                               800-464-1476 (tour times and directions)

Location: 84th St. S.W. Take I-5 to exit 89; go west for two miles.
Days/Hours: Monday–Friday, 9 a.m. and 1 p.m. Tickets available at 8:30 a.m.
   Children must be at least 8 years old
Admission: Free for families and individuals; $5/person charge for groups of
   ten or more
Tours: Reservations accepted for groups of fifteen or more; reserve three to six
   months in advance.
Wheelchair/Stroller Access: Yes

If we are a Boeing town, it's with good reason! The Everett plant is
considered the largest manufacturing plant in the world, and now—with
the 777 in flight—no doubt they'll retain the title for years. This is a free,
ninety-minute bus tour; you do have to be there early to get tickets, and
vacation months are by far the most popular. No still or video cameras
are allowed. You'll see firsthand (through the bus window) how the 747s
and 767s come together. You'll absorb an incredible amount of fascinating information in a short time. Boeing is Everett's main employer and
the main tourist attraction; over 128,000 toured the plant last year.

Centennial Trail

Location: Snohomish to Lake Stevens. To start in Snohomish, drive Bickford Ave. into Snohomish, turn east on 10th Ave., go north on Maple Ave., and that becomes the Snohomish-Machias Road. Look for a parking lot just past Three Lakes Road, or park near Lake Stevens at the Bonneville Field ballpark at the end of 16th Ave. N.E.
Days/Hours: The trail is always open, but it is unlighted at night; best to use between dawn and dusk.
Wheelchair/Stroller Access: Yes

It's amazing how many different modes of transportation can be seen on this modest, six-and-a-half-mile paved trail. Bicycles, tricycles, walkers, strollers, roller skaters, skateboards, and even horses share this Snohomish County trail. It's safe and flat, allowing youngsters learning to ride a small measure of security. The trail winds through farmland, past horses and cows grazing in fields, and around waterways. The eventual destination is Arlington.

Everett Aquasox   206-258-3673

Location: Games played at the Everett Memorial Stadium, 39th at Broadway
Days/Hours: Home schedule is generally June–August
Admission: $5/ages 13 and over; $4/children 3–12; free/children 2 and under
Wheelchair/Stroller Access: Yes

As the Class A farm team for the Seattle Mariners, the Aquasox continue to grow in stature and popularity. The lure of an outdoor game in a small ballpark—replete with hot dogs and hot chocolate and some pretty funky between-inning games and contest—is almost addicting. Bring a mitt—you never know when a foul ball may come your way. The concession stands have just the right snacks and treats. What's also special about this park and team is that owners Bob and Margaret Bavasi run a tight ship and work hard to keep the park environment comfortable for families. It's great fun. Catch a game—you might recognize a budding star at the beginning of his career.

Everett Farmer's Market

Location: Just off West Marine View Dr., north of Navy Home Port and Marine Village
Days/Hours: June 1–September 28: Sundays, 11 a.m.–4 p.m.
Wheelchair/Stroller Access: Yes.

This open-air market is a nice stopping point on a Sunday afternoon. Good selection of cut flowers, fruits, vegetables, herbs, honey, and some crafts. Walk through once before selecting; prices will vary. All Washington-grown produce.

Forest Park   425-257-8300

Location: 802 Mukilteo Blvd.
Days/Hours: Dawn to dusk
Wheelchair/Stroller Access: Strollers enter from north parking lot; wheelchairs from south parking lot.

This is a lush green park with tempting paths. In summer, the playground is a wonderful place for kids, while the rest of the family lounges on the grass. Lots of attractions here: ball fields and tennis courts, an indoor pool plus outdoor wading and sprinkler pools. One favorite is the Animal Farm and Petting Zoo. Pony rides are available in the afternoon.

The Concerts in the Park series is a wonderful summer program for the family. Here are some special programs that families can take advantage of:

- **Barnyard Birthdays.** Saturday or Sunday, 2 p.m.–4 p.m., fee is $65 for eight children and $8 for each additional child. The staff provides an afternoon of festivities, including the Animal Farm, plus cake, ice cream, and punch.
- **Bunny Bank.** Families can borrow a bunny for three days. For a $10 fee, everything is provided for the bunny's stay; you provide the T.L.C. By appointment; call 257-8303.
- **Animal Farm Educational Tour.** Weekdays by appointment; call 425-257-8300. Fee is $1 per child; adults are free. You'll learn all about the barnyard animals.
- **Peter Rabbit Tea Party.** Includes cookie-frosting and a visit with the bunnies. For ages 4 to 8; minimum of four, maximum of twelve. Call for specific dates; fee is usually $10.
- **Breakfast with the Animals.** Kids can be a farmer for a morning and help the staff care for the animals, then do some easy farm chores, and enjoy a continental breakfast. Must be 3 or older. Call for details.

Farmer's Markets such as this one in Bellingham are fun for both children and adults. PHOTO COURTESY BELLINGHAM/ WHATCOM COUNTY CONVENTION AND VISITORS BUREAU

Horse Country—Ponies Too!   360-691-7509; 425-335-4773

Location: *8507 Hwy. 92 in Granite Falls. Take I-5 to exit 194; turn left onto Hwy. 204, left again onto Hwy. 9, and right onto Hwy. 92. Horse Country is six miles up on the right. Look for a green fence and long driveway.*

Days/Hours: *Winter: Wednesday–Saturday, 9 a.m.–7 p.m.; Sunday, noon–7 p.m. Closed holidays.*

Admission: *Guided rides: $17.50/one hour, $25/ninety minutes. $5/fifteen minutes (ponies)*

Wheelchair/Stroller Access: *No*

Horse Country covers 111 acres on the Pilchuck River. The guided trips go up into the Cascades; families often vacation together this way.

There is no age minimum to ride the ponies, and staff will help if needed. In case of rain, there's a spacious indoor riding arena. Western and English riding lessons are offered, plus there's a summer day camp for kids ages 7 to 16.

Jetty Island Ferry   *425-257-8304; 425-257-8300, ext. 3079*

Location: Free ferry departs from the 10th St. boat launch and Marina Park (ten blocks north of the Naval Base)
Days/Hours: July 5–August 31: Wednesday–Saturday, 10 a.m.–5:30 p.m.; Sunday, 11 a.m.–5:30 p.m.
Wheelchair/Stroller Access: Ferry does; island does not

A free ferry is a wondrous adventure, especially to Jetty Island in the summertime. The five-minute ride goes very quickly, and warm shallow water and a sandy beach are the reward. Jetty Island offers nature walks up to two miles, crafts projects, and survival adventure games, most appropriate for 5 to 10 year olds. Guided nature walks are at 12:15 p.m. and 3:15 p.m. The ferry sails every half-hour and fills up very quickly. If you choose to arrive on your own craft, you may have to pull up on the beach as the nearby dock has limited space. Special note: There is no running water on Jetty Island. Restroom facilities are floating portable toilet stalls. Pets not allowed. Another note: During peak summer hours, the wait can be up to two hours. Parking adjacent to the boat launch.

Store to Browse

Display and Costume Supply   *425-353-3364*

Location: 5209 Evergreen Way
Days/Hours: Monday–Friday, 9 a.m.–8 p.m.; Saturday, 9:30 a.m.–6 p.m.; Sunday, 10 a.m.–5 p.m.
Wheelchair/Stroller Access: Yes

An absolute haven for the party-giver, party lover, and party-goer. Costumes for all occasions, decorations, paper supplies, and balloons, specialty items—everything but the invitations. Helium tank rentals available, too.

WHIDBEY ISLAND

Places to Go

City Beach Park   *360-679-5551, ext. 234*

Location: At the end of 80th St. N.W. in Oak Harbor, off Hwy. 20
Days/Hours: Daily, year-round; overnight camping allowed
Wheelchair/Stroller Access: Yes

The town's Dutch influence is quite evident here, with ornamental windmills and gardens alive with tulips. For children, there are two playgrounds with swings and a sliding board, a baseball field, a wading pool, and a swimming lagoon (with a full-time lifeguard in summer). The park is the stage for many community events; local families spend lots of time here.

Deception Pass State Park   *360-675-2417*

Location: On Hwy. 20, ten miles north of Oak Harbor
Days/Hours: Open year-round for overnight camping
Wheelchair/Stroller Access: In some places

This has become one of the most popular parks (and campgrounds) in the state, and for good reason. From thirty miles of hiking trails to an underwater park for divers, there's a wealth of activities. Statistics tell us that close to 4 million people a year enjoy the variety here. Don't be misled by the bridge; half the park is on Whidbey Island, the other on Fidalgo Island, but there are parking areas on both ends of the bridge to accommodate passenger vehicles. If you're hiking, the suggested route is the Discovery Trail, which begins at the Environment Learning Center on Whidbey and has side trails to Goose Rock. Other, more makeshift trails, can be quite dangerous for children.

Fort Casey State Park   *360-678-4519*

Location: Off Hwy. 20, three miles south of Coupeville
Days/Hours: Open year-round for camping
Wheelchair/Stroller Access: Yes

For Washingtonians, Fort Casey is part of a romantic, historical story. The fort was built in the 1850s and is said to be a corner of the "Triangle of Fire," a strategic defense against enemy ships attempting to sail through Admiralty Inlet in the late 1880s. With Fort Warden and Fort Flagler, Fort Casey was fortified against this and later military ploys. To the disappoint of some—and relief of many—no ships ever appeared. Fort Casey did host training troops during World Wars I and II. Today the old cannons and bunkers provide a perfect opportunity for imaginative, energetic kids. But don't miss the park's water-view trails; two of these lead to Admiralty Head Lighthouse, which opened in 1861 and is now the park's interpretive center.

Fort Ebey State Park   360-678-4636

Location: *Off Libby Road, south of Partridge Point, eight miles south of Oak Harbor*
Days/Hours: *Open year-round for overnight camping*
Wheelchair/Stroller Access: *In some places*

Originally intended as an antiaircraft base, Fort Casey saw no action and is now a 640-acre park with fifty-six campsites. There are some old bunkers, perfect for hiding and seeking. For hikers, there are several paths down to Point Partridge; near the park's north end is Lake Pondilla, noted for good bass fishing.

Places to Eat

Chocolates for Breakfast   360-675-2141

Location: *530 S.E. Barrington Dr.*
Days/Hours: *Monday–Friday, 6:30 a.m.–5:30 p.m.; Saturday, 8 a.m.–3 p.m.; closed Sunday*
Wheelchair/Stroller Access: *No*

If you love chocolate, you'll feel right at home here. In one room, you can relax with a steaming hot espresso and a pastry; in the next room they sell Northwest jams, jellies, candies, and other goodies.

Mike's Place   360-221-6575

Location: *219 First St., in Langley*
Days/Hours: *Summer–Labor Day: Sunday–Thursday, 8 a.m.–3 p.m.; Friday–Saturday, 8 a.m.–8 p.m. Winter: Sunday–Thursday, 9 a.m.–2 p.m.; Friday–Saturday, 9 a.m.–8 p.m.*
Wheelchair/Stroller Access: *Yes*

A very popular place is Mike's and not just for kids' stuff . . . but they do offer a bear-face shaped pancake for breakfast. Kid's menu at lunch include pb and j and grilled cheese. Dinner is served on Friday and Saturday only, but it's worth the trip! On Friday, kids can do the all-you-can-eat thing with fish and chips; cost is 35¢ per year. Kids' dinner menu includes chicken and clam strips. Dessert is always a big surprise; the choice changes daily. If you're lucky, you'll choose the day they're offering blackberry cobbler or pie, bread pudding, chocolate cheese cake—don't bring willpower.

SKAGIT VALLEY

Stanwood

Places to Eat

The Cookie Mill   360-629-2362

Location: 9808 SR 532; just follow the main road into Stanwood.
Days/Hours: Monday–Friday, 6 a.m.–5 p.m.; Saturday, 8 a.m.–5 p.m.;
   Sunday, 9 a.m.–4 p.m.

Great place to stop for breakfast, lunch, snack, whatever. They do sandwiches very well, also salads, soups, espresso, and cookies. It's a modest little place, but everything is freshly prepared with a smile.

Ice Cream Station

Location: 2712 First St. and Florence Rd.
Days/Hours: Summer: Monday–Thursday, noon–9 p.m.; Friday–Saturday,
   noon–10 p.m.; Sunday, noon–5 p.m. Winter: Friday–Saturday only,
   noon–9 p.m.

On a warm day in Stanwood, this is a good place to be. They've got twenty-four flavors of ice-cream and ten kinds of sundaes. Floats and malts, too, if you prefer. Looks a little like a train station, with interesting trains and photos to look out while you're relaxing over your treat. The junior counter with small, kid-size chairs is fun for the smaller ones.

La Conner

Places to Go

Deception Pass Viking Cruise   360-466-2639

Location: 109 N. First St., in the Lime Dock building
Days/Hours: Cruises year-round
Wheelchair/Stroller Access: No

They guarantee you'll spot whales, and they're probably right. From May through October, several families of Orcas play and feed in and around the San Juan Islands. Viking Cruise will take you there.

The Gaches Mansion
360-466-4288

Location: 703 Second St.
Days/Hours: Summer: Friday–Sunday, 1 p.m.–5 p.m. The rest of the year:
   1 p.m.–4 p.m.
Admission: $3/adults; free/children 12 and under
Wheelchair/Stroller Access: No

With its hundred-year history, this classic old mansion imparts a feeling of elegance to its visitors. Over the years, the mansion has been a home in high society, a hospital, and a boardinghouse. A major fire destroyed the first floor, which has been restored by the La Conner Landmark Society; the upper floors are also used for displays.

Museum of Northwest Art
360-466-4078

Location: 121 First St.
Days/Hours: Tuesday–Sunday, 11 a.m.–5 p.m. (best to call to verify)
Admission: $3/adults; free/children 17 and under with an adult
Wheelchair/Stroller Access: Yes

Somewhat new to La Conner, the museum is—as its name implies—dedicated to Northwest art of many kinds. There is a permanent exhibit by regional artists and changing exhibits to pique curiosity and a glass gallery dedicated to Northwest artists. There are special programs for children, including fish painting—with real fish! Take time to shop the museum store—you'll find some kids' toys and games among the choices.

Skagit County Historical Museum
360-466-3365

Location: 501 South 4th St.
Days/Hours: Tuesday–Sunday, 11 a.m.–5 p.m.; closed Thanksgiving,
   Christmas, and New Year's Day
Admission: $2/adults; $1/seniors 65 and over and children 6–12; $5/family
   (two adults plus children); free/children 5 and under and Historical
   Society member
Wheelchair/Stroller Access: Yes

One of the highlights of this delightful little town, the museum is a reflection of the rich history of the rural Skagit region. Perched on top of the hill, the views from the observation desk are as enjoyable as the excellent exhibits inside. Some exhibits are permanent, others change regularly, so there's always something interesting to see. Most of the items in the collections have been donated—and used, worn, or owned—by local families. From the observation desk, you'll see Skagit farmland, Skagit

Bay, the Cascades, and Mount Baker. During tulip season, you'll have a commanding and expansive view of these colorful gems. Don't miss the museum store; if you visit just the store, no admission is charged.

Swinomish Native American Community

Location: Just across the channel from La Conner

Cross the Rainbow Bridge (visible from First St.) and follow the road. Points of interest include the Native American totem pole, Pioneer Cemetery, and Native American Community Center.

Places to Eat

Calico Cupboard

360-466-4451; 360-293-7315 (Anacortes); 360-336-3107 (Mount Vernon)

Location: Three locations: 720 S. First St.; 901 Commercial, Anacortes; 121-B Freeway Dr., Mount Vernon
Days/Hours: Daily, 8 a.m.–5 p.m.
Wheelchair/Stroller Access: Yes

No trip to La Conner is complete without breakfast or lunch at the Calico Cupboard. During the summer months, expect a half-hour wait. Their home-baked breads and homemade soups are just part of the draw here; the sandwiches are generous, fresh, and hearty. Breakfasts are country-style; bring an appetite. Everything in the bakery is made fresh daily. Take something home for the freezer.

Lighthouse Inn

360-466-3147

Location: 512 First St.
Days/Hours: Daily, 11:30 a.m.–8 p.m. or later (varies with seasons)
Wheelchair/Stroller Access: Yes

You can enjoy a delightful meal overlooking the channel; the dining room has a view of everything happening on the water. Special menu items for children include fish and chips, chicken and clam strips, and burgers. High chairs, boosters, and bibs are available. During summer months, they barbecue salmon over alder logs on a street-side open pit; the aromas are wonderful!

Stores to Browse

Bunnies by the Bay   1-888-BAY-LEEE (229-5333)

Location: 617 E. Morris
Web Site: www.bunniesbythebay.com
Days/Hours: Daily, 10 a.m.–6 p.m.
Wheelchair/Stroller Access: No

This is another retail outlet for the original Bunnies in Anacortes, where the manufacturing is done. But the La Conner store is charming and worth the visit, just to get acquainted with these often irresistible creatures.

O'Leary Building   360-466-2971 (Cascade Candy Company); 360-466-1305 (O'Leary's Books)

Location: 609 First St.
Days/Hours: Generally open daily; winter hours will vary. Best to call to
   verify.
Wheelchair/Stroller Access: Yes

A great combination of candy and books. On the candy menu, home-made fudge, truffles, and chocolate suckers look tempting, or maybe chocolate Easter bunnies. Next door on the "book" menu, lower shelves filled with kids' books are just as tempting.

Tillinghast Seed and Mercantile Company   360-466-3329

Location: 623 Morris St.
Days/Hours: Monday–Saturday, 9 a.m.–5:30 p.m.; Sunday, 11 a.m.–6 p.m.
Wheelchair/Stroller Access: By ramps on the first floor only

This is a shop that deserves exploring. Housed in a building that hides its 113-year-old history well, this is the Northwest's oldest operating retail and seed store. In one room the shelves from floor to ceiling display hundreds of flower and vegetable seed packets—an amazing variety. There is garden art and assorted tools to browse through; upstairs is a year-round Christmas attic filled with everything the season has to offer. A kitchen shop and a florist are also part of this eclectic collection

Mount Vernon
Places to Go

Chuckanut Drive

Location: Between Bellingham and Mount Vernon
Driving Directions: Heading south on I-5 (from Vancouver), take exit 250, south of Bellingham's historical Fairhaven district and the northern entrance to Chuckanut Drive. Heading north, take exit 231 (sixty-two miles from Seattle) marked Chuckanut Drive, Bow Edison, which leads to the southern entrance.

What used to be a four- or five-hour trip by horse and buggy to Bellingham over a rough gravel road is now a smooth, black-topped two-lane highway. Still narrow and definitely winding, Chuckanut Drive is one of the oldest scenic drives in the state. From top to bottom the drive can take only fifteen minutes, but it's hard to resist at least one stopping point. The view of Guemes, Cypress, Lopez, Eliza, and Sinclair Islands is quite breathtaking; add the Olympics and coast ranges and Puget Sound and it becomes an arresting and extraordinary sight. On the way down, Larabee State Park is the oldest park in the state and offers overnight camping and a railroad tunnel that has an enticing echo. Alert the kids to watch for a road sign that reads: "Please drive quietly. Meadowlarks singing."

Lang's Pony and Horse Rides   360-424-7630

Location: 4565 Farm Mountain Rd., Mount Vernon. Heading north, take I-5 to exit 225; turn right on Anderson Rd.; go a quarter block and take an immediate left on Cedardale Rd. Heading north and running parallel to I-5, go right at Blackburn Road; travel about one mile. Road makes a ninety-degree turn to right and becomes Little Mountain Rd. Lang's is one and a half miles ahead on the left hand side; look for a large wooden sign. Drive up the driveway to the parking lot (near the horse barn). Heading south, take exit 225 and turn on Anderson; cross over I-5, go a quarter block, and turn left onto Cedardale and proceed as listed above.
Days/Hours: Open year-round. Hours vary; call for information
Wheelchair/Stroller Access: Yes

If you love horses, Lang's offers you a full menu of activity, including lessons, birthday parties, group trail rides, and therapeutic riding. Trail rides are available for both individuals and families. Covered picnic facilities add to your day's outing. Some of their specialty services include Girl Scout Badge programs and one-day and overnight camps. Their traveling ponies will come for school carnivals, birthday parties, and other special events. Rides are by reservation only; be sure to call ahead, and plan to arrive at least fifteen minutes prior to your scheduled riding time (for check-in and preparation).

Padilla Bay National Estuarine Sanctuary/Breazeale Interpretive Center   360-428-1558; 360-757-1549 (TDD)

Location: 1043 Bay View-Edison Road, Mount Vernon. Take exit 231 off I-5; head toward Anacortes, and follow the signs to Padilla Bay.
Web Site: www.inlet.geol.sc.edu/pdb/padilla.html
Days/Hours: Breazeale Interpretive Center: Wednesday–Sunday, 10 a.m.– 5 p.m., except holidays
Wheelchair/Stroller Access: Yes, at the center

Padilla Bay is the only National Estuarine Research Reserve in Washington state. The large sea-grass meadows and mudflats support many invertebrates and migratory animals as well. In the Interpretive Center, kids can reach out and touch the bones, teeth, feathers, and pelts representing the inhabitants of the estuary. These hands-on exhibits and presentations are put together with kids' curiosity in mind and meant to show children how the delicate balance in the bay is a natural wonder. There are tanks here full of marine life such as sea perch, sculpins, flounder, and salmon. Much of the research done here is to monitor the plant and animal populations, protect water quality, and understand better the ecological processes. Outside, you can walk or bike the 2.2-mile trail along the shoreline, or absorb the view from the observation deck.

Roozengarde   360-424-8531; 800-732-3266

Location: 1587 Beaver Marsh Rd.
Web Site: www.roozengaarde.com
Days/Hours: March–May: Monday–Saturday, 9 a.m.–5:30 p.m.; Sunday, 10 a.m.–5 p.m. June–February: Monday–Saturday, 9 a.m.–5 p.m.
Wheelchair/Stroller Access: Limited. The fields are not hospitable, but the retail store and display gardens are accessible.

Roozengarde is the place to be when the tulips bloom, but don't overlook the daffodils. The tulip festival happens the last weekend of March through the second week of April. The flowers in bloom depend strictly on the weather, but it is a magnificent sight and a huge tourist attraction. You can purchase daffodil, tulip, crocus, hyacinth, and iris bulbs here or just enjoy the brilliant color of the display gardens. Daffodils usually start blooming in March; the tulips erupt in late March or early April and continue until early May.

A beached log on North Puget Sound is a perfect place to read a book.
Photo courtesy Bellingham/Whatcom County Convention and Visitors Bureau

Places to Eat and Stay

Benson Farmstead   360-757-0578

Location: 1009 Avon-Allen Rd., Bow (just west of Burlington)
Web Site: www.bbhost.com\bensonbnb
Days/Hours: April–September for daily overnight accommodations; week-
ends only for remainder of year
Wheelchair/Stroller Access: No

If you're into bed and breakfast with your kids, here's the place to do
it! The Farmstead, owned by Sharon and Jerry Benson, is a seventeen-
room Scandinavian farmhouse with a large playroom in the granary.
Outside, a large English garden is inviting and, if you're lucky, perhaps
Jerry Benson will show you around the farm. There's a hot tub for a relaxing soak. The full farm breakfast in the morning includes homemade
breads.

Big Scoop   360-424-3558

Location: 327 E. College Way, Mount Vernon
Days/Hours: Sunday–Thursday, 11 a.m.–10 p.m.; Friday–Saturday, 11 a.m.–
   11 p.m.
Wheelchair/Stroller Access: Yes

Although a franchise, Big Scoop's a downscale version of the old-fashioned ice cream parlor. Loads of choices here, especially in burgers and sundaes. They do birthday parties in a special area; there's no age minimum, and they provide party hats, decorations, and place mats as well as a free sundae for the birthday person. High chairs and boosters available. Easy, casual stopping point.

Sedro Wooley

Places to Go

Wooly Prairie Buffalo Company   800-524-7660; 360-856-0310

Days/Hours: Tours daily, April 1–September 15
Admission: $8/adults; $6/children 3–11 and seniors. Group rates: $6/person
   in a group of six to nine; $5/person in a group of ten to fifteen; $4/person
   in a group of sixteen. Reservations required.
Wheelchair/stroller access: You'll ride on the "Prairie Schooner," which is
   wheelchair accessible. Strollers can be folded up.
Special Notes: No smoking; no pets; please no children under 3; late arrivals
   might be rescheduled.

If you've noticed, there's no address. That's because this teacher-turned-buffalo rancher wants no drop-ins, for a very good reason. There are some big bison here, and people wandering around without invitation could cause problems. It's a great place for a birthday party, which would include a hayride among the herd, a free gift for the birthday child, and activities such as the Tipi Village, Buffalo Trading Post, trampoline, and bean-bag golf. There's a hay barn for rainy days. This is a rather unique experience. For classroom presentations and ranch visits, your guide uses video and visual aids to help tell the story.

Places to Eat

The Farmhouse Inn
360-466-4411

Location: At Hwy. 20 and the La Conner-Whitney Rd., Mount Vernon
Days/Hours: Daily, 7 a.m.–9 p.m.
Wheelchair/Stroller Access: Yes

The Farmhouse Inn has been a local favorite since 1980. Farm-style meals are the ticket here, generous portions of everything. The specialty of the house: fifteen kinds of homemade pies. The kids' menu (for those under 12) has nine entrees to choose from, and includes a choice of soda. The collection of Tulip Festival posters on the wall is quite eye-catching. This is the heart of the tulip country, after all. Note: The inn is located on the highway to Anacortes; you may want to plan your stop accordingly.

SAN JUAN ISLANDS

Anacortes

Places to Go

Causland Memorial Park

Location: 8th St. and N Ave.

This park is on the National Register of Historic Places, but you'll enjoy it for its unique walls and gazebo, all constructed of rock and decorated in mosaics of colored rock. Be sure to walk around the entire park—there are hidden facets waiting to be discovered.

Guemes Island Ferry
360-293-6356 (ferry schedule);
360-336-9400 (Skagit County Dept of Public Works)

Location: Just off 6th St.
Days/Hours: Daily; hours subject to change on holidays
Fee: For walk-ons: $1.25/adults; 50¢/children under 6
Wheelchair/Stroller Access: Yes

This little ferry could almost be called "cute," but I'm sure they wouldn't appreciate it. It's a mini-ferry with a flatbed that holds up to a dozen cars and takes you from Anacortes to Guemes Island in a five-minute shuttle. You can walk on, ride over, and ride back (all fares are round-trip), or walk off and spend some time on the beach next to the landing, where kayakers launch their island explorations. You can enjoy the view and boat traffic, then ferry on back. Kids will get quite a kick out of the experience. Something different, that's for sure!

The Steam Train   360-293-2634

Location: *Departs from The Railroad Depot, 7th and R streets (right next to the* W. T. Preston*)*
Days/Hours: *Mid-June–Labor Day: Saturday, Sunday, and for community events, noon– 4:30 p.m.*
Fare: *$1*
Wheelchair/Stroller Access: *No*

Tommy Thompson's popular steam train is on vacation while Tommy is recuperating, but we've been assured it will be running again in June of 1998. The train departs from the Depot with four passenger cars pulled by a bark-burning steam locomotive; it chugs through town and makes a circle (turns around) at 9th and Commercial. Passengers can embark (or disembark) at this point, also. You can check with the Visitors Center to confirm operations (see Helpful Phone Numbers at end of the chapter).

W. T. Preston   360-293-1915

Location: *703 R Ave. (James Rice Civic Park)*
Days/Hours: *Memorial Day - Labor Day: daily. September and April: weekends only. October–March: closed. Tours by appointment only in winter months.*
Wheelchair/Stroller Access: *Ground floor only.*

The *W. T. Preston*, a steam-wheeler snagboat, cruised Puget Sound and tributary rivers to clear the waterways of navigational hazards. Big and not particularly lovely, she and many other snagboats performed an invaluable service for Puget Sound marine transportation. When retired in 1981, the *Preston* was the only large, active sternwheeler remaining in the Sound. Now stationary at the James Rice Civic Park in Anacortes, you can tour all summer long. It's a self-guided tour with an excellent brochure and some interesting side notes. A trip to the Pilot House up top is worth the climb.

Stores to Browse

Bunnies by the Bay   360-299-9194 *(store);* 360-293-8037 *(workshop)*

Location: *Retail Store: 2320 Commercial; workshop: 3115 V Pl. To reach the workshop: Take the R Ave. exit of Hwy. 20; make a right turn at 30th St.; continue three blocks toward the waterfront; turn right on V Ave.*

Days/Hours: Tours: Monday–Friday, 10 a.m. and 2 p.m. (at the workshop)
Wheelchair/Stroller Access: At the workshop, but not at the retail store

If you're not attracted by the whimsical birdhouse fence made of delightful recyclable material, you'll most certainly be drawn to the fantasy within. Bunnies and more bunnies, elegantly dressed, stylishly costumed, playfully plumaged; these are really collectibles but you can find modestly priced, more huggable versions as well. At the workshop, you'll have a personally guided tour through the whole process and meet a bunny as it acquires its name and becomes "real." There's a second retail shop in La Conner.

Marine Supply and Hardware   360-293-0314

Location: 302 Commercial
Days/Hours: Monday–Saturday, 8:30 a.m.–5 p.m.
Wheelchair/Stroller Access: Yes

From glass floats to Greek fisherman hats to a Russian diving helmet, this is almost a museum. With an unbelievable variety of merchandise, this is a throwback to the old days when you could find anything at the local hardware store. The kids may not get as big a kick out of this place as their parents, but its worth the look-in. There's enough history here for you to spin a dozen stories and help your kids learn about their grandparents' lives in new ways.

Places to Eat

Village Pizza   360-293-7847

Location: 807 Commercial Ave.
Days/Hours: Monday–Saturday, 10 a.m.–midnight; Sunday, noon –10 p.m.
Wheelchair/Stroller Access: Yes

They do dine-in, take-out, and delivery. Most amazing—their pb-and-j pizza. Plus mini-pizzas for kids, with choice of one topping (additional cost extra). They do child's portions for pasta, and lots of beverages and desserts. Pretty quaint and fun.

Orcas Island
Places to Go

Moran State Park   360-376-2326; 360-753-2027

Location: Take Horseshoe Hwy. north from ferry terminal to Eastsound;
drive east another thirteen miles.
Days/Hours: Daily; camping year-round
Wheelchair/Stroller Access: In some places

Even with 165 campsites, reservations are required to secure a place.
It's very popular. Moran is not on the Sound, it's inland—with children's
play equipment and thirty-one miles of hiking trails. Cascade Lake has
freshwater swimming beaches and rowboat rentals; Mountain Lake has
trout fishing and a 3.9 mile walk around its perimeter. Also for hikers
and walkers is the quarter-mile hike to the hundred-foot Cascade Falls.
For the hardier, bicycle to the top of Mount Constitution, where the road
climbs two thousand feet in six miles. At the summit, you can climb the
winding staircase to the top of a four-story observation tower modeled
after a twelfth-century mountain fortress. The view is incredible.

The ferry deck provides bird's-eye views of the San Juan Islands. PHOTO
©MARGE AND TED MUELLER

Places to Eat and Stay

Rosario Resort and Spa   800-562-8821

Location: *On Orcas Island: Drive seventeen miles from the ferry terminal, north and around East Sound to Rosario.*
Days/Hours: *Open year-round for overnight accommodations*
Wheelchair/Stroller Access: *Yes*

One of the charms of the San Juans, Rosario is a majestic mansion set on a rocky bluff. Visitors are delighted with its old-style charm. This eighty-five-year-old estate was once the home of shipbuilder Robert Moran; today it houses a restaurant and exercise and relaxation facilities. There are close to 200 rooms on the adjacent hillside where guests can relax on their balconies and enjoy the water view, with boats moving in and out of the marina, and seaplanes approaching and leaving the water. Friendly deer will often appear to munch on the grass. For kids, there are indoor and outdoor swimming pools, but no lifeguards.

San Juan Island

Places to Go

Lime Kiln State Park   360-378-2044

Location: *On Haro Strait, the west side of San Juan Island*
Days/Hours: *Year-round, dawn to dusk*
Wheelchair/Stroller Access: *No*

In the 1880s the lime quarries attracted big limestone manufacturing business to the island. Today the quarries are mostly good for whale-watching. The pods of Orcas, or killer whales, frolic and dine on salmon and other marine life in these waters, generally in late summer and fall. Their antics are highly visible as they plunge and surface in the Strait; quite captivating for children, who love to learn about the whale families and their relationships. There are rough trails to the bluff, with a few picnic tables. Sorry, there's no running water or flush toilets.

Whale Cruises

There are a number of reputable charter operations that will take you close to the whales without interfering with the pod. Charter trips vary in length and price; some set an age minimum of 6 years old. When

checking out the companies, be sure to inquire about bathroom facilities.
Here are some resources :

San Juan Visitors Information Center:

Orcas Island Eclipse Charters; 800-376-6566; 360-376-4663 (Orcas Island)

San Juan Boat Tours: 800-232-6722 (Friday Harbor)

Western Prince Cruises: 800-757-6722 (Friday Harbor)

Deer Harbor Charters: 800-544-5758 (Deer Harbor)

Whale Museum

800-562-8832 (hotline for beachings); 360-378-4710

Location: First and Court streets, Friday Harbor
Web Site: www.whale-museum.org
Days/Hours: June–September: daily, 10 a.m.–7 p.m. October–May: daily, 11 a.m.–5 p.m.
Admission: $4/adults; $3.50/seniors 62 and older; $1/students with ID and those 5–18; free/children under 5
Wheelchair/Stroller Access: No

The humming sound inside the museum's blue interior might be the whales talking to you. The gigantic whale skeletons on display give you a very keen sense of the size of these mammals—and healthy respect for what they can do. Explore the children's room and take time to see the video, a delightful story of how the whales feed and care for their young.

Places to Eat

San Juan Roasting Company

360-378-4443

Location: First and Court streets in Friday Harbor
Days/Hours: Daily, 9 a.m.–6 p.m.
Wheelchair/Stroller Access: Yes

This used to be the San Juan Chocolate Company and, for those of us who care, they still offer lots of chocolate choices. Espresso is another choice, plus ice cream cones, sandwiches, and desserts. Weather permitting, the picnic tables outside are inviting.

WHATCOM COUNTY
Bellingham

Bellingham Antique Radio Museum

360-671-4663 (for messages)

Location: 1315 Railroad Ave.
Web Site: www.antique-radio.org
Days/Hours: Daily, 9 a.m.–5 p.m.
Admission: Free
Wheelchair/Stroller Access: Not really

Not really? Because it's a 10 by 90 storefront with 750 to 1000 old radios and related items stacked from floor to ceiling. If you remember sitting on the floor, next to the radio, listening to *The Shadow Knows, Gene Autry,* or *Allan's Alley*—you'll be amazed to find your old family radio

Bellingham parks are always a hit with the active crowd. PHOTO COURTESY BELLINGHAM/WHATCOM COUNTY CONVENTION AND VISITORS BUREAU

again. Owner Jonathan Winter has a love affair with radio, and he's been collecting for thirty-two years. The oldest piece is a Marconi Cohere. Others include an early radio detector, and early radio tubes and valves. The history is fascinating and he loves to share it. You can learn more by checking his Web site.

Bellingham Hatchery/Department of Fish and Wildlife
360-676-2138

Location: 1700 Silver Beach Rd. Take I-5 exit 253 (Lakeway); follow past Woburn and Yew streets, past Bayview Cemetery; at Kenoyer intersection turn left onto Silver Beach Rd.
Days/Hours: Daily, 8 a.m.–4:30 p.m. Groups coming on weekends should call ahead to book tours.
Wheelchair/Stroller Access: Yes

Formerly known as the Whatcom Falls Park and Hatchery, there are interurban trails around the park, swimming holes, Whatcom Creek, tennis courts, baseball . . . and of course the fish. The hatchery raises fish for release into Whatcom, Skagit, and San Juan waters. Nine outdoor ponds and seven raceways house about 100,000 trout annually. Guided tours are an option, but call at least two days ahead for reservations.

Fairhaven Park
360-676-6985

Location: 107 Chuckanut Dr.
Days/Hours: Daily, 8 a.m.–dusk
Wheelchair/Stroller Access: Yes

This is a sprawling park with lush greenery, especially dedicated to families with young children. A wading pool (summers only) for toddlers and preschoolers is open between noon and 6:30 p.m. The playground has swings and equipment for older children. It's a short stroll to the fish ladders nearby, and in spring and summer the Rose Garden is quite beautiful.

Marine Life Center

Location: HarborPort at Squalicum Harbor
Days/Hours: Daily, 8 a.m.–9 p.m.
Admission: Free, but your donation helps to feed the fish
Wheelchair/Stroller Access: Yes

Visiting the harbor is a treat, but the Marine Life Center makes it more so. There's a Touch Pool, with hardy, small marine life that can accept the attention of young hands. You'll find hermit crabs, three kinds of starfish, anemones, sea cucumber, and snails. In the Observation Pool, there are larger versions of these animals, plus more protected specimens, including white and orange anemone, leather stars (yes, they feel like leather), copper rock fish, red rock crabs, quill bark rock fish, kelp crabs, striped sea perch, and even a thorny-headed rock fish. All the fish here are from local or Pacific waters. The tank water comes from the Bellingham Bay, through four filters. Three large aquarium tanks hold very young coho, rocky habitat critters, and "Surprising Fish Names."

Mindport   360- 647-5614

Location: 111 Grand Ave.
Days/Hours: Wednesday–Sunday, 10 a.m.–5 p.m.
Admission: Free
Wheelchair/Stroller Access: Yes

This is a winner—and you'd least expect it. Mindport is the brainchild of three enterprising people who hope to challenge your perception of how the world really works. Using the basic theorems from physics and related sciences, they have developed incredibly basic—but incredibly interesting and amazing—mini-exhibits that challenge your sense of reality. There are things to push and squeeze and holes to peer through. Exhibits include: Wave Music, pushing a paddle in a round tub filled with water creating new music patterns; Crossed Polarizes, a simple box, a special light, and plastic objects, which together create polarized light (making its waves vibrate in only one direction); a Concave Mirror; Moire Patterns; a Box of Penrose Tiles; and a Mobius Strip. Here adults can become children for a space of time.

Western Washington University   360-650-3440; 360-650-3000

Location: Visitors Center is on South College Dr. at the main entrance to
   campus.
Web Site: HYPERLINK http://www.wwu.edu www.wwu.edu
E-mail: HYPERLINK mailto:admit@ccadmit@cc.wwu.edu
Tours: Monday–Friday, 11 a.m. and 2 p.m. (except for holidays and school
   breaks)
Wheelchair/Stroller Access: Yes

Guides for the one-hour tours are university students. Included are several academic buildings and a residence hall, but the highpoints are the campus viewpoints of Bellingham Bay and the San Juan Islands, and the nearly two dozen pieces of contemporary outdoor sculptures.

Whatcom Children's Museum 360-733-8769

Location: 227 Prospect St.
Web Site: HYPERLINK http://www.cob www.cob.org/museum.htm
Days/Hours: Tuesday, Wednesday, and Sunday, noon–5 p.m.; Thursday–
 Saturday, 10 a.m.–5 p.m. Closed Mondays. Mornings are reserved for
 school groups.
Admission: $2/per person
Wheelchair/Stroller Access: Yes

This delightful place is strictly for children, especially those ages 2 to
8, and they feel very much at home here. The only permanent exhibit is
the model train. Large exhibits are on display for longer periods, while
smaller exhibits change and evolve throughout the year. "Our Town" is
here for quite a while; other facets of the exhibit will be developed soon.
Nice clean restrooms with a changing table.

Whatcom County Museum of History and Art
 360-676-6981

Location: 121 Prospect St.
Web Site: HYPERLINK http://www.cob www.cob.org/museum.htm
Days/Hours: Tuesday–Sunday, noon–5 p.m., except major holidays
Admission: None, but they encourage donations
Wheelchair/Stroller Access: Yes

This is an outstanding museum, well-known for its excellent exhibits of Northwest Coastal Native American artifacts. Also intriguing are
the timber industry dioramas, telling the local story in a more multidi-
mensional manner. Equally attractive is the ornate, hand-carved staircase you ascend from the first floor—an elegant and artistic reminder of
an earlier Victorian era. The museum has expanded, both into the nearby
ARCO Building, which houses works by local artists, and into the adjacent former firehouse, allowing for more attention to children's exhibits.

Places to Eat

Bergsma Café and Gallery 360-733-1101

Location: Just off I-5 at exit 253, across from the Visitors Center
Days/Hours: Daily, 7 a.m.–7 p.m.
Wheelchair/Stroller Access: Yes

A nice stopping point for a light lunch or snack, the café offers lots of
beverage choices, sandwiches (halves available), and soup. Pb and j is an

option, too. The gallery is mainly Bergsma art, but there is a Kid's Room with stuffed animals and toys.

Store to Browse

Village Books and Colophon Café

360-671-2626 (bookstore); 360-647-0092 (cafÉ)

Location: 1210 11th St. in Old Fairhaven
Web Site: HYPERLINK http://www.villagebooks www.villagebooks.com
Days/Hours: Summer: Monday–Saturday, 9 a.m.–10 p.m.; Sunday, 10 a.m.–
    10 p.m. The rest of the year: Monday–Saturday, 9 a.m.–10 p.m.; Sunday,
    10 a.m.–8 p.m.
Wheelchair/Stroller Access: Yes

Oh, they do love kids here. There's a cozy reading corner for kids to settle in with a new book or old favorite while the older folks browse. They have a number of special events: monthly and bimonthly Saturday programs, bookmark contests, and writing contests. Over in the café, a "mug a mocha moo"—steamed milk with hot fudge and whipped cream—is spectacular on a cold or rainy day. Ice cream in waffle cones are another specialty. It must work—they've been there a long time!

NORTH WHATCOM COUNTY

Places to Go

Berthusen Park
360-354-2424

Location: 8837 Berthusen Park. Take I-5 to exit 270 west on Birch Bay-
    Lynden Road; drive eight miles to Berthusen Road; turn north.
Days/Hours: Dawn to dusk; both day use and overnight camping available;
    call ahead for reservations
Wheelchair/Stroller Access: Limited

This 236-acre park is rich with opportunities for families to enjoy hiking, stream fishing, a playground, and an old homestead barn with vintage farm equipment. The park is named for the Berthusens, an immigrant Norwegian family of parents and ten children, who left the acreage to the city.

Hovander Homestead Park   360-384-3444

Location: 5299 *Nielson Rd. in Ferndale. Take I-5 to exit 262 west; less than a mile ahead you'll take a hard left under the railroad trestle.*
Days/Hours: Dawn to dusk
Admission: $3/for the park; $1/for the house
Wheelchair/Stroller Access: Yes at the park; no at the house

Adjacent to the Tennant Lake Natural Interpretive Center, Hovander is a delightful place for kids to spend time. The equipment they play on is from the turn-of-the-century lifestyle lived by the Swedish immigrants who used to farm. There are farm animals here, goats, rabbits, pigs, and peacocks, all cared for by 4-H club members, and a viewing tower over-looking the Nooksack River. Inside the farmhouse, vintage woodwork and décor is another reminder of earlier times.

Mount Baker Vineyards   360-592-2300

Location: 5535 Hillard Rd.; 4298 Mount Baker Hwy. In Deming
Days/Hours: Daily, 11 a.m.–5 p.m. Appointment required for tours.
Wheelchair/Stroller Access: Yes, but the parking lot is rough gravel.

Even though it's a small winery, they crush some of the area's finest grapes and the tour is very interesting. After the walk through the facil-ity, wine-tasting for adults and fresh juice (when available) for kids is the finale.

Mount Baker Wilderness Area   360-734-6771

Location: On Hwy. 542, fifty-six miles east of Bellingham
Web Site: HYPERLINK http://www.mtbakerskiarea
   www.mtbakerskiarea.com
Days/Hours: Varies: some roads will be closed in winter due to snow
Wheelchair/Stroller Access: In some areas

The west side of North Cascades National Park and Recreation Area (at Mount Baker Wilderness Area) is very popular with skiing families. You can downhill and cross-country daily in winter, mid-November through December, and on weekends during the rest of the season. After the snow melt, it's a spectacular hiking area; you can even find blueber-ries in late summer and early fall.

The Heather Meadows Visitors Center is open daily, July through September, from 10 a.m. to 5 p.m. Nearby are two half-mile hikes, Fire and Ice Trail and Picture Lake Path, that are wheelchair and stroller friendly. For more information call the Glacier Public Service Center, 360-599-2714, open daily from 9 a.m. to 5 p.m.

Snow in the middle of summer brings on a spirited snowball fight at Mount Baker. PHOTO ©MARGE AND TED MUELLER

Peace Arch State Park   *800-624-3555; 360-332-4544*

Location: On I-5 at the U.S.–Canadian border
Days/Hours: Daily, dawn to dusk
Wheelchair/Stroller Access: Yes, at the gardens

It's difficult to leave the car if you're trying to get through the border, so stopping here requires you to park off to the side. The sixty-seven-foot Peach Arch is a monument to over 200 years of peaceful relations (most of the time) between our two countries. The span is placed in the middle of the forty-acre park, resting one column in Canada, the other in the U.S. Seasonally the flowers are quite beautiful and, if it's been a long ride, this is a good place to let the kids get out and run. On the second

Sunday in June, the annual Peace Arch celebration takes place, in which thousands of American children are invited to exchange flags and other friendship symbols with Canadian children. A touching ceremony, if you can be there.

Pioneer Park 360-384-6461

Location: At the end of First St., Ferndale
Days/Hours: Tours given from mid-May–mid-September
Wheelchair/Stroller Access: Yes

This is a large expanse of play and recreation area, but the fascinating part is the collection of authentic pioneer homes, reconstructed from those originally in the area. Most were built to withstand lonely, isolated environments. Along with the homesteads are a general store, a schoolhouse, a printer's shop, and a church (which still accommodates weddings).

North Puget Sound beaches inspire all sorts of activities. Photo courtesy Bellingham/Whatcom County Convention and Visitors Bureau

Tennant Lake Natural Interpretive Center   360-384-3444

Location: 5236 Nielsen Rd., Ferndale
Days/Hours: Late June–Labor Day; hours might vary
Wheelchair/Stroller Access: Yes

The Fragrance Garden is a must. You'll develop a keener sense of smell and a deeper appreciation for the incredibly diverse scents to be found in nature. Expect bees! My favorite: the chocolate mint, of course. The plants are tended in raised beds within cement walls; running along the top of the cement wall, the full length of the garden, is a wooden rail. On the inside of that rail are Braille signs for those visually-impaired; visitors are encouraged to feel the plants. The gardens were begun in 1985; today the collection is quite mature and the variety amazing. Late spring and summer are best times to visit. For strolling or walking, take the half-mile boardwalk as it loops around the 200 acres of marsh. You might spot hawks, beavers, or muskrats as you go. The Interpretive Center is the old Neilsen farmhouse, preserved and adapted for present use.

Wet 'N Wild Waterpark   360-371-7500 (recording); 360-371-7911

Location: 4874 Birch Bay-Lynden Rd., in Blaine. Take I-5 to exit 270; turn
  west and drive four miles to Birch-Bay Lynden Rd.
Days/Hours: June–Labor Day: 10:30 a.m.–7:30 p.m.
Admission: $10.75/ages 6 and older; $7.50/children 3–5; free/children 2 and
  under
Wheelchair/Stroller Access: Yes, in the public area (for observing only)

There's something for all ages here and it is exciting! The admission covers an all-day outing. The little ones can start in the shallow pool; for the older kids, any of the four 400-foot slides are fun, especially the Twister or the Snake. Adults can relax in the hot tub. There are concessions on-site, or you can picnic with your own lunch.

Places to Stay

Inn at Semiahmoo   *800-822-4200; 360-371-2000*

Location: 9565 Semiahmoo Parkway, Blaine. *Take I-5 to exit 270; follow Lynden-Birch Bay Road for four miles; turn right on Harborview Road, then left on Lincoln Road.*
Web Site: HYPERLINK http://www.semi www.semi-ah-moo.com
Days/Hours: Open year-round for overnight accommodations
Wheelchair/Stroller Access: Yes

Generally considered a pretty upscale place to take your children, there are nearby condominium rentals that might be a more comfortable experience for families with younger ones. At the Inn, there are sufficient activities to keep most kids interested: an outdoor swimming pool, exercise facility, tennis courts, biking paths, boat rentals, kite flying, beach walking, and a kids' day camp with organized activities. You can check out kids' movies, board games (from the health club), and play Ping-Pong. All of these activities are part of their Kids' Club program; what activities are actually available will depend on how many kids are visiting that week. Close by is Semiahmoo Park, with a small provincial museum that details the salmon cannery life here in the late 1800s. Also nearby is an excellent golf course.

Helpful Phone Numbers:

Chambers of Commerce:
   Arlington: 360-435-3708
   Bainbridge Island: 206-842-3700
   Birch Bay: 360-371-0334
   Central Whidbey / Coupeville: 360-341-4545
   Edmonds: 206-670-1496
   Everett: 206-252-5181
   Ferndale: 360-384-3042
   Greater Oak Harbor: 360-675-3535
   La Conner: 360-466-4778
   Langley: 360-221-6765
   Burlington: 360-755-9382
   Lummi Indian Nation: 360-734-8180
   Lynden: 360-354-5995
   Marysville: 360-659-7700
   Mount Baker Foothills: 360-599-1205
   Port Orchard: 360-876-3505
   Poulsbo: 360-779-4848

Sedro-Wooley: 360-855-1841
Silverdale: 360-692-6800
Snohomish: 360-568-2526
South Snohomish County: 425-774-0507

Other:

Anacortes Visitor Information: 360-293-3832
Bellingham/Whatcom County Convention/Visitors Bureau: 800-487-2032; 360-671-3990
Blaine Visitors Center: 800-624-3555; 360-332-4544
Bremerton/Kitsap County Visitor/Convention Bureau: 360-479-3588
North Cascades National. Park Visitors Information Center: 360-856-5700
San Juan Islands Bed and Breakfast Inns: 360-378-3030
San Juan Islands Visitors Information Service: 360-468-3663
Snohomish County Visitors Center: 425-745-4133
Washington State Ferry Information: 206-464-6400; 800-84-FERRY (800 is in-state only)

All aboard! You can ride the train all around Leavenworth's Icicle Junction. PHOTO COURTESY OF ICICLE JUNCTION

CHAPTER
7

North Cascades and North Central Washington

• •

The North Cascades Highway is just one of the links between western and eastern Washington, but probably the most scenic, especially in fall when trees burst into glorious autumn colors. The Highway began in 1896, two separate wagon roads inching their way twelve miles up on both sides of the mountain. Now Highway 20, this two-lane route hooks through Chelan country, the Wenatchee Valley and Stevens Pass; some of the most popular stops are Leavenworth, Winthrop, Wenatchee, and Lake Chelan. One of winter's most enjoyable family trips is a pilgrimage to Leavenworth for the Christmas Lights Festival.

- **North Central Washington:** Coulee Country is a part of Washington state that has its own distinct and fascinating culture. Odessa is located in Lincoln County. This little town honors its German heritage with "Deutschesfest," a three-day festival famous for its authentic sausage and polka music. Soap Lake, just west of Odessa, is perhaps best known for the medicinal and curative powers of the lake itself (from excessive alkaline content), but is also popular on Memorial Day weekend for the Greek Panayiri Festival. Moses Lake is a Mecca for water activities—skiing, boating, fishing, swimming, and camping.

- **Lincoln County:** Almost completely surrounded by a national forest and a state range, the Methow Valley has a four-season climate. It is a hugely popular destination for a multitude of activities: mountain biking, horseback riding, hiking, cross-country skiing, snowshoeing, helicopter skiing, and river rafting, to name some. In summer, swimming, camping, tennis, and golf are primary attractions as well. In Winthrop, the wooden sidewalks and western-style turn-of-the-century buildings here qualify the town for "fascinating," if not quaint—but definitely delightful. One of the tourist attractions here is the Shafer Museum, previously a log cabin in which author Owen Wister wrote his famous Western novel, *The Virginian*.

- **Northeastern Washington:** The northeast corner of Washington state seems remote and the towns are small, but the range of activities is big! The counties here are Ferry, Stevens, and Pend Oreille (pronounced Pend-o-ray), and this is the destination for those who love the wild, unspoiled outdoors. This is home to a major moose population, grizzly bears, bighorn sheep, and woodland caribou. It may be remote, but the beauty of the country commends it to families looking for a unique experience.

NORTH CASCADES

Places to Go

Lake Chelan Boat Company
509-682-2224 *(recording):*
509-682-4584 (reservations for groups of fifteen or more);
509-682-4494 (reservations for the North Cascades and Stehekin Lodge)

Location: One mile south of downtown Chelan, off Hwy. 97A
Web Site: www.ladyofthelake.com
Days/Hours: Lady Express: May: Saturday–Sunday. June–October 15: daily. November–December 19: Monday, Wednesday, Friday, and Sunday. December 19–April 15: daily except Tuesday and Thursday. April 15– May: daily. May–October: departure at 8:30 a.m. November and April: departure at 10 a.m.
Admission: Lady II: $22/adults; $11/children 6–11; free/children under 6. Lady Express: $41/adults; $20.50/children 2–11; free/children under 2. Two-Boat Combination (a day trip, leave on one, return on the other): $41/adults; $20.50/children 6–11; $13.25/children 2–5; free/children under 2.
Wheelchair/Stroller Access: Yes

Whichever cruise you select, the trip will be rich with scenery and natural beauty. Destination for the 350-passenger Lady of the Lake II is Stehekin, located somewhat remotely in the foothills of the North Cascades National Park. The trip takes about three hours with several stops.

Planning should include bringing along some snacks and / or food and beverage (there are bathrooms on board). Lady Express, a smaller vessel, holds 100 passengers, makes fewer stops and arrives in Stehekin in about half the time; reservations are recommended. If your plan is an overnight trip, adults can carry up to seventy-five pounds of gear, children up to forty. Bicycles can be transported for an additional $13.

Lake Chelan National Recreation Area
360-856-5700, ext. 340 or ext. 14

Location: *In Stehekin at Golden West Visitors Center*
Web Site: *www.nps.gov/noca*
Days/Hours: *Recreation area is open year-round. Visitors Center: June–September: daily, 7:30 a.m.–4:30 p.m. Mid-May–mid-June and mid-September–October: daily, noon–2 p.m.*
Wheelchair/Stroller Access: *In some areas; there is a wheelchair elevator at the lodge.*

If you're looking for wilderness, or a remote getaway, Stehekin is the place. Situated at the west end headwaters of Lake Chelan and the east end of the North Cascades National Park, you can only reach it by boat or floatplane. There are a number of accommodations (bed and breakfast inns, cabins, or the North Cascades Stehekin Lodge); call 509-682-4494 for more information.

Camping families pitch their tents in the more remote areas of the park. Day hikes and backpacking climbs for preteens and teens, short jaunts for younger ones are all part of the mystique here.

Lake Chelan Parasailing
509-687-SAIL

Location: *Ticket office near Chelan Marina; riders are picked up at any dock on the lake*
Days/Hours: *June–August: daily, 9 a.m.–dusk. Reservations advised.*
Wheelchair/Stroller Access: *Wheelchairs and strollers must be left on the dock.*

Actually a great experience for kids. Children can ride the wind over Lake Chelan beneath a colorful parachute, sailing behind the boats that are towing their lines. There must be at least 80 pounds in the harness, so lightweight youngsters must accompany another child rider or an adult. The maximum combined weight is 250 pounds. The view is glorious and riders never get wet, they tell us, even when the boat slows down in order for parasailors to experience the "atomic drop." Rates are about $39 for single riders, $2 discounts for groups of three or more riding separately. Tandems pay $68.

North Cascades National Park Visitors Center

360-856-5700 (call weekdays in winter)

Location: In Newhalem. Take I-5 to exit 232 to Hwy. 20; drive east for about sixty miles.
Web Site: www.nps.gov/noca
Days/Hours: Open weekends only
Wheelchair/Stroller Access: Yes

You'll be delighted to find this family-friendly visitors center; they provide an excellent educational introduction to the North Cascades National Park. There's a twenty-five-minute film presentation and a twenty-minute slide presentation, each with a different focus and message. The exhibit room is designed to take you through each life zone of the forest; the hands-on displays for kids include dark cubbyholes to feel (and identify) some animal hide or fur. Fortunately, nothing bites back. There are Junior Ranger Programs offered at the center, and campground programs on Saturday and Sunday evenings in summer.

Seattle City Light Skagit Dam Tour

206-684-3030 (Skagit Tour Desk); 206-233-2709 (office in Diablo)

Location: In Diablo. From I-5, take the Cook Road exit (232) about four miles north of Mount Vernon; follow state route 20 (North Cascades Hwy.) for seventy miles to Diablo; signs in Diablo direct you to the Tour Center.
Days/Hours: Tours run mid-June–September: Thursday-Monday. September: tours weekends only. Closed July 4 and Labor Day.
Admission: For the four-hour tour: $25/ages 12 and older; $22/seniors over 62; $12.50/children 6-11; free/children 5 and under. Group discounts available. Reservations strongly recommended.
Wheelchair/Stroller Access: Accommodations are available with advance request.

If your kids have ever wondered where the power for their video games, televisions, and boom boxes comes from, this tour explains it quite well! You can take a fully guided tour to Ross Dam that will include a spectacular 560-foot ride up Sourdough Mountain on the Incline Railway and a twenty-five-minute cruise across Diablo Lake to Ross Powerhouse. Dinner is included (or box lunches for outdoor picnics). If you prefer a shorter tour, the ninety-minute Diablo guided tour covers the project highlights. No reservations are required for this tour; cost is $5 for ages 12 and older; free for those 11 and under.

Slidewaters

509-682-5751; 206-821-1796 *(in winter)*

Location: 102 Waterslide Dr., Chelan
Web Site: www.kozi.com (link there)
Days/Hours: Open Memorial Day–Labor Day: 10 a.m.–6 p.m., until mid-June; 10 a.m.–8 p.m., mid-June to closing
Admission: All Day: $10.95/adults; $7.95/children 4–7; free/children 3 and under. After 5 p.m.: $7.95/adults; $4.95/children 3–7; free/children 2 and under. Season passes and group rates available also.
Wheelchair/Stroller Access: For observation only

You won't have far to look to find Slidewaters; it's just up the hill as you enter town. The water park features nine rides and slides for waterbugs of all ages. There's also a nice relaxing hot tub for parents along for the ride. Those 7 and under must have an adult along. Shower rooms and are lockers available as well as outside picnic areas.

Places to Stay

Sun Mountain Lodge

800-572-0493; 509-996-2211

Location: Patterson Lake Rd., seven miles west of Hwy. 20
Web Site: www.travel-in-wa.com/ADS/sun-mtn-html
Days/Hours: Overnight accommodations available year-round. Two-night minimum stay on weekends; three-night minimum stay on holidays.
Wheelchair/Stroller Access: Yes

Sunday Mountain Lodge has recently added twenty-four new guest rooms to accommodate its ever-growing clientele. Located on the east side of the North Cascades, there is a plethora of family-type activities to be enjoyed here. Not the least of these are horseback riding, whitewater rafting trips on the Methow River, mountain bike tours, guided hikes, and fly fishing classes. There are special programs for kids during summer months and on holidays. You'll also find tennis courts, two playgrounds, a swimming pool, and a hot tub. In winter months, more than fifty miles of cross-country ski trails start just outside the lodge's front door. The general price range here is $100 to $240. On Patterson Lake there are thirteen cabins with cooking facilities, which are very popular with families: five are two-bedroom; seven are one-bedroom.

Leavenworth
Places to Go

Icicle Junction
800-789-8177; 509-548-2400

Location: 565 Hwy. 2
Web Site: www.travel-in-was.com/ads/junction.html
Days/Hours: April 1–June: daily, noon–9 p.m. July–August: 9 a.m.–
  midnight. September–October: noon–7 p.m. November: Saturday and
  Sunday, noon–9 p.m.
Admission: Park itself is free; each activity has a separate admission fee.
Wheelchair/Stroller Access: Yes

Icicle Junction is a welcome addition to this delightful town—a place dedicated to kids of all ages! There's an eighteen-hole miniature golf course (with a Bavarian church, a castle, and a barn), a Bumper Boat Lagoon with remote control boats, and Excursion Train that runs around the outskirts of the amusement center (to the delight of those on board) and—especially for the older kids—an indoor Interactive Game Center with videos galore. Snack bar and concessions also. Book the Birthday Party room for special occasions. If you're looking for getaways, ask about their overnight package with the Icicle Inn. Note: Pets are not welcome here.

Leavenworth National Fish Hatchery
509-548-7641

Location: 12790 Fish Hatchery Rd. At the west edge of Leavenworth, turn
  south from Hwy. 2 onto Icicle Road; continue for one and a half miles;
  turn left at the fish hatchery sign.
Days/Hours: Daily, 8 a.m.–4 p.m.
Wheelchair/Stroller Access: Yes

The adult salmon return to the hatchery in June and July; spawning takes place from late August through early September, and the young salmon are released in April.

Displays in the hatchery lobby describe the salmon's environmental needs. In good weather, try the Icicle Creek Interpretive Trail, a one-mile loop that explores the history, environment, and wildlife of the hatchery and the creek. Watch for the Wenatchee River Salmon Festival in September.

Places to Eat

Gingerbread Factory   509-548-6592

Location: 828 Commercial St.
Days/Hours: Winter: daily, 7 a.m.–5 p.m. Summer, daily, 7 a.m.–7 p.m.
Wheelchair/Stroller Access: No

Just as the name implies, this sweet-smelling bakery specializes in gingerbread treats, along with lots of other freshly baked cookies. You can buy cookie cutters here for gingerbread hula girls, trains, and gecko lizards. In summer, the gingerbread people are dressed in bikinis and trunks.

Hansel and Gretel Deli   509-548-7721

Location: 819 Front St.
Days/Hours: Summer: Sunday–Thursday, 7 a.m.–9 p.m.; Friday–Saturday,
    7 a.m.–10 p.m.
Wheelchair/Stroller Access: Yes

Most appropriately named, given the town's ambiance, this deli serves good homemade soup, sandwiches with imported German meats and cheese, and tempting ice cream waffle cones in lots of flavors.

Strolling Front Street

Christmas and Bavarian Ice Festival Trains

Location: Round-trip from Seattle to Leavenworth, with stops in Edmonds
    and Everett
Days/Hours: Early December weekends and Martin Luther King Jr. birthday
    weekend in January. Leaves Seattle at 8 a.m., arrives in Leavenworth
    around 12:30 p.m.; leaves Leavenworth at 5:30 p.m., returns to Seattle at
    10 p.m.
Admission: $109/adults; $99/children 12 and younger. Prices subject to
    change; call for verification.
Wheelchair/Stroller Access: Yes

It's a festive daylight train ride over Stevens Pass to Leavenworth, with a continental breakfast and exhilarating music from an oompah band. In Leavenworth, you can browse through the shops and just enjoy wandering. It'll be cool; dress warmly. In December you'll see a beautiful lighting ceremony; in January you can join in snow games as part of the

Bavarian Ice Festival. On the return trip, you can relax over dinner. Leavenworth's wonderful Bavarian theme is really appealing in the winter months.

The Hat Shop

Location: Front St.
Days/Hours: Seasonal; hours vary
Wheelchair/Stroller Access: Yes, but very narrow aisles here

If you have a thing for hats, you'll get lost in here, with over 1,000 to search through, including one that is the Cat in the Hat. There's lots for kids to choose from on the back wall, but be sure to look up—that's where the surprises are!

The Nutcracker Museum   *509-548-4708; 800-892-3989*

Location: 735 Front St.
Days/Hours: May–October: daily, 2 p.m.–5 p.m.; November–April: weekends only, except by appointment.
Admission: $2.50/adults; $1/children 6-12; free/children under 6
Tours: For groups; by appointment only
Wheelchair/Stroller Access: No.

Some people miss this phenomenal museum simply because it's not on the street level, but up a flight of stairs (near the Soup Cellar). But don't miss it—it's an amazing collection of over 3,500 nutcrackers from all over the world, from Karl at six feet to the tiny carving on the head of a matchstick. An interesting fifteen-minute video tells about the world of nutcrackers: their history and their success. The oldest dated nutcracker dates from 1569 and depicts Francis I; the oldest known nutcracker is a stone believed to be between 4000 and 8000 years old. If you're in a buying mood, some are for sale.

The Wood Shop

Location: Front St.
Days/Hours: Seasonal; hours vary
Wheelchair/Stroller Access: Yes

The walls are crammed with wooden items of all kinds. This shop is perfect for browsing and tourist gifts.

Places to Eat

Rocky Mountain Chocolate Shop

Location: Front St.
Days/Hours: Varies from winter to summer
Tours: Yes, mostly weekends, some weekdays. Reservations requested; call at least one week in advance. No age minimum; groups up to twenty, families welcome.
Wheelchair/Stroller Access: Yes

They make 40 percent of their fudge; caramel apples are a big favorite here with flavors such as apple pie, apple with cinnamon and sugar, white chocolate, M&Ms, Rocky Road, and more. On the tour, the kids get to help make fudge and then taste it!

For little ones, they'll find other activities to enjoy. Look for the chocolate bears here—dark, milk, and white—and their peanut-butter bucket. 'Nuff said.

The Soup Cellar   509-548-6300

Location: 725 Front St.
Days/Hours: Daily for lunch and dinner
Wheelchair/Stroller Access: No; access is down a steep stairway

A good stopping place for something quick and hot (or in summer, cool). They have soup and salad combos (no sharing) and sandwiches, with German potato salad and German sausage. The Child's Plate can be a hot dog or pb and j with chips, applesauce and carrot sticks for those 12 and under. A real curiosity here are the dollar bills on the beams, over 5,000 of them, mostly written on. If you're sitting in a booth, the story of the bills is on the wall over your table. Service is cafeteria style. The specialty here is white chili.

The Taffy Shop   509-548-4857

Location: Front St.
Days/Hours: Seasonal; hours vary
Wheelchair/Stroller Access: Yes

If you time it just right, the taffy-pulling machine in the window will pull the sticky stuff right in front of your eyes. There are barrels and barrels of saltwater taffy, and buckets of other sweets. If you're looking for decorated cans and tins, there's shelves full, with all shapes and sizes, some replicas of bygone food labels and well-known food purveyors. Perfect for gifts.

More Outdoor Fun

Art in the Park: In downtown Leavenworth, from May to October, this ongoing art festival brings out some pretty amazing talent.

Blackbird Island: This is where the locals go swimming in summer. No lifeguard here, just common sense. Also enjoy an easy two and a half mile walk, along the Wenatchee River. Driving directions: Drive west on Hwy. 2; turn left at the yellow blinking light. Turn right on Commercial St; go two blocks to the parking lot.

Eagle Creek Ranch   509-548-7798; 800-221-7433.

Location: Eagle Creek Rd; call for driving directions.

You can take guided trail rides in spring, summer, and fall, some taking you 4,000 feet above the ranch, into alpine terrain. Spectacular views; lunch provided. Pack trips in "cowboy style" include the back country on horseback and crackling campfires. You can be a beginner and still have fun! Ask about their wagon trips for the slightly less adventurous. Guided rides: five miles for $27 (includes tax), eight miles for $35; an all-day ride for $75 includes lunch. Call for information about overnight pack trips (includes guide, cook, saddle, pack horses, meals, and outfitting equipment). Sleigh rides from November through March; hayrides from April till September, for groups of ten or more (kids 12 and under half-price; children 2 and under free).

Red-Tail Canyon Farm   509-548-4512; 800-678-4512.

Location: Two and half miles north of Leavenworth. From downtown Leavenworth, take Chumstick Hwy. 209 to the left turn on Freund Canyon Road. Turn right at Red-Tail Canyon Farm sign.
Web Site: www.redtailcanyonfarm.com.
Admission: Sleigh rides: $12/adults, $6/children 12 and under. Hayrides: $10/adults; $6/children 12 and under. Minimum number may be required. By reservation only; call at least two weeks ahead.

This farm offers old-fashioned hayrides using big Belgian draft horses. Sleigh rides, too, from Thanksgiving through early March. They can accommodate from twelve to sixteen riders and the trips are forty-five minutes into scenic Box Canyon. In cold months, you'll get hot chocolate after the ride, in warm months a barbecue (for an additional charge).

Others

Icicle Outfitters and Guides: 509-763-3647 or 669-4909. Open from May 1–September 30, they offer two-mile guided trail rides for $16/person and five-mile rides for $32/person. Please call for special prices for kids or families.

Mountain Springs Lodge: 509-763-2713. Offers guided trail rides, priced individually. For little ones, pony rides for $5. The sleigh rides are on weekdays during the holidays, and weekends December through February. To book a hayride, you need a minimum of ten people; you must reserve in advance.

A winter sleigh ride at Red-Tail Canyon Farm. Photo courtesy of the Red Tail Canyon Farm

Wenatchee
Places to Go

Lake Wenatchee State Park   509-763-3101

Location: Twenty-two miles north of Leavenworth, twenty miles east of
Stevens Pass
Web Site: www.parks.wa.gov
Days/Hours: Overnight camping accommodations year-round
Wheelchair/Stroller Access: Yes
*Driving directions: From U.S. 2 turn north on Hwy. 207 North. Drive
another four miles to the park.*

This park is very popular, largely because it offers an incredible variety of activities year-round. In winter, cross-country skiers, snowshoers, and snowmobilers take over. Come spring, horseback riders, campers, hikers, and picnickers come roaring in to enjoy the area. At the lake's southeast corner, there's swimming, water-skiing, fishing from boats and the bank, scuba diving, and windsurfing. Warning: Bring mosquito repellent for the summer months.

Lincoln Rock State Park   509-884-8702

Location: Seven miles north of East Wenatchee
Web Site: www.parks.wa.gov
Days/Hours: Overnight camping accommodations year-round
Wheelchair/Stroller Access: Yes

Outdoor activities for everyone makes this one of the ten most popular parks in the state. There are baseball and soccer fields for older kids and children's play equipment for the younger ones. Lake Entiat, created from the Columbia River by the building of Rocky Reach Dam, offers water-skiing, a swimming area that has a shallow wading section, and a large number of picnic tables nearby. Within walking distance of the water are three loops with close to ninety campsites. Someone with a good imagination thought the nearby basalt cliffs look like Abraham Lincoln. Do you agree?

Mission Ridge   509-663-6543; 800-374-1693

Location: Twelve miles southwest of Wenatchee
Web Site: www.missionridge.com
Days/Hours: Mid-December–April: daily, 9 a.m.–4 p.m.
Admission: 1997–98 weekend lift tickets: $32/adult; $17/children 7–15; free/
    children 6 and under. Midweek: $24/adults; $17/children 7–15; free/
    children 6 and under.
Wheelchair/Stroller Access: No

Located on the eastern slope of the Cascade Mountains and easily one of the state's most popular ski areas, Mission Ridge now offers thirty-five designated ski runs. Most are at least one mile or more, the longest nearly three miles. Their Kids' Club Ski School for ages 4 to 12 has been called the best in the Northwest by The Seattle Times. Programs are designed for both half-day and full-day activities; price range is $45 to $74. For skiing parents, there is child care for ages 3 months to 6 years ($35/day) at the lodge For beginners, plenty of mild-as-can-be areas. Wenatchee is so close that there are a number of good lodging and skiing packages to choose from; most of the lodging properties allow children 12 and under to stay free. Nearby, Squilchuck Bowl has sledding and inner tubing for alternative snow fun.

North Central Washington Museum   509-664-5989

Location: 127 S. Mission St. in Wenatchee; two blocks west of the Columbia
    River
Days/Hours: Monday–Friday, 10 a.m.–4 p.m.; Saturday–Sunday, 1 p.m.–
    4 p.m. Closed weekends in January and most holidays.
Wheelchair/Stroller Access: Yes, from the loading dock between the two
    buildings. You'll have to go inside to alert them that visitors are waiting
    at the loading dock.

The coin-operated miniature Great Northern Railway is a major attraction here. The museum is housed in two buildings, with a skybridge linking the main museum to an annex featuring art exhibits. Silent movies, concerts, and traveling exhibits are frequent offerings on their entertainment schedule. Displays include a walk through a pioneer home with turn-of-the-century furnishings; elsewhere you'll see a pioneer workshop and trading store. On the museum's upper floor you'll find fossils that have been excavated locally. The museum has another claim to fame, as well: a certificate declaring that as of November 10, 1997, Wenatchee holds the record for the world's largest apple pie. The museum staff organized the event; the finished product weighed in at over 34,000 pounds. They hope to hold the record long enough to be included in the 1999 Guinness Book of World Records. When you visit the museum, there is free parking off Kittitas St., one block south of the museum.

Ohme Gardens   *509-662-5785*

Location: 3327 Ohme, right near the junction of U.S. 2 and U.S. 97
Days/Hours: April 15–October 15: 9 a.m.–7 p.m.
Admission: $5/adults; $3/students 7-17; free/children 6 and under with parents. Season passes: $20/individuals, $50/families.
Wheelchair/Stroller Access: No

Herman Ohme created lush, bountiful green abundance on a hillside dramatic for its stark natural earth tones. The walk through the gardens is 400 feet short of one mile and takes about an hour, but there are stone benches and rest facilities. The emphasis is on greenery, with trees, plants, and existing rock formations creating effects, from a lush rain forest and shaded fern-bordered pools to an alpine meadow. Ohme started his gardens in 1929 as a family retreat. In 1939, the gardens were opened to the public and now belong to the state of Washington. It's easy to see why one would want to visit this peaceful place often. The spectacular view of the valley, the Cascade Mountains, and the Columbia River is another reward. Ample free parking. Of special interest—the Ox Yore Lodge, under renovation in summer of 1997.

Riverfront Park

Location: 2 Fifth St. Going north on Wenatchee Ave., turn right on Fifth; it runs right into the park.

There's a Farmer's Market here from June through October, open Wednesday and Saturday from 8 a.m. to noon, always a worthwhile weekend family activity.

The Wenatchee Ice Arena is also located in the park. It's open from October to May, $3/skaters, $2/rentals. They feature a teens' night. Call 509-664-3396 for family rates, season passes, etc. If you're in town for winter activities (especially skiing at Mission Ridge), this is a great evening activity for the family.

During the day, Riverfront Park is especially appealing for walking, biking, and skating, for the wonderful views of the Columbia and surrounding mountains, and for great tree-climbing for kids on some grand old maples with huge limbs, not too high off the ground. You might have a conversation with Captain Alexander Griggs; his statue depicts him walking from home to work (his shipyard was located nearby on the river). The Apple Loop Trail (a fourteen-mile bike loop) runs through the park.

Rocky Reach Dam   *509-663-8121, ext. 6645*

Location: On Hwy. 97A, seven miles north of Wenatchee, on the Columbia River
Days/Hours: February–December: daily, from 8 a.m. Closing times vary; call for information.
Tours: Self-guided tours the norm; guided generator tours available during summer months and by special request.
Wheelchair/Stroller Access: Yes

Rocky Reach can hold your interest for a half-hour or a half-day, depending on the time of year. There are several areas for which to reserve time. In the auditorium, you can ask to see any film in their library; most are about ten minutes. They even have some with Disney characters. Downstairs, the Fish Ladder is fascinating. You can view the fish swimming in river water as they make their way through the Columbia River project on their way upstream to spawn. You'll see eels and other marine life, as well. The four types of fish most commonly seen here are coho, sockeye, Chinook, and steelhead trout. The best times to visit to see the fish are: steelhead in September, Chinook in May and August, sockeye in July. The museum is located in the Powerhouse. On the fourth floor, the Gallery of the Columbia and Gallery of Electricity depicts early life along the Columbia and a chronological development of electricity. As you walk from the main building to the museum, the outlook from the walkway is spectacular, overlooking the grounds, the River, the dam, and the surrounding scenery. But we've saved the best for last. Your first stop might be at the very entrance, where the low juniper grove houses a multitude of domesticated bunnies (and guinea pigs and even small mice) who live there year-round. You're welcome to stop and say hello. Lots of photo opportunities here. No pets allowed anywhere on the grounds, and no food or drink inside the building or the museum. The grounds at Rocky Reach are extensive, with beautiful floral displays, two well-kept picnic shelters, and a play area with new play equipment for smaller children.

Washington Apple Commission Visitor Center

509-663-9600 (weekdays); 509-662-3090 (weekends)

Location: *2900 Euclid St. in north Wenatchee (near Rocky Reach Dam and Ohme Gardens)*
Web Site: *www.bestapples.com*
Days/Hours: *May 1–December 23: weekdays, 8 a.m.–5 p.m.; Saturday, 9 a.m.–5 p.m.; Sunday, 10 a.m.–4 p.m. Closed from December 24–April 30.*
Wheelchair/Stroller Access: *Yes*

The center is compactly designed to offer something to everyone: a fifteen-minute video, samples of apple juice and fresh apples, and an interactive display telling you everything you could want to know about Washington's apple industry. Is Red Delicious your favorite? If so, you're right there on top. Washington's favorites are Red Delicious, Golden Delicious, Granny Smith, Gala, and Fuji, in that order. What's a Gala? A cross between a Golden and a Kid's Orange Red (sometimes called the mutt of the group). Plenty of apple-type giftware and clothing. Strangely enough, Los Angeleans eat more apples than we in Washington do!

Cashmere

Places to Go

Aplets and Cotlets Candy Kitchen/Liberty Orchards
509-782-4088

Location: *117 Mission St., one block off Cottage Ave. (about ten miles east of Leavenworth, off Hwy. 2)*
Days/Hours: *April–December*
Tours: *Daily, every twenty minutes on the hour, 8:40 a.m.–4 p.m.*
Wheelchair/Stroller Access: *Yes*

Two Armenian immigrants began this Washington landmark, mixing up the first batch of Aplets and Cotlets (known then as Turkish Delights) in an aluminum kettle on their kitchen stove. Today there are more than twenty different flavors (now including pb and j!), some nut-free and sugar-free, and the third generation in the family is running the business. Tours start in the sorting room where the nuts are carefully culled (the candy is guaranteed 100 percent shell-free!); next you'll see the huge kettles that hold 256 pounds of candy. The hot mixture is then poured onto wooden trays and rolled out to level, cooled for up to ten hours and cut into bite-size pieces. And then the best part—rolling the candy in powdered sugar! In the packing room they pack up to 5000 pieces an hour. At the end of the tour, you'll get delicious samples and a chance to purchase their products. Ask questions! The tour guide loves that. Up to 400 people daily tour the plant. And while they do tours on weekends, there is no production then.

Chelan County Pioneer Village and Museum 509-782-3230

Location: 600 Cottage Ave.
Days/Hours: Open year-round for tours of ten or more. March 1–October 31: Tuesday–Sunday, 9:30 a.m.–5 p.m.
Admission: $5/families; $3/individuals; $2/seniors and students; free/ members
Wheelchair/Stroller Access: Yes

The admission is small, considering they are almost entirely self-supporting through the Chelan County Historical Society. Consider a donation—it's worth it. The guided tours include docents dressed in pioneer garb; minimum time is one hour. Outside, there are twelve cabins in the village, a fascinating look into their history. You may see the old print shop in action or try your hand at using a goose-quill pen. In the museum, you'll find a rare and extraordinary collection of Native American artifacts reflecting their lives and environment. The wildlife, geology, and natural history of North Central Washington is illuminating. This museum well fits the phrase "a well-kept secret." Plan your trip around a visit.

The Walking Arboretum of Cashmere

This is a one-and-two-thirds-mile self-guided tour, beginning and ending on Cottage Ave. It takes in picturesque streets and homes, enough to give you an appreciation of this lovely little town. There are actually sixty different trees to be identified on the walk, but some are on private property. Pick up a "Walking Arboretum" brochure at the Visitors Center or stores in town.

NORTH CENTRAL WASHINGTON
AND COULEE COUNTRY
Grant County
Places to Go

Grant County Historical Museum and Village

509-754-3334

Location: 742 Basin St. N.W. From Seattle, take I-90 to exit 151 to Hwy. 283 to Ephrata. From Spokane westbound, take I-90 to exit 179 (Hwy. 17) to Ephrata.
Days/Hours: Daily: Monday-Saturday, 10 a.m.–5 p.m.; Sunday, 1 p.m.– 4 p.m.
Admission: $2/adults; $1.50/children 6–15; free/children 5 and under
Wheelchair/Stroller Access: Yes

On the second weekend of June and the last Saturday of September this becomes a living museum, with pioneers plying their trades in the village's twenty-eight cabins and public buildings. Some have been moved here from their original sites; the village includes a church, one-room school house, jail, bank, print shop, blacksmith, even an old-time saloon, with a completely authentic pioneer homestead. You can wander in and out of the buildings at your leisure; grandparents can talk about the "good old days." On those weekends, there is also a petting zoo.

Okanogan County
Places to Go

Omak Stampede and Suicide Race

509-826-1002; 800-933-6625

Location: Omak is sixty miles north of Chelan on U.S. 97, or sixty miles southwest of Grand Coulee Dam via Hwy. 155.
Days/Hours: Annually, second weekend in August
Admission: Tickets required for many events; call ahead.
Wheelchair/Stroller Access: In some areas

The Stampede is a week-long event featuring four performances by real cowboys (members of the Professional Rodeo Cowboys Association), grand and kiddy parades, a carnival, river-raft races, and a

Native American encampment and tribal dance competition. And, of course, the well-publicized, death-defying Suicide Race. Whatever your personal attitude, it's a colorful and unusual experience. Visitors are welcome to browse around the teepees at the Native American village. The town of Omak is small enough that almost all the events are within walking distance. There are 1,000 campsites at nearby Omak Eastside Park.

Lincoln County
Places to Go

Grand Coulee Dam

509-633-3074 (Chamber of Commerce); 509-633-9265 (the dam)

Location: *Ninety miles west of Spokane on U.S. 2 and Hwy. 174. Ninety miles northeast of George from I-90 on Hwys. 283, 28, 17, and 155.*
Web Site: *www.televar.com/~cowlee/chamber/*
Days/Hours: *Daily, 9 a.m.–5 p.m. Nightly laser light shows during summer only.*
Tours: *Free ninety-minute self-guided tours*
Wheelchair/Stroller Access: *Yes*

Perhaps the most memorable part of a Grand Coulee visit in summer months is the forty-minute laser light show that is projected nightly onto the dam's face. It starts at sunset, opening with startling quiet as blue lights illuminate the spillway, then water starts gushing downward. This 4,000-foot long dam seems to become a larger-than-life movie screen, complete with some animated cartoons during the show. There are some good choices for viewpoints of the display: in town, grab a bleacher seat across from the Coulee House motel; stake out a spot on the lawn at the Visitor Arrival Center; or watch from the parking lot at the Third Powerhouse. All three have stereo systems which broadcast music synchronized with the light show.

For a good photo vantage point, the Crown Point Vista overlooks the dam, Lake Roosevelt, and the town of Coulee Dam. You can see the laser show from here, also.

For tours of the dam itself, start at the Visitor Center with a thirteen-minute introductory video. The ninety-minute tour includes five stops at the dam and powerhouse, and an exhilarating ride in the glass-enclosed incline elevator at the Third Powerhouse. Bathroom stops advised before starting out.

For those considering extended visits, you can rent a houseboat or camp on Lake Roosevelt, behind the dam.

Sun Lakes State Park and Dry Falls Interpretive Center   509-632-5583 *(park)*; 509-732-5214 *(center)*

Location: On Hwy. 17, seven miles southwest of Coulee City
Web Site: www.parks.wa.gov
Days/Hours: Park is open daily; overnight camping year-round. Interpretive
  Center is in jeopardy due to funding; call ahead.
Wheelchair/Stroller Access: Yes

Spring, summer, and fall months are most popular here. The desert-like environment is great for horseback riding, swimming, trout fishing, and boating. The state operates the campground and swimming beach south and east of Park Lake; much of Park Lake is privately managed. For those who like some amenities, there's a golf course, Laundromat, general store, and concessions near by. The Interpretive Center is relatively new but already dealing with funding problems, which means that hours may change drastically. Center naturalists give daily talks about the mammoth ice sheets which covered the land a million years ago, forcing the Columbia River to carve a new channel. On exhibit at the center is a fossilized baby rhinoceros trapped in a pre-Ice Age mudflow. Dry Falls, three-and-one-half-miles wide with a 400-foot drop, is the skeleton of one of the greatest waterfalls in geologic history.

Places to Eat

Rock 'n Robin Drive-In   509-633-1290

Location: Bridgeport and Hwy. 174 in Grand Coulee
Days/Hours: Summer: daily, 10 a.m.–10 p.m. Winter: 10 a.m.–7 p.m.
  (sometimes closed on Mondays).
Wheelchair/Stroller Access: Yes

This place will push your nostalgia button. In summer months, the waitresses zip up to your car window to take your order—on roller skates! Hamburgers, milkshakes, and French fries are the main menu items here.

NORTHEAST WASHINGTON

Places to Go

Gardner Cave at Crawford State Park   *509-238-4258*

Location: North of Metaline, take Hwy. 31; turn west on Boundary Road; drive twelve miles
Days/Hours: Summer: 8 a.m.–dusk. Closed in winter.
Tours: May–mid-September: Thursday–Monday, 10 a.m., noon, 2 p.m., and 4 p.m.
Wheelchair/Stroller Access: No

This 1,055-foot-long limestone cave has a story worth listening to, assuming it's true. Seems it once housed moonshine stills, but the owner/bootlegger lost the tunnel in a card game to a Metaline storekeeper who then gave the property to the state parks department. Only the upper 494 feet of the cave are explorable; steel walkways and stairs keep visitors away from the precious 9,000-year-old stalactites which grow only a half-inch a century. Natural oils in our hands would kill further growth, so no touching is allowed. The quiet drip, drip, drip you hear is water falling from the stalactites. It can get very cool (low 40s); warm clothing recommended.

Manresa Grotto   *509-445-1147 (Tribal Center)*

Location: Off LeClerc Road, on the Kalispel Indian Reservation. Take Newport Hwy. to Hwy. 211; follow seventeen miles over the railroad tracks, across the bridge and another six miles north into Kalispel.
Days/Hours: Monday–Thursday, 7 a.m.–5 p.m.
Wheelchair/Stroller Access: Yes, but difficult

This hillside cave was used for religious ceremonies by both the Kalispel Native Americans and settlers. Inside are a stone altar and pews, outside a wonderful view of the Pend Oreille Valley. On the third weekend in September, a priest celebrates mass with the public. For more information about the Kalispel Native Americans, call the Tribal Center Monday to Thursday from 7 a.m. to 5 p.m.

Pend Oreille Valley Train Rides

*509-442-3397 (this number is in operation
two weeks prior to first scheduled train ride)*

Location: Ione and Metaline Falls
Days/Hours: Weekends only, 11 a.m., 1 p.m., 3 p.m. Trips are ninety minutes
Admission: $5/per person; free/children under 1 year; reservations strongly
  recommended
Wheelchair/Stroller Access: Yes for wheelchairs; no for strollers. Babies and
  toddlers may be carried aboard.

Schedules do vary from year to year for this exhilarating excursion,
but they generally start their season around Father's Day Weekend and
continue until mid-October. Most trips originate in Ione; only one weekend ride begins in Metaline Falls. There are both open and covered cars;
if you want lots of fresh air and the wind in your air, request an open car!
The train winds along the Pend Oreille River and makes a breathtaking
stop on the trestle at Box Canyon Dam some 180 feet above the water.

The autumn excursions are most popular for the brilliant fall colors
along the way. They will be open for reservations in early June.

Stonerose Interpretive Center   509-775-2295

Location: 15 Kean St. in Republic, one block west of Main St.
Days/Hours: May–October: Tuesday–Saturday, 10 a.m.–5 p.m. Mid-June–
  mid-September: Sunday, 10 a.m.–4 p.m. Group and field trips by
  arrangement.
Admission: To dig: $2/ages 12 and over; free/children 11 and under
Wheelchair/Stroller Access: Yes, but bumpy

About 10 million years after the dinosaurs roamed the earth, im-
pressions of plants, insects, and fish were left in the ground at these fossil
beds. The layers of shale simply split apart "like pages in a book," telling
the story of the Eocene Epoch. Today you can see those fossils at the
Stonerose Interpretive Center, which draws almost 10,000 visitors annually, or find some yourself by doing your own digging. After registering
at the center, you can go out to hunt for your own organisms using your
own tools or by renting theirs. The digging tools are usually hammers
and cold or nonwooden chisels (but putty knives and screwdrivers work,
too). Long pants and goggles are suggested. You're limited to three pieces
per person per day; with a family, that can add up to quite a collection!
Please bring them back to the center for identification and cataloging.
Finding one to keep is a real treasure. But be advised, the center reserves
the right to retain any fossil that is of real scientific value or significant to
the Stonerose collection.

Helpful Phone Numbers:

Chambers of Commerce:
  East Wenatchee: 509-884-2514
  Ephrata: 509-754-4656; 800-345-4656
  Grand Coulee Dam Area: 509-633-3074
  Leavenworth: 509-548-5807, ext. 21
  Marblemount: 360-873-2250
  Metaline Falls: 509-446-4415
  Moses Lake: 509-765-7888; 800-992-6234 (Washington only)
  Lake Chelan: 800-424-3526, ext. 201
  Newport: 509-447-5812
  Cashmere: 509-782-3513

Other:
  Colville National Forest: 509-684-3711
  Douglas County: 800-245-3922, ext. 2
  Odessa Visitor Information Center: 509-982-0188
  Okanogan National Forest: 509-826-3275
  Okanogan Tourism Council: 800-225-6625; 509-826-1880
  Omak Visitor Information Center: 800-225-6625
  Republic City Hall: 509-775-3216

CHAPTER
8

Greater Spokane

• •

It's been called the "Capital of the Inland Empire," and its Native American name —"Spokan"— comes from an Native American tribe who considered themselves "Children of the Sunday." It has a fair share of firsts: one as the site of the first white settlement in the Northwest; second as the smallest city to host a World's Fair. Riverfront Park was the World's Fair site; today it is home to a sparkling selection of family-oriented activities, including the Looff Carousel. Popular events here are the Lilac Festival and Bloomsday Run, early in May. Winters are verrrrry cold in Spokane, summers very warm, and not much in between. The environment sparks lots of indoor and outdoor activity; high on the list are kayaking and canoeing, recreational running, cross-country skiing, biking, walking, camping, golfing, fishing, and horseback riding. You won't be bored in Spokane; it's a rich and vital city.

Places to Go

Audubon Park   509-625-6200

Location: W. 3000 Audubon
Days/Hours: Daily, dawn to dusk
Wheelchair/Stroller Access: Yes

Shade's the magic word here, and there's lots of it. It's a spacious park with some grand old trees that provide relief on hot summer days. For kids, there's a wading pool and play equipment, plus baseball fields and tennis courts.

Rides at Riverfront Park. Photo courtesy Spokane Area Convention and Visitor Bureau

Bumpers Fun Centers (two locations)

509-489-4000 (North Town); 509-624-6678 (Riverfront)

Location: 4750 N. Division at North Town Mall; Riverfront Park
Days/Hours: Riverfront: hours same as the park. North Town: daily, 10 a.m.–
9 p.m. except Sunday, 10 a.m.–6 p.m.
Admission: Entry is free; miniature golf is $4.30. Children 6 and under play
free.
Wheelchair/Stroller Access: Yes

It's a medieval-style indoor fun forest, with fountains and greenery and an eighteen-hole miniature golf course, bumper cars, and a Ferris wheel (rides are $1.50 each). Parties are a big deal here, with two party rooms to accommodate groups and four different party packages. In the Throne Room, arcade and virtual reality video games keep everyone busy; they provide pizza, soft drinks, and the birthday cake. Party details must be arranged in advance; prices begin at $19.95 (flat rate for twelve youngsters) and go up. Call for specific details.

Cheney Cowles Memorial Museum and 1898 Campbell House
509-456-3931, ext. 101 or 122

Location: West 2316 First Ave. in historic Browne's Addition
Days/Hours: Tuesday–Saturday, 10 a.m.–5 p.m.; Wednesday, 10 a.m.–9
p.m.; Sunday, 1 p.m.–5 p.m. Closed Mondays and major holidays
Admission: $4/adults; $3/seniors 65 plus; $2.50/students with ID and kids
6–16; $10/immediate families. Wednesday is half-price from 10 a.m.–
5 p.m., free from 5 p.m.–9 p.m.
Tours: Guided tours available by reservation
Wheelchair/Stroller Access: Yes

A visit to the museum includes recently renovated exhibitions about the development of the Inland Northwest region and the Plateau Native American cultures. The adjacent Campbell House is an interesting feature, beautifully restored and furnished. At the museum, the permanent exhibits tell the stories of the Native Americans who lived here, along with the missionaries and fur traders who arrived nearly a century ago, while the changing exhibits showcase art, history, and current issues. For older children studying state and local history, this is a rich resource.

Comstock Park 509-625-6200

Location: W. 800 29th, southwest Spokane
Days/Hours: Daily, dawn to dusk
Wheelchair/Stroller Access: Yes

Comstock is one of the favorite warm-weather destinations in Spokane. In summer the swimming and wading pools are very popular, but there's also a year-round playground, groomed baseball diamonds, tennis courts, and many picnic tables.

Eastern Washington University

509-359-6555, ext. 2397 (Admissions Office/Tour Desk)

Location: In Cheney, seventeen miles west of Spokane
Web Site: www.ewu.edu
Days/Hours: Tours given afternoons, October–July, by appointment only
Wheelchair/Stroller Access: Yes

"Eagle Ambassadors" are the tour guides, students who know the university well and can share information with prospective students and their families. The tours are about ninety minutes and usually stop at the business school, a lab, a residence hall, and "The Fase"—the student athletic facility built by the Seattle Seahawks when they used it as a summer training camp. Overnights in the dorm for visiting students run $10 per night.

Fairchild Air Force Base Heritage Museum 509-247-2100

Location: Off U.S. 2, twenty miles west of Spokane
Days/Hours: Monday, Wednesday, Friday and Saturday, 10 a.m.–2 p.m.
Tours: Free; self-guided; takes about an hour
Wheelchair/Stroller Access: On ground level only

The tours here are interesting, yet leave lots of room for imagination, especially on the B-52 flight simulator. You can pull the throttles, flip the switches, and take flight above the clouds. Outside, there are nearly 700 planes and exhibits from more than 100 years of military history to explore, with artifacts from the Civil, Spanish-American, and Vietnam wars, World Wars I and II, and even Desert Storm. You'll enter through the main gate; simply show a driver's license and proof of vehicle insurance for admission.

Manito Park
509-625-6200 (Park Department)

Location: Grand Blvd. and 18th
Days/Hours: Daily, dawn to dusk
Wheelchair/Stroller Access: In most places

There are several "rooms" in this park, different gardens with lots of running space. The rose garden and Japanese garden are favorites, with their highly aromatic flowers and plantings. The big hill makes for terrific sledding in the winter months. At the duck pond, you'll be expected to share bread crumbs.

Mount Spokane State Park
509-238-4258

Location: Thirty miles northeast of Spokane; drive north on U.S. 2; at Hwy. 206 turn east; drive another sixteen miles.
Days/Hours: Closed to camping in winter months when it becomes a snow park. Summer hours: 6:30 a.m.–dusk. Overnight camping accommodations June-September
Wheelchair/Stroller Access: In some places

Although camping closes down in winter, Mount Spokane is a major ski destination. There are thirty-two runs with five chairlifts for the downhill addicts, and twenty-five kilometers of groomed cross-country trails, plus several miles of groomed snowmobile routes. Sports equipment can be rented nearby. During summer months, fifty miles of park trails are shared by hikers and horseback riders.

Riverfront Park
509-625-6600; 509-456-4FUN (recording);
509-625-6632 (administration)

Location: 507 N. Howard St.
Days/Hours: Call for general and/or specific information; hours vary with each venue.
Admission: Check prices by phone; park admission is free, but each activity has its own fee. Winter Day Passes and Winter Season Passes available at Guest Services/Gift Shop
Wheelchair/Stroller Access: Yes

As the site of the 1974 World's Fair, Riverfront has the right to be the destination for family fun! The IMAX Theatre with its six-channel sound system and a screen five stories tall looks huge to kids. The Gondola Skyride soars high over the Spokane River and its frenetic waterfalls. Other attractions: bumper cars, the Bounce Castle, the Caterpillar Train, SR-2 Ride Simulator, the Looff Carrousel (now boasting one of only five

Reaching for the brass ring on the Looff Carrousel, Riverfront Park. Photo courtesy Spokane Area Convention and Visitor Bureau

working Ruth organs in the country), and Bumpers Fun Center. You can ride the carrousel on any of fifty-four horses, a giraffe, a tiger, or a Chinese dragon. The Radio Flyer is a giant replica of an old favorite, the little red wagon. This one is big enough to climb up to the top, slide down the handle, and play on the gym bars underneath. The Ice Palace is a Mecca for budding Olympiads or beginners (it closes January to March for annual maintenance). But there are quiet places here, too. You can feed the ducks on the steps next to the Spokane River or relax on the terrace benches near the gondola ride. You can see the fairgrounds on the tour train (seasonal). In summer months, the Spokane Symphony presents free outdoor concerts; some performances take place on an anchored stage floating in the river. A great family experience.

Riverside State Park

509-456-3964 (park);
509-466-4747 (Spokane House); 800-452-5687 (camping reservations)

Location: *Six miles northwest of Spokane. From I-90, take exit 281 to Hwy. 2 (Division St.); continue to Hwy. 291, turning west on Rifle Club Rd.; go half a mile and turn south on A. L. White Parkway. Riverside is about two miles away.*

Days/Hours: *April 1–September 30: daily, 6:30 a.m.–dusk. October 1–March 31: daily, 8 a.m.–dusk. Year-round overnight camping accommodations available by reservations.*

For Spokane House: Mid-May–Labor Day: Wednesday–Sunday, 10 a.m.–6 p.m.

Admission: *Free*
Wheelchair/Stroller Access: *No*

Two centuries ago, this was the meeting place for Native Americans and white fur traders negotiating business. Today, 101 campsites, great

Riverfront Park boasts a garbage eating goat. PHOTO COURTESY SPOKANE AREA CONVENTION AND VISITOR BUREAU

hiking trails, and horseback riding attract active families. While the views of the gorge are wonderful, the Bowl and Pitcher area of the river is a deceptive place, with a very strong and dangerous undercurrent and treacherous rapids nearby. Much more harmless and definitely still interesting is the park's Spokane House Interpretive Center. Exhibits include displays from local archaeological digs regarding life before white settlers arrived and a diorama showcasing the story of the thriving 1810 fur trading post that eventually lost its business to Kettle Falls. East of the Center, off Rutter Parkway, is Indian Painted Rocks, colored traces of petroglyphs. Kids can stretch their imagination trying to decipher the messages.

Spokane Chiefs   509-328-0450

Location: Spokane Veterans Memorial Arena, W. 701 Mallon,
Days/Hours: Season is September–March (some years extended through
*   May); game time is 7:00 p.m. except Sundays at 6:00 p.m.*
Admission: Ranges from $6–$12, depending on seat location.
Wheelchair/Stroller Access: Yes

Ice hockey is a big sport in this city and the Chiefs are the hockey club. They play against cross-state rivals, the Seattle Thunderbirds, and several other Northwest and Canadian teams. The young men are hopefully working their way on to a slot on an NHL squad.

Spokane Indians   509-535-2922

Location: Interstate Fairgrounds; North 602 Havana
Days/Hours: Season is June–September; game times vary
Wheelchair/Stroller Access: Yes

The Indians are part of the cross-state baseball rivalries and play in the same league with the Everett AquaSox (Class A farm team for the Mariners). Because the closest big league team is many miles away in Seattle, local enthusiasm for the sport is high. It's a great family "thing" — bring your mitt, because you never know when one of those foul balls might drop in your lap for a souvenir.

Spokane River Centennial Trail   509-456-3964

Location: East from the Opera House at Riverfront Park to the Idaho border;
   west from Riverfront to Carlson Rd. near Nine Mile Bridge
Days/Hours: Daily
Wheelchair/Stroller Access: Yes

The trail was dedicated in 1989 to celebrate Washington's 100th anniversary of statehood. Stretching for more than thirty-nine miles, the paved route is ideal for children learning to bike or skate in-line, for parents pushing strollers, for walkers, joggers, and bicyclists. When the trail passes Gonzaga University, continuing north along the river through Mission Park; the jogging path will follow the river bank while the bike route stays near the road shoulder. Benches along the way are ideal resting places "just for the moment." The trail stretches across the Washington–Idaho border.

Wonderland Golf and Games   509-468-4386

Location: N. 10515 Division; from I-90, take the exit to Hwy. 2/Division St.;
   continue for seven miles.
Days/Hours: Monday–Thursday, 11 a.m.–11 p.m.; Friday, 11 a.m.–12:30
   a.m.; Saturday, 9:30 a.m.–12:30 a.m.; Sunday, 9:30 a.m.–11 p.m.
Wheelchair/Stroller Access: Yes at the miniature golf outdoors; not inside

Wonderland offers activities for kids ages 2 to 18 in any kind of weather. The miniature golf course is enhanced with castles, shipwrecks, and mysterious old mansions. There's another golf course indoors, plus softball and baseball batting cages, and nearly eighty video games (best for preteens and youth). For younger ones, the Rock-a-Fire Explosion Pizza Theater has animated, mechanical animals performing while you munch on pizza.

Places to Eat

Azteca   509-456-0350

Location: 200 W. Spokane Falls Blvd.
Days/Hours: Weekdays, 11 a.m.–10 p.m.; Friday–Saturday, 11 a.m.–
   10:30 p.m.
Wheelchair/Stroller Access: Yes

The best deal here is Sunday, when kids' menu items are just 95¢. The meals comes with rice, beans, and a choice of enchilada, taco, or burrito. Their "Little Amigos" menu has other choices, too. At the table, crayons and place mats to color can stave off hungry energy, along with tortilla chips and salsa. High chairs and boosters available.

Chuck E. Cheese Pizza Time Theater   509-327-6623

Location: 100 Shadle Center, near Alberta and Wellesley
Days/Hours: Daily, 11 a.m.–10 p.m.
Wheelchair/Stroller Access: Yes

Mechanical musicians, a healthy salad bar, lots of pizza, and other kid-type foods make this place a popular family gathering place, especially for birthday parties and end-of-the season sports team parties.

Old Spaghetti Factory   509-624-8916

Location: 152 S. Monroe
Days/Hours: Sunday–Thursday, 5 p.m.–9:30 p.m.; Friday–Saturday, 5 p.m.–
11 p.m.
Wheelchair/Stroller Access: Yes, into the building, but not into the rest-rooms

Tables can't be reserved here, but when you arrive, ask if you can be seated at a table in the train. That, plus the hardwood floors and vintage collectibles on the walls give this restaurant an entertaining ambiance. Children can order off the menu with smaller portions for a few dollars less.

The Onion (two locations)

509-747-3852 (Riverside); 509-482-6100 (Division)

Location: W. 302 Riverside; N. 7522 Division
Days/Hours: Sunday–Thursday, 11:15 a.m.–11:30 p.m.; Friday–Saturday,
11:15 a.m.–1:30 a.m. (both locations).
Wheelchair/Stroller Access: Yes

Deep-fried onion rings large enough to wear as bracelets. Chocolate cake in slabs, not slices. And specialty hamburgers to suit almost any appetite. This place is a big draw for local folks. Items on the children's menu range from $2 to $4; included are fish sticks, chicken, hot dogs, hamburgers, and pb and j sandwiches. High chairs and boosters available.

Helpful Phone Numbers

City of Spokane Parks and Recreation Department: 509-625-6200

Spokane Visitor Information Center: 800-248-3230; 509-747-3230

Washington State Parks: 800-233-0321

CHAPTER
9

Southeast and South Central Washington

• •

Early on the Columbia River's travels through Washington, the powerful waterway moves through the triangle known as the Tri-Cities—Kennewick, Pasco, and Richland—where the sun shines nearly 300 days a year. The cities are nestled at the convergence of three major rivers: the Columbia is joined by the Yakima and the Snake. This makes for some major water sports activities, including water-skiing, Jet-ski riding, fishing, and jet boat tours. About fifty miles east is Walla Walla, and farther north is Pullman. The Blue Mountains and Umatilla National Forest are great hiking, fishing, and camping destinations; the Snake, Touchet, and Tucannon rivers offer river-rafting adventures. This interesting landscape of mountains and rivers challenges and tempts families who love the outdoors. Part of this country is a fertile wheat land known as the Palouse.

Moving right along via U.S. 195 to Highway 270, you'll come to Pullman, home of Washington State University and source of one of the state's major rivalries. The Apple Cup pits the WSU Cougars (who went to the Rose Bowl in 1997 after a sixty-seven-year dry spell) against the Washington Huskies. Emotions and loyalties run very high at this annual football frolic.

- **Tri-Cities:** Once considered a secret city, Richland today is a leader in nuclear energy production and waste disposal. Pasco and

Making fire with flint. PHOTO COURTESY OF THE YAKAMA NATION CULTURAL HERITAGE CENTER

Kennewick have historical significance related to the Lewis and Clark exploration. In 1805, Meriwether Lewis and William Clark camped in Pasco on their trek west and passed through what is now Kennewick, which means "winter haven" in Chemanpum Native American language.

- **Walla Walla:** Walla Walla is fifty miles east of the Tri-Cities on U.S. 12 and hovers on the Idaho border. In Native American it means "many waters," and its fame centers around the fields of Walla Walla sweet onions. The harvest season is a busy one and somewhat brief, but the onions are incredibly popular across the country. The weather here has been described as "tongue-sticking cold," but families with the love of the outdoors will feel at home. The mountains are home to elk, deer, bighorn sheep, black bear, and cougar, and assorted collections of phenomenal wildflowers.

- **South Central Washington:** Some of Washington's most fertile country is to be found here. From Ellensburg, moving southeast through the Yakima Valley on to Toppenish, the crops are abundant and delicious, from apples to asparagus. There's a rich ethnic blend of people, too. An emerging Hispanic population in Yakima has created the Hispanic Chamber of Commerce, and Native American history is celebrated in a number of areas. The names of the counties are enticing: Skamania and Klickitat. The cities are equally mysterious: Zillah, Wapato, Toppenish, Yakima, Naches, and Selah. The Yakima and Columbia rivers are responsible for this opulent landscape.

SOUTHEAST WASHINGTON

Tri-Cities

Places to Go

Columbia River Exhibition of History, Science, and Technology (CREHST)
509-943-9000

Location: 95 Lee Blvd., Richmond
Days/Hours: Monday–Saturday, 10 a.m.–5 p.m.; Sunday, noon–5 p.m.
Admission: $3.50/adults; $2.75/seniors 62 and older; $2.50/children 7–16;
  free/children 6 and under
Wheelchair/Stroller Access: Yes

Formerly Hanford Museum, this is now CREHST. Considered a museum and a science center, the focus here is the dynamic story of the

Columbia Basin. They've created a number of entertaining and interactive exhibits and displays, with topics ranging from hydropower, agriculture, and salmon restoration to advanced science and technology. There's a gift shop for browsing as well. This area continues to be a very provocative source of information; the museum is another step forward in bringing the story to the public. CREHST shares its parking lot with the Three Rivers Children's Museum.

The Golf Club (formerly Longest Drive/Shortest Putt)

509-735-6072

Location: 6311 W. Clearwater Ave.
Days/Hours: Daily, 10 a.m.–9 p.m.
Admission: $3.50 per person for either golf or basketball; kids 4 and under
play mini-golf free
Wheelchair/Stroller Access: The facility proper is accessible, also one of the
miniature golf courses and the Bankshot Basketball.

Now a Nevada Bob franchise, The Golf Club can accommodate multitalented families. The driving range is covered and heated in winter, misted in summer. There are two eighteen-hole miniature golf courses and for the basketball addicts, an eighteen-station basketball course called Bankshot Basketball. Each station increases in difficulty.

Ice Harbor Dam and Locks

509-547-7781

Location: On Snake River and Lake Sacajawea; from Pasco, take U.S. 12
across the Snake River Bridge about ten miles; turn onto Hwy. 124.
Days/Hours: Dam: year-round. Visitors Center: April–September: daily,
9 a.m.–5 p.m.
Tours: Self-guided
Wheelchair/Stroller Access: Limited

Built in the 1950s, Ice Harbor Dam houses one of the largest navigational locks in the world. The dam retains the Snake River which in turn forms Lake Sacajawea. While the tours are self-guided, there's interesting history about the dam and its impact on hydroelectric power. You can stop inside the powerhouse and watch fish jumping up the ladder. Near the dam, you'll find a small Native American petroglyph; this marks the tribal grounds inundated by the lake when the dam was built.

Northwoods Restaurant and Storyland Golf

509-786-6900 (Storyland); 509-786-2002 (restaurant)

Location: *At exit 80 off I-82 in Prosser; twenty miles west of Richland*
Days/Hours: *Restaurant: daily, 10 a.m.–6 p.m.*
Wheelchair/Stroller Access: *Yes for the restaurant; limited at the golf course due to gravel paths.*

The restaurant and miniature golf course are adjacent, but you'll quickly know the difference. A thirty-foot tall dinosaur greets you at Storyland, and the embellishments around the course are handmade, including the green giant and castle. The golf course closes in winter. Next door, the restaurant offers children's menus with meals under $5. High chairs and boosters available.

Oasis Waterworks

509-735-8442

Location: *6321 W. Canal in Kennewick*
Days/Hours: *Memorial Day–Labor Day: Sunday–Thursday, 10 a.m.–6:30 p.m.; Friday–Saturday, 10 a.m.–9:30 p.m.*
Admission: *$12.40/all-day session; $9.25/half day (after 2:30 p.m.); free/ seniors over 55 and children under 4*
Wheelchair/Stroller Access: *Only for observation*

What a great place to cool off in the summer! Eleven outdoor water slides, a 5,000 square foot swimming pool, outdoor courts for basketball and volleyball, and special kiddy slides for the younger ones—adds up to something for everyone. Suggested age is 4 years and up. And adults are welcome, but they don't have to get in the water.

Sacajawea State Park/Sacajawea Interpretive Center

509-545-2361

Location: *Tank Farm Road. Take U.S. 12; four miles southeast of Pasco, you'll turn southwest onto Tank Farm Road; go one more mile and—at the Y-intersection—follow the road east for another mile. Parking nearby.*
Web Site: *www.parks.wa.gov*
Days/Hours: *Dawn to dusk; closed in winter months*
Wheelchair/Stroller Access: *Yes*

Named after the courageous Shoshoni woman who played such an important part in the Lewis and Clark expedition, the park and center offer much of interest. In the park, play spaces, swimming, water-skiing, fishing, and boating abound. In the Interpretive Center, videos about the expedition tell the extraordinary story; elsewhere exhibits tell the story of local Native Americans' lifestyle through tools, bowls, and other artifacts.

Three Rivers Children's Museum   509-943-5437

Location: 650 George Washington Way, Richland
Days/Hours: Tuesday–Wednesday, 10 a.m.–8 p.m.; Thursday–Saturday, 10 a.m.–5 p.m.; Sunday, noon–5 p.m.
Admission: $2.50/visitor; free/children under 1
Tours: Yes; minimum of ten people; $1.50/per person; reserve one week in advance
Wheelchair/Stroller Access: Yes

A group of parents opened this museum in 1991, and it's been popular ever since. There are lots of hands-on activities, and a main exhibit that is on display for a year at a time. Junior scientists can hatch chicks from eggs and butterflies from cocoons; toddlers have climbing ramps and blocks especially for them. Saturday mornings are designated for art activities. They'll do private parties here, too. Note: They share a parking lot with the CREHST Museum.

Tri-City Americans   509-736-0606

Location: 7100 W. Quinault, Kennewick
Days/Hours: Season is September–March with thirty-six home games; starting time 7 p.m. except for Sunday at 6 p.m.
Wheelchair/Stroller Access: Yes

Hockey's the game here, and the team is part of the Western Hockey League. Composed mainly of older teens with eyes on the National Hockey League, the competition is quite exciting. They skate hard and love what they do. The Americans are the closest thing to a professional sports team in this area, and it's a popular family spectator sport.

Places to Eat

Red Robin Burger and Spirits Emporium

(two locations)

509-943-8484 (Richland);
509-736-6008 (Kennewick)

Location: 924 George Washington Way (Richland) ; 1021 Columbia Center
Blvd. (Kennewick)
Days/Hours: Sunday–Thursday, 11 a.m.–10 p.m.; Friday–Saturday, 11 a.m.–
midnight
Wheelchair/Stroller Access: Yes

Yes, you know the name—it's the same. Nice to know you can count
on a familiar place! With over a dozen hamburger choices for hungry
kids, onion rings and potato skins for snacks, they also specialize in some
neat nonalcoholic fruit and ice cream concoctions. High chairs and boosters available (no pb and j here).

Walla Walla

Places to Go

Fort Walla Walla Museum

509-525-7703

Location: 755 Myra Rd. in Fort Walla Walla Park (west side of Walla Walla
near College Place)
Days/Hours: April 1–October 31: daily except Mondays. Closed the remainder of year.
Admission: $4/adults; $3/seniors and students; $1/children 6–12
Tours: $2.50/adults; $1/children under 18. Tours last one hour; reservations
necessary—call at least one week ahead.
Wheelchair/Stroller Access: Strollers, yes; difficult in places for wheelchairs
but you may call ahead for golf-cart transportation. They have cement
trails.

There's a great challenge and hands-on learning experience for kids
here. When they try to pack a doll-house-size wagon with miniature versions of pioneer necessities, they quickly realize how challenging it was
for Northwest settlers to pack their covered wagons. But this is just one
part of an Oregon Trail exhibit at the museum, and it's easy to pretend,
with log cabins and an 1867 schoolhouse to roam through. New in spring
of 1998, an Italian Heritage Farmstead, complete with vineyards. Other
displays feature a combine with a Shenandoah hitch and thirty-three life-
size mules. During special events, pioneer craftspeople and tradespeople

are busy working, blacksmithing, and baking. Exhibits in other nearby buildings tell stories about the Marcus and Narcissa Whitman missionary party, local Native Americans, and early farming in the region.

Whitman Mission

509-522-6360 *(National Park Service)*;
509-522-6357 *(library)*

Location: Off U.S. 12, seven miles west of Walla Walla
Web Site: www.nps.gov/parks.html
Days/Hours: Daily, 8 a.m.–4:30 p.m. Closed only on Thanksgiving, Christmas, and New Year's Day.
Admission: $2/person; $4/family; free/children under 16 and to those with Golden Age Passports
Wheelchair/Stroller Access: Yes, except at approach to the monument

One of the earliest settlements on the Oregon Trail, the mission is now a memorial to the Native Americans and missionary settlers who lost their lives here. If you have time, hike up to the monument on the hill and watch the sunset.

Demonstrations are a popular feature at the Yakama Nation Fall Festival.
PHOTO COURTESY OF THE YAKAMA NATION CULTURAL HERITAGE CENTER

Places to Eat

Ice Burg Drive-In

509-529-1793

Location: 616 W. Birch St. (corner of W. Birch and Ninth)
Days/Hours: Monday–Thursday, 7:30 a.m.–9 p.m.; Friday, 7:30 a.m.–
   10 p.m.; Saturday, 11 a.m.–10 p.m.; Sunday, 11:30 a.m.–9 p.m.
Wheelchair/Stroller Access: Drive-in only

Nothing changes here, including the marvelous milkshakes made with fresh seasonal fruits. In summer and fall, strawberry, cherry, and blackberry are good choices; other months banana or pineapple. Of course we prefer chocolate. Locals claim these are the best burgers in the Northwest.

Clarkston and Pullman

Places to Go

Chief Timothy State Park/Alpowai Interpretive Center

509-758-9580

Location: Take Hwy. 12 and—eight miles west of Clarkston— turn north
   onto Silcott Road; cross the bridge onto the island in Lower Granite Lake.
Web Site: www.parks.wa.gov
Days/Hours: Overnight camping year-round with limits: Winter: weekends
   only from December 1–April 1, no reservations necessary. Spring and
   summer: reservations necessary; campground open daily. Alpowai
   Interpretive Center: June–August: Wednesday–Sunday, 1 p.m.–5 p.m.
Wheelchair/Stroller Access: Yes

The Lower Granite/Snake River behind the Lower Granite Dam offers a graduated sandy beach, safe for wading and swimming. The children's play area and picnic tables nearby are tree-shaded for summer comfort. The Alpowai Interpretive Center tells the story of the Nez Perce Native Americans who lived here. On display are artifacts recovered from archaeological digs before the dam's waters flooded the area. The Nez Perce played an important role in the Lewis and Clark expedition.

Ferdinand's

509-335-4014; 509-335-2141 (for tours)

Location: In the Food Quality Building on WSU Campus (South Fairway)
Days/Hours: Monday–Friday, 9:30 a.m.–4:30 p.m.
Tours: Self-guided tours anytime. Guided tours are thirty minutes, given
from 10:30 a.m.–12:30 p.m.; reservations required; call ahead one to two
weeks.
Wheelchair/Stroller Access: Yes

This is indeed a working university, and Ferdinand's is an important part of the campus. You stop here for delicious ice cream, milk shakes, and Cougar Gold cheese made in their own dairy. In fact, you can watch the process via a video and window in the Observation Room. You can take a self-guided tour anytime which might include just the video; on guided tours you will see the cheese being made, and their marvelous antique milk bottle display. Tours of the dairy farm are also available with advance planning.

Palouse Falls/Lyons Ferry
State Park

509-549-3551; 509-646-3252

Location: West of Pullman and north of Walla Walla, just off Hwy. 261,
eight miles northwest of Starbuck, is Lyons Ferry State Park. Palouse Fall
is six miles north of Lyons Ferry on Palouse Falls Rd.
Days/Hours: Overnight camping April–September; day-use only remainder
of year at Palouse Falls, closed at Lyons Ferry.
Wheelchair/Stroller Access: No

A great adventure occurs here. As the 198-foot Palouse River waterfall rushes to the Snake River through hardened lava flows, the rising mist creates a mysterious but colorful aura. If you want to hike up the hillside, which is layered with columns of basalt, ask a ranger about the best climbing route, as the steep hike is daunting for younger children. Nearby, Lyons Ferry State Park offers fifty-two camping sites. These are located on the west side of Hwy. 261; on the east side of the highway are the park's waterfront activities. A roped-off swimming beach is protected by a breakwater. The fishing dock is actually the old open-deck Lyons Ferry, used for river crossings more than thirty-five years ago. North of the breakwater, a dirt road takes you to a one-mile gravel path leading to a historical overlook. A nearby Native American burial site contains prehistoric human bones known as Marmes Man, thought to be at least 10,000 years old.

Washington State University

509-335-3581

Location: In Pullman.
Web Site: www.wsu.edu
Days/Hours: Monday–Friday, 1 p.m., when school is open
Tours: Free; one hour guided tours start at Room 442, French Administration Building
Wheelchair/Stroller Access: Yes

The tours are a great opportunity to climb the hills and see this popular campus. You'll stop inside the Conner Museum, which has the largest collection of birds and mammals in the Pacific Northwest. Next, the WSU Museum of Art, and then the Webster Physical Sciences Building where you'll see the Jacklin Collection, one of the world's largest petrified wood collections. If you're there during the week, a swing by Ferdinand's is a must. One of WSU's strong points is the vast number of students whose parents are alumni.

SOUTH CENTRAL WASHINGTON

Skamania and Klickitat Counties

Places to Go

Columbia Gorge Interpretive Center

509-427-8210

Location: 990 S.E. Rock Creek Drive; off Hwy. 14 in Stevenson
Days/Hours: Daily, 10 a.m.–5 p.m. except New Year's, Thanksgiving, and Christmas
Admission: $6/adults; $5/seniors; $5/students 13 and older; $4/children 6–12; free/children under 5
Wheelchair/Stroller Access: Yes

This $10.5 million center houses displays and exhibits that tell the story of the people and activity that shaped the Columbia Gorge. It's an important historical saga for our state: the Native Americans and white pioneers, the industries—fishing and forestry—the geological events. There are centuries-old artifacts and a new fishing wheel, the Corliss. Children particularly enjoy the nine-project slide show with the potent sounds dramatizing the floods, lava flows, and other geologic forces that shaped the gorge, and the replica of an Native American fishing platform next to a indoor working waterfall. Youngsters 10 and older are most receptive to the history to be learned here.

Goldendale Observatory State Park and Interpretive Center

509-773-3141

Location: 1602 Observatory Dr. In Goldendale on Hwy. 142, turn north on N. Columbus Ave. at the light, drive one mile to the Y-intersection, then follow the road up the hill for another mile.
Web Site: www.parks.wa.gov
Days/Hours: Park: April–September: Wednesday–Sunday, 2 p.m.–5 p.m. and 8 p.m.–midnight. October–March: Saturday, 1 p.m.–5 p.m. and 7 p.m.– 9 p.m., Sunday, 1 p.m.–5 p.m.
Wheelchair/Stroller Access: No

The telescope sits in a metal dome on top of the hill; the scope peers through a rotating opening. It's a twenty-four-and-a-half-inch reflecting Cassegrain, the largest of its type accessible to the United States public. You can see planets and stars in daylight, but evening viewing is by far the best experience.

Horsethief Lake State Park

509-767-1159

Location: On Hwy. 14; two miles east of Hwy. 97, thirty-three miles west of Goldendale
Web Site: www.parks.wa.gov
Days/Hours: Overnight camping April–September; closed remainder of year
Wheelchair/Stroller Access: No

Years ago, coastal and interior Native American tribes gathered here to trade and socialize. Their artists and storytellers left petroglyphs on rock walls (next to the trail west of the south parking lot). Later, in the 1800s, Lewis and Clark passed through and noted the importance of the area as a meeting place. Today, there are twelve sites for campers and a lake full of trout beckoning to fisher-persons. The lake's name still remains a mystery to us.

Ice Caves at Gifford Pinchot Forest

509-395-2501

Location: On Forest Road 24, about six miles west of Trout Lake
Days/Hours: Daily until they are snowed out (or in)
Tours: Self-guided; stop at the Trout Lake Ranger Station for maps and information sheets.
Wheelchair/Stroller Access: No

It's the maze of icy stalactites dripping from the ceiling and stalagmites growing from the floor in the Mount Adams Ice Cave that keep children entranced as they climb up and down the ladder steps. It takes a strong climber to maneuver this experience; most visitors are 8 and older. This eerie sight is something they won't soon forget. The ice cave is located in the Mount Adams Ranger District at the south end of the forest; inside the cave the atmosphere is cold and dark. Come equipped with flashlights, warm jackets, and sturdy climbing shoes. The ladder steps in the cave's upper area descend to an underground level which is slick and often narrow (making backpacking difficult in places). The cave was formed by basalt flows from an ancient volcano.

Maryhill Museum
509-773-3733

Location: 35 Maryhill Museum Drive; off Hwy. 14, south of Goldendale
Days/Hours: Mid-March–mid-November: daily; 9 a.m.–5 p.m.
Admission: $5/general admission; $4.50/seniors 62 and older; $1.50/children 6–16; free/children 5 and under. Members free any time. Groups welcome; reservations necessary for ten or more.
Wheelchair/Stroller Access: Yes

Amazing to find this extraordinary museum tucked away in the southeast corner of our state, but here are permanent collections of great value, as well as a variety of special exhibitions. Originally it was to be the home of entrepreneur Sam Hill, who envisioned a 7,000 acre Quaker community on the property. When his personal vision failed to attract enough followers, the home became the museum. After his death, the museum was completed through the efforts of Alma Spreckels of the San Francisco sugar family. Among the permanent collections at the museum are the Auguste Rodin Sculpture and Drawings; the Queen Marie Gallery containing memorabilia and the possessions of the Romanian Queen; the miniature Theatre de la Mode of French fashion mannequins; the Native American Collection with rare prehistoric rock carvings; and—especially popular with youngsters—the Chess Set Collection with over 100 antique and unusual sets from around the world. The Café Maryhill offers lunch and light refreshment from 10 a.m. to 4:30 p.m. Children especially enjoy exploring the landscaped grounds and sculpture gardens filled with wild peacocks.

Three miles east of Maryhill, just off Hwy. 14 is Stonehenge, the first monument in the country to honor the dead of World War I. A replica of England's famous memorial, this too was built by Sam Hill as a tribute to the men of Klickitat County.

Maryhill State Park

509-773-5007;
800-452-5687 *(camping reservations)*

Location: On Hwy. 97, twelve miles south of Goldendale
Web Site: www.parks.wa.gov
Days/Hours: Open year-round for overnight camping; reservations neces-
sary, April 1–September 30.
Wheelchair/Stroller Access: Yes

Only three miles east of the Maryhill Museum, overlooking the Columbia River, the park has two stone breakwaters creating a sheltered swimming area with a gravel beach. From here you can watch the adventurous (and skilled) windsurfers as they catch a breeze and skim across the river on their sailboards. It's a tricky sport at best. Nearby, there are fifty utility campsites and twenty tent sites for overnighters. Note: There is no running water here during winter months.

Places to Eat

Baker's Dozen-n-More

509-427-7808

Location: 310 S.W. Second St., Stevenson (Skamania County)
Days/Hours: Monday–Saturday, 7:30 a.m.–5:30 p.m.; Sunday, 8 a.m.–2 p.m.
Wheelchair/Stroller Access: Yes

If you've eaten one of their Bigfoot cookies, maybe you, too, believe they make them from a mold of a real Sasquatch paw print. The furry monster may not have any connection at all with these delicious sugar cookies, but it makes for a good story. There's lots of other tempting goodies in the case.

Yakima Valley
Places to Go

Darigold Dairy Fair

509-837-4321

Location: 400 Alexander Rd., Sunnyside
Days/Hours: Daily, 10 a.m.–8 p.m.
Tours: Self-guided
Admission: Free

If grilled cheese sandwiches are a favorite in your family, you'll enjoy the view from the window, watching the cheese machines in action. You can see the curds being salted, then the forty pound blocks of cheddar as they roll off the assembly line. The lessons in pasteurization are interesting, but most certainly the acrobatic cows swinging from the rafters will catch your child's attention. There is free cheese tasting at tour's end; you'll find some wild ice cream flavors in the gift shop, as well.

Fort Simcoe State Park   509-874-2372

Location: On Hwy. 220, thirty miles west of Toppenish
Web Site: www.parks.wa.gov
Days/Hours: Summer months: daily, dawn to dusk. Winter months: week-ends only, 8 a.m.–dusk. No camping here. Tours of grounds by appointment.
Wheelchair/Stroller Access: Yes, at the Interpretive Center and most grassy picnic areas; not at historic barracks

Fort Simcoe is another good history lesson for students of Washington state. Once a campsite for the Yakama Indian tribe, it became a military post in 1855 as a result of conflict between the tribes and white settlers. When the fighting subsided, the fort was given to the Bureau of Indian Affairs, which began farm and carpentry training for the tribal members in the 1920s, and taught them to read English. Today Fort Simcoe showcases both stories: ten soldiers' barracks have been restored, and the Interpretive Center depicts the Native Americans' role in the saga. Located at the end of a thirty-mile dead-end street, the park has numerous picnic tables, a covered picnic shelter, and playground equipment for youngsters up to age 10.

Washington's Fruit Place Visitor Center   509-576-3090

Location: 105-S. 18th St., Ste. 103, Yakima. Take exit 33 off I-82 to Yakima Ave.; follow road to 18th St., along the Yakima River.
Web Site: www.bestapples.com
Days/Hours: Monday–Friday, 9 a.m.–5 p.m.; Saturday, 10 a.m.–5 p.m.
Admission: Free

Exhibits here are designed so that even the youngest can manipulate the equipment on display. Children can test their skills at the cherry bouncer, apple sorter, and pressure testers—all used in the harvesting of Washington apples. You'll learn how our farmers grow delicious fruits, then you can sample some. The apples, cherries, plums, pears, peaches, and apricots are all grown here in Washington. The center is related to the Wenatchee Apple Commission's Visitors Center.

White Pass
509-672-3100; 509-453-8731

Location: Fourteen miles southeast of Mount Rainier National Park, fifty
   miles west of Yakima
Days/Hours: Late November–mid-February, 8 a.m.–4 p.m. Mid-February–
   mid-May, 9 a.m.–5 p.m. Extended hours of night skiing in late December,
   4 p.m.–10 p.m.
Wheelchair/Stroller Access: Limited

There are four chairlifts to the top of several challenging downhill runs; lower slopes are good for beginners. For cross-country skiers, there are more than twelve kilometers of groomed, double-track trails. Parents can take advantage of the child-care services available daily between 8:30 a.m. and 4:30 p.m. for youngsters 2 to 6. At the base of the hill, there's a restaurant, general store, and service station.

Yakama Nation Tribal Cultural
Heritage Center
509-865-2800; 800-874-3087 (RV Park)

Location: On Hwy. 97, one mile north of Toppenish, twenty miles south of
   Yakima
Days/Hours: Monday–Saturday, 9 a.m.–6 p.m.; Sunday, 9 a.m.–5 p.m.
Admission: $4/adults; $2/seniors and students 11 and older; $1/children 7–
   10; free/children 7 and under. Family admission is $10.
Wheelchair/Stroller Access: Yes

The difference in the spelling of their name is their heritage. A decision to return to their roots prompted action in 1994 by tribal leaders to readopt the original spelling. The colorful culture of the Yakama Nation is the focus of the museum and cultural center. The tribal history is recounted from the perspective of the elders and other tribal members; photographs and dioramas are a grim reminder of the effect white settlers have had on this way of life. This is an important part of Washington students' history lessons. Despite a troubled history, the Yakama are a very proud people, working to retain their heritage. Native American powwows are held here, attracting participants from throughout the region. Next to the cultural center, the Yakama Nation Recreational Vehicle Park rents sites for vehicles, tents, and teepees.

A Native American guide welcomes you to the Yakama National Cultural Heritage Center. PHOTO COURTESY OF YAKAMA NATION CULTURAL HERITAGE CENTER

Yakima Bears
509-457-5151

Location: Yakima County Stadium on Pacific St., near S. 10th—on the
Central Washington State Fairgrounds
Days/Hours: Season is June–September; game time is 7:05 p.m., except
Sundays, 6:05 p.m.
Admission: $4/adults; $2.75/seniors and children 12 and under
Wheelchair/Stroller Access: Yes

Affiliated with the Los Angeles Dodgers, the Bears are a Class A home
team with a Class A following here. The minor leaguers play against in-
state rivals such as the Everett Aquasox and Spokane Indians. This is one
of the best family experiences around; bring the kids out early to watch
batting and fielding practice. Bring a mitt—souvenir balls are easy to
catch! You'll love their mascot, Boomer the Bear.

Yakima Interurban Trolley Lines
509-575-1700

Location: Round-trip to Selah, leaving from Yakima Electric Railway
Museum in Yakima
Days/Hours: May–mid-October: weekends and holidays, 10 a.m., noon, 2
p.m., and 4 p.m.
Fares: $4/adults; $3.50/seniors; $2.50/children 6–12; free/children 5 and under
Wheelchair/Stroller Access: Yes

This two-hour round-trip between Yakima and Selah is an imaginative excursion aboard the Yakima Valley Transit System's original electric
streetcars. The route follows city streets, winds past fruit orchards, across
the Naches River, and past Convicts Cave. Criminals in the 1920s sentenced
to hard labor were forced to break rocks here—an eye-opener for those old
enough to understand. During the trolley's operating hours you can also
take a free self-guided tour of the Yakima Electric Railway Museum.

Yakima Valley Museum and Historical Association
509-248-0747

Location: 2105 Tieton Dr. in Yakima
Days/Hours: Wednesday–Friday, 10 a.m.–5 p.m.; Saturday–Sunday, noon–
5 p.m.
Admission: $2.50/adults; $1.25/seniors and children 11 and older; free/
children 10 and under
Wheelchair/Stroller Access: Yes

From a covered wagon to the office of a Supreme Court justice, you'll
find much of interest in Yakima's history and diversity. Justice William

O. Douglas was a native of Yakima, and his Supreme Court office is here in replica. There are several hands-on activities for kids: a vintage general store and claims shop and a "match the animal with its fur" exhibit. The horse-drawn vehicle collection is quite extensive (no riding allowed), including a Conestoga covered wagon, mail coaches, and the Overland Express wagon. Lots of room for vivid imagination here.

Places to Eat

Deli de Pasta   509-453-0571

Location: 7 N. Front St. in Yakima
Days/Hours: Monday–Thursday, 11:30 a.m.–8:30 p.m.; Friday–Saturday,
*   11:30 a.m.–9:30 p.m.*
Wheelchair/Stroller Access: Yes

It's strictly Italian here, and the locals voted it their favorite restaurant in 1993. You can "do your own" here by choosing a pasta, then deciding which sauce will top it off. Both pasta and sauce are homemade. There is no children's menu, but half portions can be ordered for about $1 less than full price. Desserts are appealing: homemade ice cream, tira misu, and major chocolate chip cookies.

Yakama National Heritage Inn   509-865-2551

Location: On U.S. 97, one mile north of Toppenish
Days/Hours: Monday–Wednesday, 7:30 a.m.–8 p.m.; Thursday–Saturday,
*   7:30 a.m.–9 p.m.; Sunday, 8 a.m.–2 p.m. for brunch, dinner till 8 p.m.*
Wheelchair/Stroller Access: Yes

You'll have to drive around behind the Winter Lodge to find the restaurant and its surprising menu. The inn serves buffalo, genuine Native American fry bread, barbecued salmon, and juicy huckleberry pie, for starters. If you have children with adventurous appetites, they'll really enjoy the opportunities for new foods. Breakfast is served Monday through Saturday, brunch on Sunday.

Kittitas County
Places to Go

Central Washington University   509-963-1215

Location: 400 E. 8th Ave., Ellensburg. Enter campus at the corner of 8th and D streets.
Web Site: www.ewu.edu
Days/Hours: Reservations necessary. To go into classrooms, make the request when you call for reservations; they will need to make arrangements.
Tours: Forty-five minutes
Wheelchair/Stroller Access: Yes

Usually teens are most interested in this, especially if they're considering Central as their next educational challenge. The tour is an outdoor walk past some fairly modern structures—the library, fine arts building, and dormitories—but just off campus, you'll see the more historical side of Ellensburg in turn-of-the-century homes. Of special interest here is the "Chimposiums," one-hour educational workshops involving the university's well-known signing chimpanzees. Four primates—Washoe, Loulis, Moja Dar, and Tatu—have learned to sign using the ASL (American Sign Language) vocabularies. Tuition is $10 per adult, $7.50 per student (CWU students and youth under 18); the Chimposiums take place on Saturdays at 9:15 a.m. and 10:45 a.m. and Sundays at 12:15 p.m. and 2:00 p.m. Prepaid reservations are recommended. The CHCI facility is located at the corner of Nicholson Blvd. and D St.

Children's Activity Museum   509-925-6789

Location: 400 N. Water, corner of Fourth and Main in Ellensburg
Days/Hours: Wednesday–Friday, 10 a.m.–3 p.m.; Saturday, 10 a.m.–4 p.m.; Sunday, 1 p.m.–4 p.m.
Admission: $2.50/adults and children 2 and over; free/children under 2
Wheelchair/Stroller Access: Yes

Toddlers love to come here just to play on Pleasure Island, the climbing area reserved for those under 2 years of age. For older ones, the reflection exhibit tickles their fancies as they watch themselves grow six feet tall or become triplets. Others spend their time trying on costumes and performing on a stage, budding actors and actresses no doubt. There are special drawers whose contents keep changing, a constant surprise for young ones. The unusual robotic arm and black-light room add to the magic—and in the Magic School Bus, Ms. Frizzle welcomes school field trips every Tuesday from October to June, and science experiments are available daily. They specialize in hands-on exhibits; many are changed periodically throughout the year. Along with field trips, they do birthday parties (for a nominal fee).

Ellensburg Rodeo · 800-637-2444; 509-962-7831

Location: Ninety minutes east of Seattle; off I-90, take exits 102 or 109
Days/Hours: Labor Day weekend: from Friday at 1 p.m. to noon Monday.
Kittitas County Fair opens 10 a.m.–10 p.m.
Admission: Tickets range from $8–$26; you can purchase them year-round through the numbers listed above. Discounts available for seniors and groups of twenty-five or more.
Wheelchair/Stroller Access: Special seating for wheelchair users; special parking for strollers outside the arena

One of Washington's oldest and best-known weekend winners, the Ellensburg Rodeo began in 1923 and celebrated its Diamond Jubilee in 1997. It's a uniquely American sport featuring some of the finest ropers, racers, wrestlers, and riders in the country, and a great family getaway. You can count on fireworks, barrel racing, bull-fighting, and lots of hard riding. Participants come from as far away as Mexico, Australia, and Canada. Accommodations available through Central Washington University (call 800-752-4379); free shuttles from the university and Ellensburg High School make getting there easy. Save time for the fair, with its prize-winning animal exhibits, carnival rides, and good old-fashioned food.

Gingko Petrified Forest State Park · 509-856-2700

Location: Near Vantage, east of Ellensburg.
Web Site: www.parks.wa.gov
Days/Hours: Park: year-round, dawn to dusk. Interpretive Center: Mid-May–mid-September: 10 a.m.–6 p.m.
Wheelchair/Stroller Access: In some areas, but it's difficult

It's not a rock band or a space alien or a UFO. It's a prehistoric tree, now a living fossil, that dates back about 200 million years to the Triassic period. In those day they grew abundantly near Vantage until a lava flow destroyed them. Today visitors can still find pieces of petrified wood from the ginkgo. In the Interpretive Center, you'll find information about the gingko, other minerals, and the basic geology of Washington. Outside, an interpretive trail two miles west of the center leads you through a desert marked with fossil recoveries.

Happy Trails

360-656-2634

Location: Easton; take I-90, exit 70; follow the off-ramp to north of the freeway; turn onto Sparks Road. Follow Sparks Rd. less than 1,000 feet to Silver Ridge Ranch for parking.

Days/Hours: Daily, 10 a.m.–8 p.m.; late November–early March or as long as the snow permits

Admission: $15/adults; $7.50/children 10 and younger. Reservations with a $50 deposit required. No age minimum.

Wheelchair/Stroller Access: There is access to bobsled rides for disabled people and toddlers, but equipment (wheelchairs and strollers) must be left at parking lot.

The Happy Trails wagon master leads groups on twenty-minute bobsled rides (complete with blankets and jingle bells) pulled by two-horse teams through meadows and trees to a concave snow bowl ideal for inner tubing. Bring your own inner tube or borrow one from Happy Jack, the trail master. If you want some hot beverages (cocoa, soup, apple cider, etc.), they'll build you a bonfire and boil the water. You can even roast hot dogs and marshmallows here—or warm your hands between runs. There are portable toilets near the snow bowl for your convenience. After about ninety minutes of unadulterated snow fun, Happy Jack and the horses will bring you back to the parking lot, probably very tired and very happy! Note: It can get cold for little ones here; recommended for those 3 years and older.

Olmsted Place State Park

509-925-1943

Location: At the end of North Ferguson Road, four miles east of Ellensburg

Web Site: www.parks.wa.gov

Days/Hours: Varies; call ahead

Tours: Both guided and self-guided. Reservations needed for guided tours; fee is $1/per person or $36/thirty people (schools groups)

If you're browsing on your own, the park contains a vintage 1857 cabin and a neighboring home built in 1908 that still contains most of its original furniture. The guided tours do offer more information and usually prove to be more interesting to children; the tours include a visit to a turn-of-the-century schoolhouse, an overview of early farm equipment still in working condition, and a ride in a covered wagon. The Olmsted brothers have been responsible for a number of well-known parks and recreational areas throughout the state; the land for this park was left to the state by the Olmsted granddaughters years ago. The park is now the site for several popular annual family events.

Places to Eat

Sweet Memories Bakery   509-925-4783

Location: 319 Pearl St., Ellensburg
Days/Hours: Monday–Friday, 7 a.m.–7:30 p.m.; Saturday, 8 a.m.–6:30 p.m.
Wheelchair/Stroller Access: Yes

The fragrance of fresh sourdough and cheese breadsticks will lead
you around the corner to the bakery. Located close to the Children's
Museum, sandwiches are made to order here and pb and j is a priority.
High chairs available.

Helpful Phone Numbers:

Chambers of Commerce:
  Asotin: 800-933-2128
  Clarkston: 509-758-7712
  Dayton: 800-882-6299; 509-382-4825
  Ellensburg: 509-925-3137
  Goldendale: 509-773-3400
  Greater Yakima: 509-248-2021
  Hispanic Chamber of Commerce of Greater Yakima: 509-952-7137;
    509-248-6751
  Prosser: 509-786-3177
  Pullman: 509-334-3565
  Selah: 509-697-6877
  Skamania County: 509-427-8911
  Toppenish: 509-865-3262
  Walla Walla: 509-525-0850
  Wapato: 509-877-3080

Other:
  Klickitat County Visitor Information Center: 509-493-3630
  Tri-Cities Visitor and Convention Bureau: 509-735-8486
  Umatilla National Forest's Walla Walla Ranger District: 509-522-6290
  Yakima Valley Visitor and Convention Bureau: 509-575-1300
  Reservations Northwest: 800-452-5687 (to reserve campsites)

Appendix

● ●

Trip Planning Resources In Washington State

Bicycle Program/Washington Department of Transportation: You can obtain a map and guide to bicycling in the Northwest by calling 360-705-7277.

Washington Forest Protection Association: They provide a paperback guide called *A Walk in the Woods—A Public Guide to Private Forests*, with information about the diversity of Washington's forests, the jobs forests create, and wildlife and plant preservation. Especially interesting to kids are the charts showing how to match animal, bird, and reptile life with their tracks and habitats. Call 800-459-6637.

Washington State Department of Fisheries: Call 360-902-2200 in Olympia for a packet of information about saltwater sport fishing regulations.

Washington State Department of Natural Resources: Also in Olympia, the agency sells maps and brochures describing the 135 primitive recreation sites with the 5 million acres of DNR-managed land in Washington state. Call 360-902-1234.

Washington State Department of Wildlife: Call 360-902-2200 for information on freshwater fishing and viewing.

Washington State Fair Association: This resource is located in Moses Lake; their calendar includes listings for county fairs, festivals, and special events throughout the year.

Washington State Lodging and Travel: The state tourism development division has a "Get Away Guide and Calendar" with complete listings of events and activities around the state. They also offer an information line with a calendar of current events. Call 360-586-2088, 360-586-2102, or 800-544-1800.

Washington State Park Winter Recreation Office: Their "Sno-Mobile Guide" to (commercially) groomed trails in the state is free. For more detailed info that includes maps, cost is $2.50. Call 800-233-0321.

Index

Index

ABOUT THE AUTHORS

ROSANNE COHN, the original author of *Discover Seattle With Kids*, is a graduate of Garfield High School and the University of Washington, and a leading consultant in the public relations field. Deeply involved in community work as well, she contributes time and energy to the Bellevue Philharmonic and serves on the Foundation Board at Lake Washington Technical College. Rosanne and her husband, Lawrence Kahn, live in Bellevue. Between them, they have seven grown children, six in the Puget Sound area, one in Texas.

SUZANNE MONSON is a Seattle-area newspaper reporter and freelance writer. She and her husband, Dori, have three young daughters who adore trying travel adventures. A Vancouver, Wash., native and University of Washington alumnus, she has worked for The Vancouver Columbian, the Associated Press and The Seattle Times. Her current work includes writing business, education, travel and family-focused features. She enjoys serving as president of the Shoreline Education Foundation and sharing tried-and-true getaways with other parents at her daughters' schools.

OTHER BOOKS FROM JASI PUBLISHING

The Best of Central California: Main Roads and Side Trips.
Bob Carter

The Best of Orange County California: A Guide to Scenic, Recretional and Historical Attractions. *Gregory Lee*

The Brewpub Explorer of the Pacific Northwest. *Hudson Dodd, Matthew Latterell, Lani McCormack, and Ina Zucker*

California's Gold Rush Country: A Guide to the Best of the Mother Lode. *Barbara Braasch*

Discover The Poconos With Kids: A Guide for Families, *Marynell K. Strunk*

The Essential San Juan Islands Guide. *Second Edition, Marge and Ted Mueller*

Oregon's Coast: A Guide to the Best Family Attractions from Astoria to Brookings *Carolyn & David Gabbe*

The Seattle Super Shopper: The Savvy Shopper's Guide to the Greater Puget Sound Area, Eighth Edition. *Vicki Koeplin*

Spokane: The Complete Guide to the Hub of the Inland Northwest. *M. E. Buckham*

Stepping out in Seattle. *Mandy Johnston, with Doug Feyereisen and Annie Goodgion*